IN EXILE

ALSO AVAILABLE FROM BLOOMSBURY

Lev Shestov: Philosopher of the Sleepless Night, Matthew Beaumont
Contradiction Set Free, Hermann Levin Goldschmidt, trans. John Koster
Modernism between Benjamin and Goethe, Matthew Charles
Another Finitude: Messianic Vitalism and Philosophy, Agata Bielik-Robson
Heine and Critical Theory, Willi Goetschel
Hannah Arendt's Ethics, Deirdre Lauren Mahony

IN EXILE

GEOGRAPHY, PHILOSOPHY AND JUDAIC THOUGHT

JESSICA DUBOW

BLOOMSBURY ACADEMIC
LONDON • NEW YORK • OXFORD • NEW DELHI • SYDNEY

BLOOMSBURY ACADEMIC
Bloomsbury Publishing Plc
50 Bedford Square, London, WC1B 3DP, UK
1385 Broadway, New York, NY 10018, USA
29 Earlsfort Terrace, Dublin 2, Ireland

BLOOMSBURY, BLOOMSBURY ACADEMIC and the Diana logo are
trademarks of Bloomsbury Publishing Plc

First published in Great Britain 2021
This paperback edition published in 2022

Copyright © Jessica Dubow, 2021

Jessica Dubow has asserted her right under the Copyright, Designs and
Patents Act, 1988, to be identified as Author of this work.

For legal purposes the Acknowledgements on p. viii constitute
an extension of this copyright page.

Cover design by Charlotte Daniels

Cover image: *Der Verlassene Raum*, Berlin. (Photograph © Neville Dubow Archive,
Special Collections, UCT Libraries)

All rights reserved. No part of this publication may be reproduced or
transmitted in any form or by any means, electronic or mechanical, including
photocopying, recording, or any information storage or retrieval system,
without prior permission in writing from the publishers.

Bloomsbury Publishing Plc does not have any control over, or responsibility for,
any third-party websites referred to or in this book. All internet addresses given
in this book were correct at the time of going to press. The author and publisher
regret any inconvenience caused if addresses have changed or sites have ceased
to exist, but can accept no responsibility for any such changes.

A catalogue record for this book is available from the British Library.

Library of Congress Cataloging-in-Publication Data
Names: Dubow, Jessica, author.
Title: In exile: geography, philosophy and Judaic thought / Jessica Dubow.
Description: 1. | New York: Bloomsbury Academic, 2021. |
Includes bibliographical references and index.
Identifiers: LCCN 2020029910 | ISBN 9781350154254 (hardback) |
ISBN 9781350191778 (paperback) | ISBN 9781350154278 (ebook) |
ISBN 9781350154285 (epub)
Subjects: LCSH: Jewish diaspora–Philosophy. | Geography. |
Jews–History–Philosophy. | Jews–Identity. | Jewish philosophy.
Classification: LCC DS134.D83 2021 | DDC 181/.06–dc23
LC record available at https://lccn.loc.gov/2020029910

ISBN:	HB:	978-1-3501-5425-4
	PB:	978-1-3501-9177-8
	ePDF:	978-1-3501-5427-8
	eBook:	978-1-3501-5428-5

Typeset by Integra Software Services Pvt. Ltd.

To find out more about our authors and books visit www.bloomsbury.com
and sign up for our newsletters.

For Talitha, Beth and Thomas

CONTENTS

Acknowledgements viii

Introduction: Exile at the origin 1

1 'A patch of ground between four tent pegs': Franz Rosenzweig and the time of exile 17

2 The Second Commandment in the Second Empire: Or, a small theology in Walter Benjamin's city 47

3 Liberalism pluralism and the mourning work of assimilation: Isaiah Berlin via Sigmund Freud 73

4 'Wherever you go you will be a *polis*': Hannah Arendt via Rahel Varnhagen 111

5 Posthumous place: W.G. Sebald and the displacement of landscape 141

Epilogue: Placeholding 165

Notes 174
Bibliography 213
Index 224

ACKNOWLEDGEMENTS

One of the enjoyments of completing this book is not only releasing this particular albatross from about my neck (it has hung there far too long) but realizing just how many colleagues and friends have been a part of this work and the debt I owe to them. The book cover features a photograph taken by my father, Neville Dubow, an art historian and photographer. It is of Karl Biedermann's 'The Deserted Room' (*Der verlassene Raum*): a cast-bronze table, two chairs – one toppled – and a platform of parquet flooring situated in the corner of a small, quiet neighbourhood park in Koppenplatz, Berlin-Mitte. A drama has happened here, one repeated thousands of times: a bang on the door, a hurried departure, an unoccupied place, an occupant without a place. Seeing it for the first time, I knew I wanted to write a book that shared something of its spirit and scale: somewhat larger than life size, but not by much; constellating an array of abstractions while keeping a close link to actual sites and scenes.

I am very grateful to the Leverhulme Trust which supported much of this work as well as to the Frankel Institute at the University of Michigan, Ann Arbor, which in the fall of 2015–16 granted me a fellowship in all senses of the word. The conversations and inspirations I found there were hugely important – especially with Scott Spector, Jeff Veidlinger, Guy Stroumsa, Michael Löwy, Marc Caplan, Efrat Bloom and Geneviève Zubrzycki. I owe a special debt to Geoff Eley. The generosity and rigour of his reading, his unwavering counsel and belief in this project have been extraordinary. If I have failed to 'historicize! historicize! historicize!' this is not due to a shortage of reminders.

I also thank my colleagues in the Department of Geography at the University of Sheffield – in particular Peter Jackson, Eric Olund, Richard Phillips, Jenny

Pickerill, John Flint, David Robinson. In all sorts of ways and on most days, the practical help and less than practical humour of Thomas Sullivan and Rowan Jaines cleared the fog, dissolved the worry and kept me buoyant. Phoebe and Astrid played their inimitable parts, too. I appreciate the probing criticism and encouragement from the anonymous reviewers of the manuscript. My profound thanks to Lisa Goodrum and Lucy Russell at Bloomsbury for their smooth shepherding of this book to its eventual destination.

My treasured friends in South Africa, England and Canada and my family in Brighton, Cape Town, Cambridge, Maastricht and Williamstown continue to show me that the ties that truly bind are seldom geographical or that geography is precisely what happens between places.

Introduction
Exile at the origin

1

Exodus is not, as least to begin with, a flight to anywhere. One of the distinctive features of the biblical narrative is that it sets itself against an itinerary that would allow any clear escape or point of arrival. Instead, *Exodus* presents us with a 'topological paradox':[1] a route where the 'way out' is strangely continuous with the 'way back', or one where the path to liberation might be reversed and the command to flee counter-claimed. Rather than proceeding from Egypt to Canaan via the well-trodden 'Road of the Philistine' (a journey of only a few days and the route referenced prominently at the start of the *Parshat Beshalach* 13:17), the narrative tells us the Israelites looped around towards the Red Sea and thus back in the direction of their Egyptian pursuers. The 'Book of Exile and Redemption', as Nachmanides (Ramban), the medieval Sephardic rabbi described it, is less a purposive onwards advance than a crossing back and forth over an uncertain edge, proceeding anxiously, recursively, misleadingly to liberation.

In her account of the Talmudic commentaries, Avivah Zornberg explores the curiosity of the biblical itinerary. Why, she asks, are we told so explicitly of the rejected route, the 'road not taken'?[2] And how may we interpret the second, and seemingly skewed, choice? Zornberg turns to Rashi – in particular to the emphasis that the eleventh-century Midrashic commentator places on certain words and phrasings of *Exodus* 13:7:

> God did not lead them by way of the Philistines *because it was too close*: and therefore it was easy to return to Egypt by the same road.
> For God said, *Lest* the people change their minds when they see battle and return to Egypt: they will *think a thought* about the fact that they have left Egypt; and will set their minds on returning.[3] (emphasis added)

In these and related exegeses, Rashi's argument is clear. If the straight route (in Hebrew, *peshuta*) is too direct, the desire to return (to slavishness, to servitude) might prove too irresistible and the impulse to regress (to security, to its inhibitions) might appear too compelling. The paradox, of course, recalls one of the oldest psychic snarls in political thought: that tyranny and errancy go together, that there is a kind of licence in constraint and, in reverse, an enthrallment with authority in the endorsements of freedom.[4] Whereas Rashi alerts us to the paradoxical psychic attachments of bondage, Moses Maimonides (Rambam) points up the sociological intelligence of liberating the bonded subject by way of indirection: journeying to freedom stepwise, crabwise, and by incremental degree.

> For a sudden transition from one opposite to another is impossible ... It is not in the nature of man that, after having been brought up in slavish service ... he should all of a sudden wash off from his hands the dirt [of slavery].[5]

If this is a biblical rendition of the caution against the tumults of revolutionary haste in favour of the slower-footed rewards of gradualism – 'the deity', writes Maimonides, 'uses a gracious ruse'[6] – then Moses' choice of the circuitous, 'crooked route' *(me'ukum)* is not only a cunning tactic, a contrivance of social adaptation, habituation.[7] It is also a meditation of space as it twists back on itself: a space in which the passage to redemption prompts a simultaneous regression or where the continuities between escape and return produce a torsion at the heart of freedom. For, while the crooked route might handicap precipitous action, hindering the Israelites' drive to retreat or making it fail, it also allocates a space for rebellious thought – allowing for the vitalities of doubt and revision; creating a breach, a fracture, a gap in which redemption circles around its own immeasurability. In narrative terms, as Zornberg notes, what constitutes 'thought' for the newly liberated people is precisely liberation's renounced or 'unthought' dimensions: anxieties uneasily worded, equivocations fitfully awakened, risks identified and resisted. And so they press Moses:

> Was it for want of graves in Egypt that you brought us to die in the wilderness? What have you done to us, taking us out of Egypt? Is this not the very thing we told you in Egypt, saying 'Let us be, and we will serve the Egyptians, for it is better for us to serve the Egyptians than to die in the wilderness?' (*Parshat Beshalach*, 14:11–12)

If *Exodus* is about the movement to freedom it is, then, a 'difficult freedom',[8] to use Emmanuel Levinas' famous phrase, which prepares for possibilities that are entirely other: of a discontinuous experience, an unpassable transition, an awareness of the capacity for failure. Even more, as Zornberg comments, it allows the Israelites to consider their deliverance from slavery in terms of its negation, 'as a tragedy, a story about death',[9] even of violence. ('Is it for want of graves in Egypt …? You have brought us to die … What have you done to us … ?') Even after the miraculous parting of the Red Sea and the jubilant song of thanksgiving that follows it, Moses' followers remain sceptical, querulous, concerned only with the privations of injury and loss. 'If only we had died at the hand of God in the land of Egypt, when we sat by the fleshpots, when we ate our fill of bread!' (16:3). And again, later: 'Why did you bring us up from Egypt, to kill us and our children and our livestock with thirst?' (17:3). From out of the rock, split apart by a strike from Moses' staff, water begins to flow.

But the place of the miracle isn't named for an inexplicable, unfathomable event: neither for a magical infraction of natural law nor for any divine fulfilment of human desire. It is inaugurated by the altogether more profane labour of Massah (*testing*) and Meribah (*arguing, disputing*): a self-conscious attentiveness to the function of exodus, to its structure as an indeterminate concept rather than a decisive command. 'Is this a story of redemption or of diabolical hatred'?[10] Or even, as Freud's speculations on Jewish ethnogenesis allow, of the Israelite's murderous challenge to the legitimacy of Moses' identity and thus to the power of his primal authority?[11] In its various Talmudic readings, then, there is little that makes *Exodus* a story of historical origin or an event of national origination. If it can be said to be about a beginning at all, it is one posited – and simultaneously dismantled – as a disturbance, an obscurity, a beginning grounded in – that 'begins with' – its own renunciation. Or, as Moses' crooked route out of Egypt implies, it is a beginning that pivots on a contradiction, one where a continual crisis in the locus of authority opens the way for Rashi's disordered, disputatious 'thinking of thoughts'.

Whether turning biblical scripture into a political parable is a viable move or not, *Exodus* alerts us to a certain *type* of thought, a certain *process* of thinking, that we might properly call speculative, or better yet, *subjunctive*. As with its grammatical mood, this is the state and space of a hope, a hypothetical, a stipulation, a supposable; it is a turning towards something that does not yet exist or is ever certain to happen. Like Jacques Lacan's characterization of anxiety which, in contrast to fear, never bears on a determinate or pre-formed object, to be in exile – to think exilically – is not merely to be disengaged from a settled or pre-existing place. It is rather a relation to a non-object, a kind of conditional connection with a *non-location*, an intimate liaison with something unfixed, insufficient or not yet its own.[12] But if there is an important political and philosophical principle to be gained from the biblical desert, might there be good reasons for renewing its spatial aporia? This would mean understanding exile as it yields the question of the national by virtue of being outside – and somehow against – it: a space that poses the problem of time and territory by necessarily *thinking through*, but not necessarily *believing in*, assurances of origin and arrival.

2

If *Exodus* sets up Judaic space as a problem of origin – the problem of an 'anoriginal origin',[13] to borrow Andrew Benjamin's formulation – then it also talks to a particular traversal of space central to the modern philosophical tradition: the movement between the spatial co-ordinates of Athens and Jerusalem. Positioning herself against the very different foundations of Leo Strauss and Emmanuel Levinas, the British philosopher and social theorist Gillian Rose argues against the antinomies posed by philosophy's alternative cities.[14] Which is to say, she contests any either–or separation between the logics and legacies of the Hellenic and Hebraic traditions: the former normatively characterized by secular political reason, the latter by an ethics of prophetic revelation.[15]

Addressed from both sides, Rose registers a double objection. On the one hand, to take Athens as the proxy and place name for structural analysis and the authority of social institutions means disabling the errors constitutive of modernity itself: the sense in which modernity's inadequacy to its own identity cancels any equation between reason and domination, impeding any hurry to disqualify the law on the basis of its complicity with coercion. On the other hand, to nominate Jerusalem as a wholly different city and methodology – the site of angelic anti-reason, the 'sublime Other of modernity'[16] – does not merely traduce Judaic theology by allegorizing it out of modern political history, and out of historical consideration as such. For Rose, it also sequesters biblical scholarship by turning it into a purely interiorized and irenic community, holding to a Judaism unsullied by 'rationalism, violence, the history of the world'.[17] As the imprimatur of a misguided post-modernism, as Rose reads it, the principled disengagement from metaphysical reason and the systematic actualities of power in favour of all that is relational, responsive, unknowable, alterative, has done nothing more than lay the foundations of a new city, a site consecrated by the founders and fellow-travellers of a new ethics. Indeed, in place of old Athens – its metaphysics disgraced, its first principles indicted (not least, by their incrimination in the 'totalizing' politics of the twentieth century) – there now is substituted a 'New Jerusalem': a city sufficiently chimerical to assign only difference and not identity, a destination upraised and evasive enough to relieve its pilgrims of any agency, action, outcome.

Rose's stance against a 'neo-Hebraic'[18] revival in contemporary Continental (mainly French) thought is decidedly adversarial. And her accusations are unforgiving. But while her rejection of an anti-Hellenic valuing of Judaism in late twentieth-century philosophy often rests on axiomatic reduction – Rose's accounts of Levinas' '*Buddhist* Judaism',[19] the truncation of 'Reb Derrida's' 'Judaism as writing'[20] and Jean François Lyotard's solicitations of Martin Buber are particularly distilled – it helps make sense of her broader project. That is to say, Rose aims not only to 'spoil the opposition'[21] between the dominion of Greek autonomy and the ethics of Judaic alterity but also to open the scabrous space in which they converge and collide. Between and *within* the walls of Athens and Jerusalem, there is (and, for Rose, there has always been) a middle ground – a 'middle city', we may say – in which secular reason is never just the coherence of philosophical knowledge, and ethics is never just the refuge or *ressentiment* of sacrality's failure. Accordingly, the middle in question is not any absorptive or formally reconcilable ground. It cannot culminate in any bridging movement from one discourse, one authority – or, one city – to its opposite other. Instead, the middle at issue is a 'broken middle', as Rose names it, in which Athens and Jerusalem both labour: tarrying with the inseparability of periphery and proximity, hazarding a claim to what might be ventured – and lost – in encountering their own limits and reckoning along with the 'breaches in [their] walls'.[22]

And so, in place of a fixation on origins – or rather, in place of assigning a fixed city from which to launch a critique of origins – Rose urges us to engage the difficulty of 'beginning from the middle ... [and] claiming the middle from the beginning'.[23] This entails defying the mastery of any one locus in order to assume the burden of thinking faultily, improperly, agonistically. It means allowing that we are already in the middle of the irreconcilable and, yet, indissociable. It involves thinking neither of sacred starts nor of absolute ends but returning to the incompletions built-into the break and staying on far longer than expected here: within the anxiety of the middle, occupying a space 'rended not mended',[24] anorginally, interminably. On Rose's account, then, the respective inhabitants of Athens and Jerusalem do not mutually misperceive or disable each other. The first is not an outmoded, degraded city and the second is not an exultant or expectant one. There is instead a middle city, an archaic-modern or sacred-secular space, one that is always already – from the origin and incessantly – broken. Or, in Rashi's terms, *crooked*.

Whether Rose's critique of those who would divorce Athens from Jerusalem is valid or not, her call for us to re-inhabit the middle – and to restate the anxieties of living there – alerts us to a space that we may properly call dialectical. Crucially, this dialectic is not positive. It does not culminate in any new (mega) city in which Athens and Jerusalem may be ultimately synthesized or where one might be shrunk to fit inside the other. It is dialectical in being perpetually at odds with itself. Indeed, it is a middle city whose never-endings and always-beginnings return us to the topological predicament with which this chapter began: of exile included within the question of the territorial by reason of its radical exclusion from it; a desert waiting and desert wandering whose object or anticipation – the formation of settlement, place, emplacement – is not (necessarily) to be *sought,* but is (necessarily) to be *thought through*. As such, if Rose is right to say that there is no critical advantage to be gained by keeping Athens apart from Jerusalem, there is good reason for keeping the exilic desert in play: understanding it neither as the antithesis of any city nor as an anterior, irrational space sublated *en route* to modernity but as a simultaneous excess and inadequacy which pressure them, continually constituting and disorienting both.

We began with a crooked route: a path lodged in the ambiguity of a departure that was also a possible return, and with a subject characterized by its relation to a non-location. We began, too, with no point of origin (except as the ground on which the ontology of origins might itself be displaced) and no end (except as an incalculable abeyance) but with an active rent, with an exodus as it risks the action arising out of a 'thinking of thoughts'. But if, as I have suggested, the exilic desert might be the ('broken') middle-city between the established philosophical termini of Athens and Jerusalem, might it also entail a different kind of historical intensity? Might the uncertainties of a 'crooked' space and time make a claim for the thinkability of history outside those reductions that induce us to think *either* under the warranties of territory *or* under the threat of its dispossession? The 'middle-city' I have in mind is thus not a 'middling' or mutually agreed space: tacitly neutral and neutralizing, concerned with a moderating splitting of difference. Even less is it a transitional space that would chart the passage from desert dispersion to walled city – *from* exile *to* history – but the inverse: it is a release from the very supersessions of time that expel and keep us from all that is 'originally' untimely, and so a conception of exile locatable *within* history itself.

In this, 'the Origin is [precisely] the Goal', to put Karl Kraus' famous maxim to a somewhat different use.[25] Here, there is neither any edifice built of the pull of immanent historical forces – the law of an Athens – nor any positing of an *elsewhere* and *elsewhen* to signify an overcoming of substantive, historical life – the ethics of a transcendent Jerusalem. There is only the work of returning to a founding un-fulfilment, to a non-national middle, an 'an-originality' infinitely generated and destined from the start.

3

This book is about the spatial basis of Judaic thought; about, as it were, the influence of this ancient, anxious, non-national middle on key figures in a twentieth-century Jewish European intellectual and theological tradition. And the questions it poses are these: What is the intimate entwinement of exile and Judaic philosophy, of spatial displacement and various modes of critical deliberation? How might we reassert the exilic 'middle' as a particular process or category of thought: a consciousness by which Jewish history has, in some ways, always been addressed and one which it must, in the most urgent of ways, aim to recover? Indeed, how might exilic space operate to erode those structural alliances of time and territory, identity and sovereignty, historicism and the 'true life' of the nation-state that modernity has organized under the name of history? For if space and displacement are the principal terms in these pages, they cannot be thought outside correlative relations of time – that is, without the understanding that all temporal distinctions are essentially spatial in character.

Thus, according to narrative convention, the indexical 'here' of a journey is simultaneously an insistent 'now', a 'there' is also the 'then' of a past or the expectation of a future: collocations of space and time which change a site into a source, an itinerary into a chronology, and transform distance and topography into discourse and topic. The basic point being that a Western philosophy of time is not only deeply imbued with a search for location – for a *place in time* – but that to reference space is to invoke a certain progressive, punctual idea of how time, and history, should run.

What happens, however, when it is exile and not emplacement that is at issue, and when it is loss and not linearity which orders our reckoning of time? The various ways in which this question comes to be assumed – exposed, actioned, imagined as a form of analysis – frame what I am seeking to present as a peculiarly Judaic ontology. This book, then, does not attempt to develop a historical account of Jewish uprootedness, mobility or dislocation. Nor is it a reworking of the hoary myth and metaphor of the 'Wandering Jew', a recycling of its infamies by other means. Or, if it is, my aim is to recover the possibilities and capacities of this figure: returning to the place of exile denied and required by the consolidations of modernity, grasping its currency from within Judaism's own philosophical and theological sources and, crucially, raising the stakes of exile's 'an-orginality' to convert what is usually regarded as a sign of Judaism's singularity into the work of its undecidability. For if exile – like Rose's 'broken middle' – announces a breach in spatial organization it cannot be harnessed to any exclusiveness in national, ethnic or religious emplacements. It means stumbling on (and over) the indeterminacies of place itself, being rerouted by the deviations and disorientations internal to it.

Exile at or *as* the origin – this middle space or middle city which settles nothing, proceeds nowhere, and bears no proper name – is thus the very opposite of organized or autochthonous self-beginning. Initiating the very indecisions which a declaration of origin usually allays, it also registers a certain intensification or exertion in spatial and social existence: making a case for distance and dispersion where no place or positioning may assert jurisdiction over another,[26] drawing in futures – and uncertainties – unavailable in any present. For 'the inability to tolerate empty space', as Wilfred Bion reminds us, doesn't merely defend against the contingent; it also 'limits the amount of space available'.[27] Exile, in short, is not just a specific spatial experience; it produces a form of critical surplus. 'Beginning from the middle',[28] repatriating exile back to the heart of territory, it translates disorientation into the exposure of new orientations: ones not given by any established coordinates of place or matched with an emblematic 'city' imagined as being rightfully and properly one's own.

Franz Rosenzweig, Walter Benjamin, and Hannah Arendt – over recent decades all three have accrued an astonishing library of exegetical and critical accounts, a seemingly endless run of individual studies, comparative portraits, convergences and collisions of thematic idioms and intellectual lineages, abbreviations, elaborations, revisions. Drawn from a German-Jewish background stretching from late Wilhemine to post–Second World War Germany, all continue to inspire analyses of Jewish tradition in its entwinement with the crises of European modernity and its contemporary entailments. Thus, Benjamin's unique blend of historical materialism, urban aesthetics and messianic politics has supplied rich ground for any number of interdisciplinary combinations moving between the languages of philosophy, theology, Jewish studies, art history, visual culture and urban theory. Arendt's writings on totalitarianism, revolution, the nature of freedom, the faculties of action and judgement inform a range of increasingly urgent twenty-first-century debates around citizenship, human rights, pluralism and public political being. Rosenzweig, long recognized as a key figure in the genealogy of post-structuralist philosophy, has recently been revisited in relation both to the major works of his near-contemporary Martin Heidegger and to his imprint in the writings of Emmanuel Levinas, Jacques Derrida and, more obliquely, Maurice Blanchot.

From a very different intellectual framework and geographic context (liberal-pluralist rather than critical modernist and Russo-British not German-Jewish) Isaiah Berlin, too, is once again attracting scholarly attention. In a post-imperial and late-liberal reality where identities are caught up in ever-more violent transitivities, Berlin's central questions – how to reconcile opposing ethical worlds and incompatible social spaces? how to live with the surfeits and dissatisfactions, the limits and irremediable losses, incurred by this process? – prompt me to read him under the influence of his own exilic and Judaic terms. Putting Berlin's political liberalism into dialogue with Sigmund Freud – yet another guide to German-Jewish modernity – further allows me to place exile in conversation with the spatiality of assimilation and approach it by means of its structural similarities with key themes of the Freudian project. For the liberal drama of assimilation, in my account, is less the opposite or overcoming of an exilic condition than a (therapeutic) re-description of it: a kind of 'exile-with-a-difference'[29] in Michael P. Steinberg's wonderful phrase, or what I come to identify as the labour of a 'self-limiting spatiality'. Indeed if, as Freud reminds us, our proposed solutions always tell us more about our injuries than they ever achieve in terms of survival or repair, then assimilation is perhaps the best guide for registering the full force of an 'anoriginal' exile: restating its excesses and understanding Berlin's particular brand of liberal pluralism as exile's re-routing, or self-curative redress. Thus, political pluralism and psychoanalytic practice each range awkwardly, homelessly, (un)knowingly over the incompletions of a Judaic spatiality and each, in their different ways, demand the agility – precisely, the agility of the middle – of thinking along with loss, of living within failure.

The final figure in this study, the post-war German novelist W.G. Sebald cannot be said to invoke a Jewish identity, even as he so often deals, if only allusively, with the Holocaust and the deep shadow of its belated symptoms. And nor does Sebald's peculiar literary genre easily relate to conventional forms of philosophical argument or meditation. At the same time, his eccentric spaces – especially the ways in which Sebald fundamentally reconfigures the aesthetic and geographic trope of landscape – offer a compelling course for challenging the governing containments of human space and its temporal – that is, historical – presence. In this they exemplify a specific exilic intelligence as this book conceives it: installing a distance from the defences of time and territory, disclosing the founding failures and foreignness of place, and enjoining us to inhabit them.

Sebald appears at the end of this book, then, not so much to broaden or boost the arguments developed in the preceding chapters. His presence isn't a kind of non-Jewish coda or last-minute ecumenical addition, even as his writing is expressive of an affectivity that is itself genetically related to a German-Jewish history. As with other figures in this book, Sebald's treatment of place is not merely as an ambient geography – a scene, a setting, a frame for thought – and neither can his understanding of exile be confined to the facts of this or that context – specific histories of specific people and populations displaced, dislocated, dispossessed. As such, Sebald's landscapes – or the presence of 'posthumous place', to anticipate a later turn in my argument – cast doubt on the possibility of place itself: questioning not what remains of place from the wreckage of life or the indigestible debris of its understanding, but of its capacity to ever have been knowable, communicable, orientable in the first place. Here, landscape keeps watch over its own non-compliance. All sightlines are wrong, all perspectives unhinged and planes deformed. Inhabitation is self-opposing, self-cancelling rather emplacing. In this, the paths that Sebald opens up twist back to our starting point, returning us to a beginning that, like exodus, is already a middle: 'crooked', 'broken', breached. Indeed, if Sebald belongs in the company of a Judaic tradition this is not just because his post-Holocaust landscapes lament the loss of certain places and the eviction of their histories. It is because they mark the structure of an internal 'middle', that point at which we might eliminate a place and expel its subjects, but cannot eliminate a place's own infractions, the exile immanent to it.

The figures I have selected, the aspects of their work I privilege and the use to which I put them accord with this basic proposition. Rosenzweig's theological anti-historicism, Benjamin's sacral urban aesthetics, Arendt's conception of the ancient Greek *polis* and its disruption by the figure of the

'Jewish pariah', Berlin's defence of Western liberal pluralism, and the peculiar impossibilities of Sebald's landscape imagination. In disparate languages and from often conflicting positions, all offer accounts of how we might interpret theoretical and philosophical practice in spatial terms, understanding exile less as a geographic and historical predicament than as the (pre)condition for a distinctive critical consciousness. And all draw out, or draw on, a particular Judaic understanding of space: that middle space, that desert exile, the constitutive breach in the city walls which wagers a certain type of thought, not merely extending or troubling the remit of the territorial but showing a radical imagination to be at work as distance or displacement itself.

It follows that the specific spaces examined in each chapter correspond in unusual, and sometimes inverted, ways to others that precede and follow them. For example, *The Star of Redemption*, Rosenzweig's early twentieth-century theological critique of historical time and territoriality, constellates with *The Arcades Project*, Benjamin's materialist analysis of nineteenth-century urbanism. Here, the Judaic injunction against the graven image returns – unexpectedly, anachronistically, abrasively – to expose the internal contestations of secular modernity, raising the spectre of an ancient prohibition amid the flagrant visibilities of the most modern, reasserting 'The Second Commandment in the Second Empire', as I have it. Likewise, Rosenzweig's version of the exilic 'middle' has some consonance with Isaiah Berlin's liberal pluralism which, locating the present at the centre of its social and political model, insists on the indeterminacy on which thought and action depend, as on the insufficiencies of that 'human-horizon'[30] without which, for Berlin, morality and creativity cannot survive. More discrete spaces and their temporal disjunctions speak across each other, too. The small Leningrad apartment of the dissident poet Anna Akhmatova that Berlin visited in 1945 – the *mise-en-scene* of his subsequent polemic against the theoretical foundations of modern totalitarianism – echoes with the attic room in the Jägerstrasse,

Berlin, in which Rahel Varnhagen, the subject of Arendt's portrait of German-Jewish modernity, presided over her literary salon in the closing decade of the eighteenth century. Two small rooms, two histories, two geographies and two variants of exile which, refracted through their two very different interlocutors, converge in meditations on exile, melancholia, the persistence of the past, and diverge on the politics of assimilation and pluralism that seek to resolve them.

The structure of this book is thematic, its shape is constellatory. But a specific date and event (albeit often tacit) run through it. Rosenzweig writes and dies a decade before the outbreak of the Second World War; Benjamin doesn't survive it; in their different ways, Berlin and Arendt think about and through it; Sebald, the *nachgeboren*, turns his own exile into the spatial analogue of the temporal delay of being 'born-after'. Other voices, including Maurice Blanchot, Jean-François Lyotard, Jacques Derrida and Jean-Luc Nancy, enter as more recent conversational partners, receivers and abstractors of a modern Jewish tradition and of the era's ruinous end. Throughout, the preoccupations of cultural geography (my own) intersect with the fields of Jewish studies, critical theory, philosophy and European intellectual history to track the 'middle' ground – often shifting, variable, inopportune, ill-fitting – of the shared ontology of Judaic spatiality and the critical imagination.

1

'A patch of ground between four tent pegs'
Franz Rosenzweig and the time of exile

1

In a letter to his friend, Gertrud Oppenheim, written in May 1917, the German-Jewish philosopher and theologian Franz Rosenzweig offers his own version of thinking the spatiality of the middle:

> For everything we call history happens by a volition thrusting past a compulsion and in the process becoming another compulsion, after which the whole process begins again; but here a *fragment of the ahistorical is thrown in the middle of history*.[1] (emphasis added)

Conceiving his major work, *The Star of Redemption* (1921), while serving on the Balkan Front between 1917 and 1918, completing it in the tumultuous aftermath of the collapse of the German-Imperial and Habsburg armies and at a moment when Central European political structures had definitively failed, Rosenzweig could perhaps justifiably review history from the perspective of an *ahistorical middle*. In a period when the most disintegrative features of modernity – and its definitive agent, the nation-state – were on spectacular display, Rosenzweig voiced the call of a generation seeking an alternative to a nineteenth-century model of political nationhood and the compulsions of a Hegelian vision of history which presupposed it.[2] Idealist philosophical inquiry, initially valuable to the world story and since 'carried forward to maturity', was now 'a deadening power',[3] 'an empty shell',[4] its escalating exhaustions eventuating in the crises of 1914–18. Writing his 'Concluding Remark' to *Hegel and the State* (1920), which originated with his doctoral study from 1910 to 1912 under the supervision of the National Liberal historian, Friedrich Meinecke, Rosenzweig noted:

> We are at end. We feel the extent to which we are at the end today, when the century of Bismark, at whose gate the Hegelian life stands like the thought before the deed, has collapsed [...] When the edifice of a world collapses, the ideas that had given birth to it, the dreams that were woven through it are buried under the debris.[5]

If the First World War signalled the inevitable summary of a philosophy bound to the nation-state 'as the image of the actuality of reason', in Hegel's famous formulation[6] – indeed, if the war was to finally confirm the long overdue fate of an ideal and bloodless reason in the very real and bloody death of Europe's millions – then only a turn against the 'concept of 1800'[7] (at once the highest peak and ultimate redundancy of Rosenzweig's Hegel) could re-orient the questions laid down by philosophy. Where the philosophical repudiations of Martin Buber, Ernst Bloch, Walter Benjamin, George Lukács and Gershom Scholem were imagined along with a variety of political and Messianic radicalisms, as Anson Rabinbach charts the ethos of the late Wilhemine German-Jewry, Rosenzweig's task stands under its own sign of historical redemption.[8] It meant reinvigorating theology without abandoning the philosophical merits of modernity, rejecting the morbidity of an older idealism and initiating, in its stead, 'The New Thinking' (*Das Neue Denken*): a novel methodological mix of religious faith and reason able to engage more directly with the particulars of finite, circumstantial existence.[9] A 'redemption-in-the-world',[10] a combination of belief *and* knowledge (*Glauben und Wissen*) or the supreme facticity of what he calls an 'absolute empiricism'[11] – for Rosenzweig, the world exploded by the war demanded both.

But if throwing a 'fragment of the ahistorical … in the middle of history' is Rosenzweig's challenge to the temporality of historical process – of 'a volition thrusting past a compulsion and becoming another compulsion'– its implications are fundamentally spatial. It involves living in the cracks of a national imagination and in a realm set apart from the violence of state formation: one structured in the absence of sovereign territory, or rather outside the temporal consciousness that Western thought has shaped as that space. Being in the middle, then, is not just distinguishable from those more attenuated orientations – the abstraction of origin and aim, the arithmetic of first and last – that characterize the language and legitimations of world history. It is the qualitative experience of a Judaic spatiality and, for Rosenzweig, the ground of its distinction. Indeed, conceived at the very moment when conventional dreams of Jewish self-determination were being prospectively realized, Rosenzweig's ('ahistorical') middle emerges as a kind of entreaty, reawakening the contradictions of an ancient space precisely to caution against its new secular solutions. In the 'Germ Cell' (the *Urzelle*) of the *Star* written in November 1917,[12] in the days following the publication of the Balfour Declaration, he indirectly invokes the exilic desert as a model of the incomplete and incompleting.

> The concept of order of this world is […] not the universal, neither the *arche* nor the *telos*, neither the natural or the historical unity, but rather the singular, the event, *not beginning or end, but rather middle of the world*.

From the beginning as well as from the end the world is 'infinite,' from the beginning, infinite in space toward the end, infinite in time. Only from the centre does there arise a bounded home in an unbounded world, *a patch of ground between four tent pegs that can be posted further and further out.*[13]

(last emphasis added)

In Part 3, Book 1 of the *Star* – the only part of this philosophical-theological labyrinth that deals exclusively with Judaism – the spatiality of the middle (that provisional yet delimited *patch of ground between four tent pegs*) emerges to unhinge the defences of *arche* and *telos*, countering the continuum of linear time and its imbrication in the structures of territorial statehood. Indeed, if 'all worldly history is about expansion,'[14] then what distinguishes Rosenzweig's 'middle' is a space that refuses state formation precisely because it refuses the calculus of historical time. There is, in short, no geopolitical principle of nation or sovereign territory – no boundary or border-drawing, no 'demarcating [of] a parcel of land and the definition of mine, yours, and his'[15] – without a corresponding mode of temporalization. In the preface to a proposed 1918 monograph that, according to Paul Mendes-Flohr, was intended to accompany his doctoral study of Hegel, the spatial content of historical time is made clear. Playing off the classical geographic principle of *ökumene* (the known, inhabited, humanized world) and opposing it with the call of *thalatta, thallata* ('the sea, the sea' which, as Xenophon tells us, is the cry of Cyrus' exhausted troops in sight of the Black Sea), Rosenzweig defines the first border as the commencement of world history, and its forward momentum as the border's 'ever-renewed' extension.[16] Here, an initial spatial act does not merely demarcate, define, situate. It establishes a precedent and thus also the procurements which that precedent makes, and repeatedly remakes, for the future. Thus, Rosenzweig's first border not only cues the progressive unfolding of epochs, institutions and events, but sets the tempo of a particular durability: instating a foundation that the future is bound to recite or restate, a primary habitat settled and capable of being infinitely revisited.

2

All embedded moments, as Jacques Derrida reminds us in his extended commentary on Walter Benjamin's *Critique of Violence*, entail a 'performative force',[17] one that is also always a reiterative one. For Derrida, the violence that establishes law is thus inseparable from the violence that promises to maintain it. What confirms the 'mystical foundation' of its authority is that it

> belongs to the structure that [...] founds what ought to be conserved, conservable, promised to heritage and tradition. [...] Thus it inscribes the possibility of repetition at the heart of the originary. [...] Position is already iterability, a call for self-preserving repetition.[18]

For Rosenzweig, a similar commitment to repeatability underwrites a historicist distribution of time and territory. On the one hand, the specific target of Rosenzweig's attack is the principle of historical progress and the laws, wars and revolutions that fulfil it. For Hegel, of course, it is 'history as the world's court of judgement', in Schiller's phrase, which ultimately determines the meaning of events; through the triumph or demise of willed enterprises, it is history that judges which of them is adequate to the unfolding of universal reason. On the other, as Stéphane Mosès points out, for Rosenzweig, the recent geopolitical cataclysms of Europe had already judged – and decisively condemned – Hegel.[19]

It is against this background that the *Star* sets about reversing every impetus of temporal succession and its historicist variants implicated in the inauguration and augmentation of territory. Thus, to 'calculate the years of [one's] own chronology',[20] as Rosenzweig writes, is not only proper to the 'ploughed in'[21] nature of national historical life: the ways in which to live historically means to share in the vitality of land, entrusting oneself to the soil and the prerogatives of the 'soil's dominion, territory', 'appropriate[ing] from its permanence a guarantee of [one's] own permanence.'[22] It is also this temporal assurance which supplies the autochthon's answer to life's discordant flows: capturing time's contingencies, clotting its 'uncurbed'[23] movements, stifling its singularities, 'confining [its flow] to stagnancy',[24] in order to make the historical time of the state possible. It means investing land and territory, institutions, languages and customs with the obligation to repeatability, damming up the changeable currents of time with 'standstills, small stations, crammed times',[25] punctuating the running stream of things so as to announce the very *advent of an interruption*, decreeing that 'now something is suddenly there that persists'.[26]

But the stalling of time is only the state's 'first word'.[27] Sooner or later rivers and coursings resume, contingencies resurface, life bursts the banks of the law's persistence, and 'that which lasts [law] and that which changes [life] seem to separate'. At which point sovereign authority 'raises its sword anew'[28]: it 'drops into the current of time', it 'masterfully seizes the moment, and every following moment' as it repeatedly strains to repair the lapse between law and life: resuturing them 'according to its will and its ability',[29] constraining the unprecedented by converting it into the principle and promising it to iteration. Thus the state comes to 'hang its law over alteration'.[30] It 'takes [the dissensus between life and law] in hand; in fact it is nothing other than this solving, resolved every moment, of the contradiction'.[31] In short, state-time, for Rosenzweig – what Eric L. Santner calls its 'sovereign temporalization'[32] – depends on a continual rebinding of life to the law, replying at every instant to the unruliness of their division. The result is an annulment of change in the depleting of time, submitting life to the empty ferocity of the state's lawful successions.

Under the sign of *Natural History* (*Naturgeschichte*), Walter Benjamin was later to describe the voids of historicism in similar terms: as the enervation of time paradoxically dedicated to its lifeless endurance, the temporal indifference of objects and events which, drained of their vitality, are ceaselessly, incurably – *chronically* – revived anew. Anticipating Benjamin's *Theses on the Philosophy of History* (1940), Rosenzweig similarly decries a time chained to its own extensions:

> Here events rule over time and not the reverse. Epoch is that which stands between its before and after; little does it care how many years the chronicle assigns to it; each epoch weighs the same whether it has lasted centuries or decades or only years. Events govern time here by marking their notches in it.[33]

At its foundation, then, Rosenzweig's 'law in the State'[34] is not a matter of reason, or reason's proscriptions and allowances alone. It is, primarily, a matter of temporality. It arises out of the marking of a precedent able to be repeated: transforming the singular or excessive *once* into the successive *once more*, eliminating discontinuity, encircling the 'contradiction of old and new by the violent renewal of the old, conferring upon the new the lawful force of the old'.[35] The ruinous life of nations, empires, regimes, ideologies: for Rosenzweig, all fall under the 'martial spell'[36] of time coerced into renewal; all are defined, in Benjamin's subsequent terms, by the 'law-making' and 'law-preserving'[37] tautology of foundation, conservation and re-foundation. In Rosenzweig's words:

> Since the State is violent and not merely lawful, it remains at life's heels. This is the meaning of all violence, that it founds new law. It is not a disavowal of the law, as one probably thinks, fascinated by its revolutionary conduct, but on the contrary its foundation. But a contradiction is hidden in the idea of a new law. Law is as regards its essence old law. Now it shows itself as what violence is: the renewer of old law. In the violent act law continuously turns into new law. And the State is therefore equally as much lawful and violent, refuge of the old law and source of the new; and in this double shape [...]

the State places itself above the mere flowing off of the life of the people. [...] At every moment the State violently settles the contradiction between preservation and renewal, old and new law [...] These moments confined by the State are therefore authentic 'hours' of the people's life that of its own accord knows no hours.[38]

One of the guiding intentions of *The Star of Redemption* is to suggest the ways in which Judaism, 'remain[ing] always foreign and annoying to the State',[39] opposes the calculated alliance of time and territory, history and sovereignty, historicism and the political-theological resolution of contradictions. Since the task of institutional and juridical authority is to press time into iterability – to enable the origin 'to repeat itself originarily', in Derrida's words[40] – it follows that *Judensein* ('Jewish-being', in Rosenzweig's Heideggerian idiom) is distinguished by its alternative conception of time. Indeed, in his 'New Thinking', Rosenzweig identifies a *need for time* or, which amounts to the same thing, 'the taking of time seriously':

To need time means: not to be able to presuppose anything, to have to wait for everything, to be dependent on the other for what is ours.[41]

When a beginning is no longer predictive and there is no end or abstraction to carry it forward towards an assessment, time ceases to be a formal speculation and arises only as a present contingency. And to be present and contingent is not to repeat or to live on as (deadened) persistence or perseverance. It is to step onto the risk of relations, to be exposed and receptive to the urgencies of intervention, exchange, translation. And so, for Rosenzweig, *being-in-time* becomes a mode of *being-in-relation*. Both set in motion an orientation other than (sovereign) predicate or signifying proposition. Both produce a space in which neither side of the border – origin and end, subject and object – rests on the stability of self-enclosure. And both transpire only in a non-permanent middle, 'on the narrow plank of its momentariness'.[42] To 'need time', to heed time, to take it 'seriously', then, is not only to commit to the disjointedness internal to temporal existence. It is also a commitment consciously turned towards an externality, a stranger, a neighbour, another. It means installing alterity in the middle of the moment, allowing for its appearance *in* and *as* time itself. Which is finally to say, Rosenzweig's version of Judaic anti-historicism does more than invert a model of progressivist history; it arises out of a spatiality set apart from autochthony. 'The tribal legend of the [Jewish] people', he clearly asserts, 'begins otherwise than with indigenousness'.[43] Always and only provisional, never preassigned because 'originally' displaced or misplaced, such an untimeliness withdraws Judaism from the linear violence of the law as it disrupts the self-identity of the subject: unhinging its normative coordinates, revealing it in its encounter with others in a series of new and ever-renewed moments. As such, relations – with specific others as much as with scenes of an unspecifiable otherness – are not just always and infinitely possible. They are also occasioned at every turn, they can be expected *at any time*. Perhaps right now? Perhaps 'in the next moment'?[44] 'As early as today?'[45] Being constantly vigilant to what might be unbound at such moments, a-waiting the unforeseen energies condensed there, is simultaneously our endless and immediate concern.[46] Present impossibility, in short, is the very ordeal in which the 'middle' is located. If no historical or empirical situation can conceive new capacities, none excludes the dare that now, *this time*, something else, something hidden, unbidden, might happen.

Thus, *relationality by way of temporality* – relationality arising from the rents of time, from the momentariness of the 'middle' – makes us more than the accretions of history, and more than bearers of an identity defined by the usual part-whole accounting of social formation. There is both a surfeit and an insufficiency at the heart of all 'seriously' temporalized things. For if Rosenzweig identifies a new 'need for time',[47] it is a need that can never find true release, a requirement whose tensions must overshoot or fall short of any realization. Indeed, against the periodization of 'eras, epochs, great moments' – all those sovereign summations which objectivize time or render it 'an immovable thing'[48] – it is a need for life and relations lived in the surplus – and along with the stakes – of today, in an excessive and singular state, in an exilic 'middle' without settlement or consistency.

3

A time without prediction, an identity without indigeneity, an existence that insists on the spacing of a 'middle': so, for Rosenzweig, does a Judaic time exclude itself from the horizon of a historical place or, more correctly, from any *territorial conception of time in the form of the state*. One can imagine all sorts of objections that would denounce Rosenzweig's distinction, or at least be troubled about their consequences. Certainly, positioning Judaism outside the time of the state means confronting the complications which arise from the halachic assumption of Judaic election and exemplarity.[49] Conversely, positing the enrootedness of other historical and political peoples as the source of their strength and survival – the objects of territorial statehood, for Rosenzweig, are paradoxically both constraining and 'life-bestowing'[50] – means that *The Star of Redemption* comes close to reproducing a standard trope of anti-Semitism: the Jew as a serially accursed subject, a 'fossilized' form irreconcilable with the deployments of History – the very stray and skeletal figure that Hegel, in his early theological writings, defines by a finite and *a fortiori* obsolescence, its historical function spent in refusing the *place* of Spirit.[51]

The Jew as ahistorical wanderer is the fundamental typology for Rosenzweig, too, and for not dissimilar reasons. One of the distinctive features of Judaic identity, he writes, is that 'it looks at itself in about the same way as the outside world thinks of it'. As he continues in his notes on the medieval Spanish poet Judah ha-Levi:

> A whole world asserts that the Jewish people is outcast [...] and the Jewish people does not itself, in some assertion of its own, refute this dictum, but instead merely confirms it.[52]

Endorsed from the 'inside', however, Rosenzweig's outcast Jew leads us somewhere very different. It answers the injury of an 'outside' reproach by rewriting rather than renouncing it, reshuffling the crudeness of Hegel's indictment to uphold something of its furtive truth. Thus, if Rosenzweig does little to dispute the myth of the Wandering Jew, this is not because he simply accepts, affirms or fails to oppose it. Still less is this a heroic exoneration, an internal aggrandizement of Judaic landlessness, or the kind of self-seeking admission of lack that Slavoj Žižek describes as 'a self-denigration that secretly asserts its contrary'.[53] Rather, in Rosenzweig's hands, myth itself becomes a form of *exposition*: it is not the evasion of a vulnerability or endangerment but the brink at which such things come to be enunciated, amplified, *exposed*. The distinction is important. For, whereas the reductive forces of myth-making are usually directed at an overcoming of contradiction – specifically, for Rosenzweig, the 'contradictions between national characteristics and world history, home and faith, earth and heaven,'[54] – then his Judaism has no need of myth precisely because it remains outside the 'vital drives'[55] of those antimonies that require a resolution. As an identity, it emerges only with its refusal to substitute the excesses of the moment, the middle, for any (mythic) 'power over time,'[56] and only along with the unravelling of national life defined by its 'daily, apparently conclusive, solving of all contradictions'.[57] In short, Rosenzweig's ahistorical Jew establishes its own credentials. Even as myth, it brings no relief from anxiety. On the contrary, it raises the stakes of time and territory and points up the crises of both.

It also sheds light on those instances in which Rosenzweig connects ancient narratives to the condition of a modern Jewish diaspora. In a letter addressed to his cousin, Hans Ehrenberg, later to become an eminent Protestant theologian, Rosenzweig refers to the Pharisees of the immediate post-exilic period whose refusal of membership to a national community, he suggests, might find a correspondence with the anti- or non-Zionist German Jewry of his own time.

The prophets observed an objective critical attitude toward their own state, the Pharisees toward the states of the Diaspora. In both cases it was really objectivity, not negation: it was an attitude of non-identification. The nineteenth-century destroyed both these forms of objectivity (the Pharisean in practice, the prophets' in theory) by falsifying into cosmopolitanism what, in reality, was a revolutionary criticism of their own state. It is a matter of course that Zionism finds itself impelled to restore the attitude of prophetic criticism. But it is not certain whether, and to what extent, Pharisean critical objectivity can be re-established for the Diaspora which persists even in Palestine.[58]

If Pharisean practice – and its nineteenth-century nationalist misappropriation as cosmopolitanism – refers to an ancient social movement, its problem of non-identification is wholly immediate. More than merely citing an earlier separatist attitude, Rosenzweig brings it to bear on a context in which the theoretical status of both liberal-assimilation and political Zionism posed a fundamental challenge to any idea of a de-territorialized identity. Like other German Jews working in the brief, yet vital, inter-war period of parliamentary democracy, the question of whether cultural or spiritual Zionism implied any claim to land and nation was itself inextricably linked to a complex of debates over the viability of Judaism's separation from, or participation in, a German national polity. Was Jewish faith compatible with the tenets of German idealism? Were German national culture and national Self, even in their high Fichtean sense, themselves exemplary sites of cosmopolitanism? Or had the recent horrors of European militancy revealed the ultimate paucity of liberal-assimilationism? All these concerns invest Rosenzweig's Pharisean allusion with a specific charge. Like the internal endorsement of incompleteness – Rosenzweig's 'non-mythic' Wandering Jew – it insists on a non-identification at the kernel of Judaic identity; more than enlarging the terms of historical inclusion, it derives a historical principle from alienated existence itself. As we shall see, for Rosenzweig a critical (Pharisean) attitude to the state depends on various kinds of temporal and spatial subtraction. It requires the temporality of a 'not yet there' (*noch nicht da*) that cannot be a collective 'becoming' and the persistence of an unachieved space bound to the pressures of waiting and wandering.[59] Only a redemption from the defences of national history – a historicity 'in other-than-a-historicist-sense', in Dana Hollander's phrasing – could finally unbind time from the demands of territory. Only with an existence thought of as exilic might a new kind of identity be imagined: one that neither claims nor rejects the appeal of territorial settlement but makes the faulty attachments of settling most visible.

4

Rosenzweig died in 1929, and thus too early to encounter the possibility of the National Socialist state organized for genocide. Nor could he elaborate his position on the founding of a Jewish homeland in 1948. But, as a member of that community of late Wilhemine and Weimar German-Jews, his revaluing of exile, as I have suggested, directly engages the fraught and, often highly polemicized, struggles over German-Jewish self-identity. For Hermann Cohen, heir to the culture of eighteenth-century Mendelssohnian assimilation and mentor to Rosenzweig's generation, the question of a split German-Jewish psyche was answered in the recognition that Kantian rationalism (the key concepts of the autonomy of universal law, liberty and duty) offered the deepest affinity with ethical precepts derived from Judaic historical scripture and liturgical practice. In his famous 1915 essay 'Deutschtum und Judentum' ('Germanism and Judaism') Cohen's wartime defence of Jewish allegiance to the German state, the confluence of enlightened reason and monotheistic religion were not only set in philosophical terms. Resituating Jewish faith within German culture, and proposing that an 'inner community' of a rational social ethics obtained between them, the line that Cohen draws from Plato to Maimonides also contained a kind of noumenal vision: of a German nation able to affirm the logic of a double origin and so exert the 'original power' of its cosmopolitan vocation. As he writes in the second version of his essay:

> Maybe – who can foretell the course of history? – it will one day be considered not among the least of its glories that Germany not only granted protective and civil rights to its Jews but also made them part of that spirit which informs German science, German art, and all other expressions of German creativity [...] to the benefit of the entire world.[60]

While later highly critical of Cohen's position, Rosenzweig continues to address the nature of the '*and*', imbuing the conjunction between Germanism and Judaism with the same uncanniness – precisely, the Freudian register of intimate estrangement – which, in the *Star*, he invokes to distinguish Judaism from the territorial orientations of other historical and political communities. Put another way, if the sovereign occupancy of land is inimical to Rosenzweig's conception of Judaism, then the same kind of disconnected connection is traceable in his reading of the elusive '*and*' that dramatizes the condition of Jewish European modernity. Here the conjunction is not the bifurcated subject of an earlier Enlightenment tradition – where, for Rosenzweig, the conjunction was not an *'and'* at all, but 'an insidious "or"',[61] a false choice given by assimilation's craven apologetics. Nor, as with Cohen, does Rosenzweig's *'and'* intend any equation between Judaic theology and German humanism – a potentially 'tasty dish', he concedes, but one whose integrative, and near nationalist, sentiment 'is really no more than a caricature': a transposition 'to the intellectual level ... of the social Germanism' exemplified by an aspiring, and essentially Europeanist, Jewish middle class.[62]

The *'and'*, for Rosenzweig, is an emphatic double bind: not a matter of Judaism's detachment from, or enjoining to, a national identity but the craggy facts of living in insoluble tension with it. Anything less than living the disagreements of Judaism and Germanism, any dissolving of the disjunctive *'and'* – 'the basic word of all experience, and the word the philosopher's tongue is not used to', he asserts in 'The New Thinking'[63] – would approach a modern form of idolatory, would even conclude in a form of death.[64] Writing to the art historian, Rudolf Hallo, in January 1923, Rosenzweig makes the analogy explicit.[65]

> I am perhaps especially innocent with respect to the problem of *Deutschtum* and *Judentum*. I believe that my return to Judaism [*Verjudung*] has not made me a worse but a better German. I do not view the generation before us as better Germans ... Were someone to suspend me between tenterhooks, tearing me in two pieces, I would surely know with which of these two halves my heart ... would go; I also know that I would not survive the operation.[66]

To be Jewish *and* German, as Rosenzweig insists, entails a fundamental dissymmetry in relation – a 'relationless relation' in Derrida's reading of him[67] – in which secular history might be addressed within the horizon of Judaism but without the ground of coincidence, congruity or benevolence. Being a participating citizen of a surrounding *Umwelt* and a member of a uniquely metahistorical community – 'both at the same time'[68] – thus signals less any simultaneity than an identity, *and a temporality*, without agreement, growth or any quantitative continuity of passage. In this sense, the interminable impasse of the '*and*' functions much like the 'broken middle', to revisit Gillian Rose's description of the space between the philosophical cities of Athens and Jerusalem. Available to being neither mended in origin nor ameliorated by any ultimate aggregation, it stands between Jewishness and Germanness as the mark of the irresolvable, the discontinuous, the unassimilable. Like the exilic desert, that space of 'anoriginal' origin,[69] it has to do with everything set apart from the violence of foundation and conservation which lies at the ruthlessly reiterative core of sovereign relations. In short, Rosenzweig's recalcitrant '*and*' does more than open up or aerate the hyphenated identity of German-Jewry in the early decades of the twentieth century. Re-locating the source to the middle – or better, understanding the middle as the source of Judaic space itself – it also enters the estranged as a term of belonging: not cancelling the dissymmetry of periphery and centre but establishing a space in which provisionality might itself be allowed an identity. In this, the middleness of the '*and*' also forms part of a critical uncoupling that sees through Zionist claims to Jewish territoriality.

> For the eternal people, the homeland never becomes its own in that sense; it is not permitted to sleep at home; it always remembers the lack of constraints on the traveller and is a knight truer to his land when he lingers on his travels and [...] longs for the homeland it has left than in the times when he is at home. The land is in the deepest sense its own only as a land of longing, as – holy land. And this is why for it, even when it is at home [...] this full proprietorship of the homeland is disputed; it is itself only a stranger and tenant in its land.[70]

Thus the land, even if inhabited, never quite 'takes place'. Like the '*and*' that at once entails and holds apart, it is a permanently suspended promise of place – another space, precisely, a *holy* land – where longing is not any privation defined by the absence of territory but the very commitment to such a condition. It is the resurgence of a founding absence experienced as 'ever new' and 'in the moment',[71] a future incompletion which is already, 'anoriginally' there. From this perspective, Zionism is not only a normative political ideology, a provincial attachment, 'merely one more root gripping the earth in addition to all others'.[72] It deprives Judaism of its metahistorical vocation as the sole guarantee of its eternity. Writing to Gertrud Oppenheim in May 1917, Rosenzweig's hostility to the investment of a legal and political home for Judaism is given in just these terms:

> The Zionists will attain [their] goal by managing to found their Serbia or Bulgaria or Montenegro in Palestine ... [But they] will be lost once they lose their touch with the Diaspora. Their contact with the Diaspora is the only thing that makes them hold fast to their goal, which means, however, that they must be *homeless in time*, and remain wanderers *even over there*.[73] (emphasis added)

To 'be homeless in time ... even over there' clearly upends the obligatory positings and counter-positings of national affirmation: the uprooted as the opposite of the embedded, separation as the opposite of attachment, exile as the opposite of home. However, if we take dispersion as the spacing of the middle then it is no longer an injurious realm – a depleted, minimized existence that might yet be inflated or gathered within the sum of a greater communion. Rather than a remedial temporality of a fall and a restoration, being 'in-the-middle' opens onto a new possibility – one that might ground a polity in which landlessness becomes its own form of self-preservation, and statelessness is turned into an alternative kind of sovereignty.[74] Thus, for example, when the Bible narrates the Exodus narrative, as when the Passover Haggadah commands that we annually retell it ('every individual is supposed to regard the Exodus out of Egypt as if he himself had also gone out'[75]), at issue is less a form of memorialization – precisely, the sovereign exercise of 'self-conserving repetition'[76] – than of entering into a fundamental play of tenses. Likewise, even those theological verdicts usually set into the endmost or utmost of times, the Day of Atonement and the Day of Judgement, are handed over to the immediacy of the present moment. If these are moments of profound attestation, they evidence only the most ordinary, incomplete reckoning; what is yearly returned is never a final word but only 'this the "latest" judgement'.[77]

Rosenzweig's time, then, is not a reassembly of elements already known, or a composition of conditions able to be prefigured, and accounted for, by any structural frame. It is the synchrony of things at once immemorial and prophetic, the singular insistence of a past event shot through with the 'unpredictability of the brand-new'.[78] Here, where there is no 'hiding behind history'[79] or where the place of history is itself misplaced, one does not go back to a beginning in time but experiences it, at each instant, with the uniqueness *of* a first time. Here, it is pure contemporaneity that comes to persist, not chronology. Here, separation from the order of 'origin' comes again (every year), re-instating ('now and forever'[80]) an absence always already entailed. In short, if beginning with the middle means sustaining the originary displacement that Rosenzweig's *Judensein* demands, it also determines the temporality of exile: of being outside a horizon of (lawful) expectation and within a 'not-yet happening now',[81] amid a homelessness that refuses temporal prediction even as it intensifies – and, more, *infinitizes* – the time of desire.[82]

5

The crucial point, I have been arguing, is that to deny Jews a land of birth or a participation in history is not to negate the idea of origin *per se*; it is to recast its spatial location. Not predicative and therefore non-permanent, without precedent and therefore unrepeatable, to be in the middle is, in effect, to be without the defensive, and ultimately violent, attachments of ethnic and national histories. Or better, rejecting what Santner describes as the state's 'compulsion to repeat',[83] Judaism's exilic middle enables it to enter into the unguarded, un-commanded midst of things – *beyond* the reiterations of a political temporality and thus *into* a space sustained in an infinitely sudden, infinitely present tense.

Importantly, with its stress on what might be suddenly seized upon in the present there is nothing in Rosenzweig's philosophy of 'waiting' that guarantees an ideal end or proffers an Ever or Elsewhere. While hope, like longing, might well appear in singular moments, there is nothing in its constitutive incompleteness that harbours a worldly telos or might be guided by necessity. As an *Augenblick* – literally, a glance or blink of the eye[84] – the ever-present, ever-renewed moment of the middle cannot expand to envision its fulfilment or include the gradational steps of arriving there. This, then, is not that Idealist (and nationalist) knowledge which, for Rosenzweig, sets out to rationalize those promises that theology had traditionally circumscribed to the realm of belief. And it is not any idea of Utopia in its usual sense: neither any move towards a fated, transcendent condition, nor a hoped-for event whose required or compensatory elements must be stipulated in advance.

Waiting, in short, 'does not posit anything' or 'create anything outside itself'.[85] It does not petition or postdate. Unlike the warlike time of the state – as unlike the zealot's prayer – it does not reckon with a future, with duration, or the maximalist's 'once and for all'.[86] Without temporal jurisdiction, waiting brings time to a halt, placing it in the service of a contingent and empirical humanity, making the future not a historical category but an activity folded into the terms of the present. It is the potential in-breaking of a time that cannot be prepared for, an 'opening up of something locked'[87] that makes itself present in the ordeal of *this* moment, *this* action. Conversely if, as Rosenzweig insists, knowledge and relations *take time* and therefore can never arrive at, or be restricted to, essential definitions, then what we do *not yet* know and what has *not yet* been conceived are vital to the possibility of change – or less militantly, waiting means staying attuned to the conditions in which change may appear.

Hence, Rosenzweig's struggle with Hegel. For *The Star of Redemption* is not only a critique of Hegelian state formation but an argument that, in any model of temporal succession, nothing radically new, irregular, or as-yet unthought can really occur. Indeed, to the extent that historicism annuls the unpredictable, Rosenzweig declares the history of all modern European nationalisms to encompass a kind of eschatological drama. Collapsing the borders of the immanent and transcendent, conflating the previously separate entities of factuality and belief, thus does the modern state 'fulfil what was promised in revelation'.[88] Such an eschatology not only gives the state the temporal form it is reaching for; it involves the political in an otherworldly endurance, allowing it to press on 'to eternity step by step'.[89] For Rosenzweig, the outcome is more than a concept of the nation-state shaped by the spirit of Christianity. It extends the biblical notion of Jewish election to all national peoples, transforming nationalism into a modern form of divine 'chosenness'. However secular they may appear, when ordered by points of foundation and destination, all world-historical 'peoples are chosen people, and all modern wars are holy wars', as Mosès puts it.[90] In Rosenzweig's words:

Nationalism expresses not merely the people's belief that they come *from* God [...] but that they go *to* God. [N]ow peoples do have this belief, and hence 1789 is followed by 1914–1917, and yet more 'from and to's.[91]

Thus does the logic of the eschaton – beginnings and ends, 'from's and to's' – become institutionalized in the guise of the nation-state. In experience, as in thought, however, 'to wait' is not to stop; it is to go on living and to go on thinking. 'Living time knows nothing of points', Rosenzweig insists.[92] 'As little as one could just as well begin a [...] war with a peace treaty [...] or life with death, one must learn to keep waiting until the moment comes, and not skip any moment.'[93] So conceived, being in the equivocal middle – in time lived, time spent – becomes central to *The Star*: not just a foil to the divinization and determinism of history but a fidelity to the 'pure factuality'[94] of existence, of a life defined by inconsistency because it is known only 'through and within the [finite] boundaries of the human'.[95]

It is precisely such a time that is illuminated by the 'star of redemption'. Far from adhering to some remote salvific event, Rosenzweig's star is a thoroughly proximate phenomenon. It is a 'this-wordly' incursion, a present incandescence, a kind of *exegesis of the present*. What it reveals is not any path on the long way to eternity – its route is neither the ever-onward 'way of the cross'[96] nor, as in Rosenzweig's Hegel, the course of dialectic ascent. It is, rather, the labour of rescuing or 'redeeming' a moment; setting apart a conditional happening within the actual, and actualizing, limits of time; enriching the present with its capacity for initiation – but alarmingly, unpreparedly, inconclusively so. Here, in other words, it is *kairos* not *chronos* that ushers time back in, marking the entrance of a new opportunity, or the recognition and reception of a critical demand. Weaker than a declaration or decree but perhaps strong enough to light up the cracks and gaps in the 'what is' and the 'already known', it is a 'sudden and provisional light'[97] in which history stands unhinged, an unassimilable – even *miraculous* – radiation of possibility within the horizon of profane existence. Indeed, like the divine miracle which he carefully distinguishes from the wonders of pagan magic, Rosenzweig's 'star' promises nothing; it carries no propositional content. Yet neither is it defined by its inexplicability nor is it given as the reward of 'willed prayer'.[98] It is a matter of its timing, its temporality. Even the *Book of Exodus*, he reminds us in 'A Note on a Poem by Judah ha-Levi', 'explains the parting of the Red Sea *post eventum* as something "natural"':

> Every miracle can be explained – after the event. Not because the miracle is no miracle, but because explanation is explanation. Miracle always occurs in the present and, at most, in the future. One can implore and experience it, and while the experience is still present, one can feel gratitude. When it no longer seems a thing of the present, all there is left to do is to explain [...]. The east wind has probably swept bare the ford of the Red Sea hundreds of time, and will do so again hundreds of times. But that it did at this moment when the people in their distress set foot in the sea – that is the miracle.[99]

The question of the divine event, then, is less how something 'comes to pass' – a matter of knowable causation – than 'that it comes when it does' – a practice of temporalization proper. Much like the desert scene of *Exodus* itself, it emerges less as a contravention of any temporal continuum than as an engagement with time's plurality, with a redoubling of experience such that 'what only a moment before was a coveted future becomes present and actual'.[100] Unlike the time of the state, Rosenzweig's miracle does not entail a curtailment, a blockage of flows, a violation of the ordinary and everyday. It is neither a phantastical deviation from the domain of the sensible nor an executive or exceptional power over time, whether sanctioned by a divine or politically sovereign force. Rosenzweig's miracle entails the opposite: an intensification of inhabited life, an exacerbated (but unexceptional, un-exempted, un-preserved) present, a sudden wedge – a *revealing, a presentation* – in the world whose sole precondition is the readiness to be alive to the contingencies obscured there.[101]

Here, we are far from relations as they signify indifferently – *intemporally* – in a system in which the succession of one state by another performs the tautologies of a legal-historical order. For, if Rosenzweig's miracle is about time as it pours into the present and is borne by it – or, if the revelatory arises in the excessive 'middle' of things – it is also consonant with the exilic desert with which this book began. It was along with this *an-original* scene of Exodus, as the Introduction suggested, that Judaic space emerges as a 'broken' or non-national middle: less a space beyond or without the time of history and territory than one which exposes a disordering, an un-containment, internal to them. With Rosenzweig in mind, the exilic desert – its waiting, its wandering, its unbidden possibilities – becomes a new kind of critical condition: one not merely located at the 'an-origin' of Judaism but gleamed in the obscurities of its ever-renewed present.

6

If sustaining such a middle means living incompletely, this also means that Jerusalem is never simply the antithesis of Athens, as an older geography of philosophy has it, and nor is exile an archaism absorbed by the consolidations of modernity. Instead, all coincide. How might we further explore the potential of the coincidence? By way of concluding this chapter and easing into the next, I move on from Rosenzweig and the exilic desert to focus on Walter Benjamin's analysis of the nineteenth-century city. I do this not so much to point up the affinities between the two but to read Benjamin in an allegorical mode, the very approach he champions and on which he most often insists. As allegory, might Benjamin's urban topography describe its own version of a fractured, un-mended 'middle'? Might we read it as a 'third city' between – and within – the formal divisions of Athens and Jerusalem, as Gillian Rose has it? Or, in my preferred terms, as a secular site in which an ancient Judaic space unexpectedly reappears? Indeed, if the desert and the city are no longer taken as two opposing models of thought proper to two discrete epochs of historical time and their distinct arrangements of space, then Benjamin's nineteenth-century city not only offers a framework for thinking the fragmented nature of modernity. It becomes the scene of an anterior and alternative incompletion: the Judaic desert, the chronically unfinished, accidentally re-actualized and rendered anew.

In *The Arcades Project*, his masterwork on nineteenth-century Paris, Benjamin offers his famous account of urban modernity in which time is simultaneously elevated and devalued.[102] Convolute M9.4 cites a passage in which the German-Jewish writer and journalist Ferdinand Lion describes the nature of the city's spatial and temporal shocks.

> The most heterogeneous temporal elements [...] coexist in the city. If we step from an eighteenth-century house into one from the sixteenth-century, we tumble down a slope of time. Right next door stands a Gothic church, and we sink to the depths. A few steps farther, we are in a street from out of the early years of Bismarck's rule [...] and once again climbing the mountains of time. Whoever sets foot in the city feels caught up as in a web of dreams, where the most remote past is linked to the events of today. One house allies with another, no matter what period they come from [...]. The climactic points of the city are its squares: here, from every direction, converge not only numerous streets but all the streams of their history [...]. Things which find no expression in political events, or find only minimal expression, unfold in the cities: they are a superfine instrument, responsive as an Aeolian harp.[103]

Clearly it is not the absence of temporal markers but their incomprehensible excess that defines Benjamin's city: transgressing the boundaries of the historical record, unfixing the distinctions that might localize time, puzzling any attempt to find out where the past might fit. Even the city square is not only the royal point where the phantoms of vanished histories collide. It is also where multiple temporalities contract and accelerate, reversing any pull towards generality or causality. Never quite proceeding and never quite deriving, there is no street or stream in Benjamin's city which is comparable to the one that comes before it or to the one that flows from it. Piled up with fragments and therefore without goals, teeming with significations that can never become realizations, *The Arcades Project* tempts historical time and thwarts its conciliations. If this stages a structural complexity it also enables the peculiar irresolutions of this materialist thinker. Thus, even as we strain to intuit some prefigured or final temporal propriety from which Benjamin's city has slipped away, we encounter only the malfunction of the remnant, the vestige, the remainder. Where contemporaneous modern poetics might see such temporal leftovers and their juxtapositions as the work of metonymy – the tacit agreement between one term and a generalized other – Benjamin's city involves no such settlement. It is a space that is unlocatable as it divests temporal relations of any ability to congeal into a weighty continuum. Instead it reduces history to its most fugitive expression, its temporal minimum, as it simultaneously sifts it through the gauze of the present. Like Rosenzweig's 'homeless[ness] in time',[104] Benjamin's city turns on similar temporal lawlessness:

> The constructions of [historicism] are comparable to instructions that commandeer the true life and confine it to the barracks. On the other hand: the street insurgence of the anecdote. The anecdote brings things near to us spatially, lets them enter our life [...]. The true method of making things present: to represent them in our space. It represents the strict antithesis to the sort of history which demands 'empathy', which makes everything abstract. 'Empathy': this is what newspaper reading terminates in.[105]

The significance of the passage is twofold. The 'street anecdote' of the city not only opposes the 'commandeering' of chronology in being a speech-act broken off from its chain of prior connections, an obstacle unassimilated to the comprehension of urban history. It also exposes chronology's primary aim: to drain discord, steadily eliminating – through the 'empathetic' transfer or exchange of identity – the jarrings and strangeness of temporal dis-identity. In this, Benjamin's anecdote functions as a kind of middle in Rosenzweig's exilic, incompleting sense. It doesn't just force a break in the subject's experience of time. It drives identity out of the centre of any form – and with it the illusion that anything like a continuity might pertain between thought and its object, part and whole, past and present. Even as it remains undecidable – out-of-joint, agitated, even anachronistic – the anecdote mobilizes the strategic question: How may we see the present – extracted out of chronology, as out of empathic fusion – as at once ancient and insurgently new? How does the moment, the non-historical immediate, time at its most dispossessed, always exceed a totality, shattering its self-preserving identity, detecting within it those stray shards it has been unable quite to dissolve? And what kind of historical awareness might thus be produced?

Any answer to these questions must begin with the recognition that the past, for Benjamin as for Rosenzweig, makes a demand on us now – and calls towards the future – not as a verifiable or retrievable event but as a fracture, an inadequacy, that sustains itself in the pressures of the present. One of the various formulations of that temporal claim takes the form of the allegory, which Benjamin develops in his early study of *The Origin of German Tragic Drama*, written in 1925 and published in 1928 seven years after Rosenzweig's *The Star of Redemption*. Unlike the Romantic symbol in which, for Benjamin, experience comes to be instantly perfected – and the struggle of its communication (falsely) solved – allegory attests, above all, to the indirect referentiality of history: that the past is never fully itself, that it constantly misses itself, that its meaning reveals itself precisely where immediate understanding may not. Which is to say, allegory arises not merely in reanimating a past, balking at its recalcitrant ghosts or laying them to rest. More unnervingly, it arises from the apprehension that the instance of an event and our awareness of it do not necessarily tally, that perceptions are incomplete and truths both belated and overdue, that the historicity of history can be grasped only amid the detritus and deposits secreted in the 'differentia of time'.[106] Most noted in

Benjamin's parade of allegorical figures, it is the ruin, the orphaned fragment, the funereal visage and the death's head which are especially adapted to uncover – that is, to *temporalize* – the structure of historical experience. Here, the actuality of a historical event lies not in the recovery of evidence but in the recognition of its dissolution. Here, the past is charged by an insufficiency that persists, by a lack that makes a claim on us, that points to what is *presently lacking*. Thus stands allegory in Benjamin's account: not just an image of a past but one, which in the belatedness of its presentation, means the resurgence of an original absence, the rousing of a loss, the enlivening of a lack, always already entailed. In allegory's temporal syncopations, too, resides a capacity akin to Rosenzweig's eternal 'star'. Here, lodge the splinters, the scattered sparks, of unanswered pasts: pasts that in the sphere of the actual still await redemption, and a future able to name itself as that instant.

Can we imagine Benjamin's nineteenth-century city as itself a biblical allegory? Might the city attest to the presence of a past predicament and the persistence of its founding fractures? If so, does the real historical index of his urban modernity lie not in itself – in the evidence and identity of its own phenomena – but in its allegorical doubling with another, earlier space: precisely, with the desert of Exodus? To which questions of time we might add a further, methodological one: Might the Benjaminian allegory itself be a peculiar presentation of the un-mended middle? Like Rosenzweig's 'patch of ground between four tent pegs', might it configure a *Judensein* that leads not to any security of territory but exposes the untimely gaps constitutive of it? If this is so we might also revise Rose's assertion, outlined in the Introduction, that to exchange an old Athens for a new Jerusalem is merely the misguided trait of contemporary philosophical scholarship: recasting Judaism within the intrigues of a non-coercive ethics, protecting it from the baleful effects of modern political history.[107] For allegory, as we learn from Benjamin, is neither amiable nor evasive; far from de-historicizing Judaism it serves to keep open and undecided the irreconciliations of time that distinguish Judaic history itself. Moreover, if Rosenzweig's version of Judaism not only fails to be in history but must perform or enact this failure, then Benjaminian allegory might itself be seen as one of its privileged forms. Which is finally to say, allegory does not merely subvert the opposition of past and present, the archaic and the modern, the theological and the secular, the desert and the city. Nor does it contain some kind of causal connection between the two such that the one irreversibly succeeds the other, which it then pledges to commemorate or is somehow fated to preserve. Legible only in its incompletion, apprehended only in its lack of passage and transition, it is thus, via allegory, that we might reposition Judaic exile: locating it in the disorientations that Rosenzweig calls the 'midst of time'[108] and which, in Benjamin's city, is the thwarted space which makes history thinkable.

Of course, neither Rosenzweig nor Benjamin deploys their arguments outside of specific contexts *in* which – that is to say, *against* which – they unfold. Where *The Star of Redemption* – conceived in the trenches of the First World War – ends an idea of history based on a logos that could rationally order the world, *The Arcades Project* – a concatenation of 'exiled' fragments collected by an exile on the eve of the Second World War – is a pre-history of urban modernity itself. In this, Rosenzweig and Benjamin enlist a common renunciation and resource. Both converge on an 'un-corrected' middle, both arise out of a Judaism immemorially attuned to this breach. And the same demand sounds in each. The well-known words are Benjamin's in *Theses on the Philosophy of History* written in early 1940:

> One reason why fascism has a chance is that in the name of progress its opponents treat it as a historical norm. The current amazement that the things we are experiencing are 'still' possible in the twentieth-century is *not* philosophical. This amazement is not the beginning of knowledge – unless it is the knowledge that the view of history which gives rise to it is untenable.[109]

If any response to authoritarianism is possible it depends on entering an alternative relation of time. For the expression of amazement, as Benjamin suggests, is not only 'not philosophical'; in its failure of thought, it remains politically ineffective. While it speaks of perplexity, even wonderment, it does not yet contain the effect of a circuit break, a shock, a jolt. It is not yet an 'awakening': that response which, for Benjamin, is inseparable from the structure of a temporal alarm, requiring that we attend less to the explanatory terms of past history than to its recognition in an explosive now. For Rosenzweig, as this chapter has argued, Judaism *is* this alternative conception of time, a time whose kernel – whose 'germ cell', we may say – is precisely the emphatic presence of the present.

And so the doubled image of the desert as city, or the allegory of the desertified, exilic city. As allegory, it maintains the question of a past that calls towards a future, or of how belatedness itself becomes anticipatory. Also maintained *by it*, however, is a structure of history that will have to be continually displaced if Judaism is to refuse the alliance of identity and autochthony, time and territory. Put another way, the desertified city returns us to the surplus in all that is neither Athens nor Jerusalem and still less any transition between them.[110] Here, the ever-renewed event of Exodus overleaps the time of the nations, re-attesting – with 'very old testament'[111] – not to origin or end but to what becomes possible in the space of the middle.

2

The Second Commandment in the Second Empire

Or, a small theology in Walter Benjamin's city

1

Arnold Schoenberg never completed *Moses und Aron*, the three-act opera that he worked on between 1928 and 1932, shortly before fleeing Austria and finding eventual sanctuary in the United States. Staged as an extended polemic between the biblical brothers, *Moses und Aron* deals, at its most general level, with the principle of monotheism and the problem of its representation. Schoenberg never resolves the problem, for an important structural reason. The logic of the libretto, he found, could not be completed by the musical score. But the unfinished and impaired have another measure. In the last minutes of Scene Five of Act Two, Moses – symbolic Father, bringer of the Law – cannot speak.[1] Against a muted orchestration, his voice scored in a halting bass Sprechstimme, he breaks down in distress: 'Unimaginable God', 'Inexpressible many-sided idea', the strenuousness of any thought shattered by the inability to communicate it. With 'O word, thou word, that I lack', Moses falls silent, along with the opera itself.[2]

If Moses is impotent to convert conceptual substance into symbolic form, or thought into utterance, this is only in part because we witness him struggling with the 'many sided idea' of thematizing a Jewish god: on the one hand, a problem of illegitimacy (the biblical proscription of the image) and, on the other, a problem of formal or logical impossibility (of a god which, being 'uncreated', has no image either).[3] The theological dilemma is indivisible from the musicological one. 'The insoluble contradiction which Schoenberg has taken as his project,' Theodor Adorno writes, 'is also the contradiction of the actual work.'[4] The task, then, is for a compositional mode which might defy the phantom of a reconciled or natural aesthetics, one which might refuse settlement, synthesis and the consolations of the sensuous. All of this means that Moses' maladroit speech, like the opera's fractured form from which it is inseparable, is not just about the encountering of a lack or limit. Nor is it about the frustrated desire to overcome that limit: a frustration given by the assumption that what lies on the other side of Moses' 'slowness of tongue'[5] is a preformed language not yet seized, the fulfilment of a fluency undiscovered, still to come. It is not simply that words wither in Moses' mouth or struggle to attach themselves to sonorous song. At issue is neither any deficiency in subjective expression and nor does Schoenberg refer us backwards or forwards to an ideal speech, to a 'word, thou word' of which a fallen human language is but a stumbling, fretful imitation. On the contrary, the failure is about the necessity of foreclosing any form in which continuity and compensation might appear. It is about an art that determinately negates the temptations of symbolic satisfaction as, in theological terms, it refuses the release of any apparent revelation. In Schoenberg, the two coincide: the song-less stutter is already testimony to gratification's own deficiency; every effort is its own ragged failure. Because God is 'invisible' he is 'inconceivable'; because unperceived, 'immeasurable'; because fathomless, 'everlasting', 'eternal'.[6] Moses simulates this commanded unmeaning as best he can, with speech acts pitched only on the edge of comprehension.

For his part, Moses' brother Aron believes in aesthetic reconciliation precisely because it *does* imply revelation: the appearing or envisioning of the divine, the specular meeting of an object God and a subject people. As a worker of signs and miracles, Aron insists on the communicative power of the image. Matching the vocal registers of a seductive bel canto, he argues that all ideality is ineffective unless it is brought to phenomenality, unless the unknowable is made available to identification and abstraction is exchanged for the animations of the object. 'No people can believe in what it does not feel,' he proclaims in Act One, as he defies Moses, seizing his staff, whereupon it turns into the terrifying plasticity of a serpent. While for Schoenberg's Aron the image is not inimical to the realm of the conceptual – 'images of our idea; they are one', he sings – the effects of the integration are of course incorrigibly ideological. In his role as sweet-tongued lyricist and smooth-tongued pragmatist, Aron knows that the visual is able to couple form to content in such a way as to direct and appease it. He knows, too, that it is the principle of vision as that privileged form of mediation between self and the world, which organizes the terms of knowing and belonging, allowing for an evidential relation to the object world and an apperceptive eye on what is to come. And so, Aron knowingly renounces that most supreme command of monotheism:

Thou shalt not make unto thee a graven image, nor any matter of likeness, of anything that is in heaven above, or that is in the earth beneath, or that is in the water under the earth.[7]

Moses puts Aron, the disarming idolater, under arrest, accusing him of debasing the true nature of the divine as absolute and inscrutable Idea. The libretto and music dry up. With the single scene of the third act left undone, Schoenberg gives us a Moses unable to speak or speculate, unable to image or ontologize. Held in the grip of the prohibition, however, he dramatizes the terms of a radical criticality.

Importantly, the question posed by the Second Commandment concerns the formation or fabrication of a god – its availability for use as an idol – rather than the field of visual representation more generally.[8] For what is proscribed by Judaic law is not so much figuration or the work of art itself, but a certain relationship to it: that is, the image conceived as a fixed and fully intelligible form, or as something which might fix and fulfil the terms of intelligibility itself.[9] Above all, when Exodus 20.4 forbids the making of sculpted or graven images, as when Talmudic and Hassidic commentaries later modify the motif of the Cherubim's painted faces in Solomon's Temple, the injunction is directed against the image as it makes an absolute claim for itself. Bounded and whole, solid and autonomous: it is not so much the sign of an original thing as an entity with an exigency, density, cogency, of its own.[10]

What accounts for the false character of the image's divinity, then, is less a matter of representational insubstantiality – the image in its mimetic or referential relation – than its eidetic verifiability: the assumption of a truth shaped in *praesentia*, in the power and conspicuousness of its being present, of being in place. In this, as Jean-Luc Nancy argues, the Second Commandment differs in important respects from the familiar Platonic series of bifurcations – essence/appearance, original/copy, true reality/everyday shadow – and thus from the question of the image as second-order index, a qualification at one or two removes from unqualified perfection.[11] The biblical injunction does, however, have everything to do with the consequences of the image that inhere in its presuppositions: its self-evidence and self-sufficiency, its declaration of weighty tautology rather than its existence as depleted double, its sheer steadfastness of form. Thus, as in Isaiah 46.7, the image is insensible for the same reason that it appears alive. It is the very semblance of vitality that renders it inert, unyielding, unresponsive, unconcerned. This is its bad faith and dupery: the idol may be 'spirited' – and even lead a life of its own – but it is unable *to move* or to be moved; fixed in its appointed place it must remain indifferent to those who worship it.

> They bear it, on the shoulder they carry it, and *they put it in its place and it stands, from its place it does not move*; yea he cries to it and it does not answer; from his distress it does not save him. (emphasis added)[12]

Schoenberg's opera, then, is not merely a recitation of Judaic law. Whether we see the image-ban as a question of impropriety (a wrongful kind of worship) or impossibility (how to figure that which, being infinite, has no figure?) it refers us to a certain blockage or fragmentation of visual perception: refuting truth as a presence addressed to the eye, insisting on the blindness *within* what is given to be seen. Indeed, it is the refusal to image precisely because Schoenberg's Moses acknowledges that it is only along with its own retreat that representation might have something to reveal. As both monotheist and proto-modernist, he concedes too that here – in the interdiction internal to the image, in the abeyance exposed in its 'being-there' – lies the noisy, clamorous (or, in Moses' case, the stammering) moment: the moment of remainder and interruption, a counter-visual breach. At this point, it is not the (prohibited) meaning but its *own unrealizability* that causes the image to be '*banned*'.

2

I leave Schoenberg's *Moses und Aron* aside for now, but I retain from the biblical and operatic story something of its spatial scene, its setting. For what is significant is that the struggle between the Hebraic brothers occurs in the context of *Exodus*. If, as in the previous chapter, the spatiality of Judaic exile opens onto Rosenzweig's 'homeless[ness] in time',[13] and if the biblical desert finds its allegorical doubling in Benjamin's secular city, then here we encounter the questions of another contradiction. Might we take the image denounced in *Exodus* and locate it within the incompletions of urban modernity? Indeed, if the image is idolatrous in being immobile – it '[has] feet but cannot walk', says Isaiah 46.7 – might it be 'remobilized' if we conceive the city as itself a space outside of territory and its entailment in the domain of history?[14] Finally, how might the biblical prohibition produce a new mode of visual perception – one that takes the *anti-image as its ethic* precisely because it takes *exile as its origin*?

In exploring these questions I return to Walter Benjamin's *The Arcades Project*. Importantly, I am not concerned to unearth a rudiment of theological life beneath the surfaces of Benjamin's urban modernity. It isn't a matter of uncovering buried esoteria ('depth doesn't get you anywhere at all', says Brecht. 'It's just depth – and there's nothing whatsoever to be seen in it.').[15] But nor am I attempting to reconcile Judaism's image-ban on the one hand with Benjamin's materialist critique of commodity culture on the other: a move which would rehouse the theological under the rubric of secularity, domesticating and bordering both. The aim, instead, is to find a properly dialectical – non-identical, non-reconciled, always disorienting – encounter between the two, asserting their compaction at the very site in which their antimony is most certainly announced, the modern city. In this I assign Benjamin's Judaism a specific place and time: Paris in the nineteenth century. Accordingly, what will be important is not an account of the biblical prohibition or of modernity *per se*, but the space of the city itself. Here, amid the visual at its most self-evident, the image-ban emerges at a moment of maximum jeopardy and in its most extreme disguise. Here, like an ill-timed anomaly, the Second Commandment intrudes into the Second Empire: bringing to light the invisibilities of the modern city, displaying the non-compliances of the image implicit in it. The visual oversupplies of modernity, in this sense, do not deviate from theological proscription; they illuminate its essential logic. If this involves presenting things which, according to Judaic law, cannot equal any decisive presence, it also means exposing the interdictions, the incompletions, internal to the modern itself. Which is precisely where, as Benjamin likes to say, its historical index most alarmingly strikes us.[16]

In *One-Way Street* (1928) Benjamin includes a fragment called 'Mexican Embassy' whose epigraph reads:

> I never pass by a wooden fetish, a gilded Buddha, a Mexican idol without reflecting: perhaps it is the true God.[17]

Begun as an essay laying the historical ground for *One-Way Street*, it is with the *Arcades* – 'the theatre of all my struggles and all my ideas'[18] – that Benjamin scavenges for the home-grown deities that shadow modernity and the market, and focuses the visual as the principal means of their collective identification. One of the key themes of the *Arcades*, its visual phantasmagoria, refers of course to the eighteenth-century popularization of the magic lantern show. In darkened theatres throughout Revolutionary Paris, concave mirrors and obscured light sources called up the heroic and villainous dead: at once discharging memories of the Terror and, in an age newly invigorated by utopian possibility, drafting other desired futures as well. An ingenious staging of ghosts, skeletons and demons (their forms usually back-projected onto walls, white sheets, smoke drifts or gauze screens) it is to this spectacle that Marx's chapter on commodity fetishism in *Capital* owes its inheritance and to which Benjamin's 'Exposé of 1939', his final programmatic statement of the *Arcades*, is addressed.

> Our investigation proposes to show how […] the new forms of behaviour and the new economically and technologically based creations that we owe to the nineteenth-century enter the universe of a phantasmagoria. These creations undergo this 'illumination' not in a theoretical manner, by an ideological transposition, but also in the immediacy of their perceptible presence. They are manifest as phantasmagoria.[19]

Feints of the market place, the soteriology of the commodity or, contrarily, devilish 'perspective[s] on infinity'.[20] Set ablaze by reflections and refractions of flickering light, by images and innumerable mirror-images, it is no coincidence that the arcades will be described by Benjamin as a home for spectres. Here, dead things are resurrected; the defunct, invalid and disused come back to life. This point is decisive. If urban modernity traffics in things that have acquired what Otto Ruhle, in his 1928 biography of Marx, calls a 'ghostly objectivity',[21] this is because the commodity, though mortified, refers to nothing outside its own being-present – exhibiting, imposing, and embodying a general dream of death and resurrection. In his reformulation of Marx, Benjamin will come to see the stream of historicist time as analogous to the dumb tenacity of commodity production. To what Marx famously described as the 'theological niceties'[22] of spectral attraction corresponds a Benjaminian model in which the symbolic structures of historical life, always exposed to violence, lose their viability and yet persist in parched, eviscerated, petrified form. Unvital signs, exhausted resurrections, expended repetitions: these are the strange ruinations conjured up in Benjamin's reading of Natural History (*Naturgeschichte*). That is to say, they belong to the contradictory slippage of properties between biological nature and human history born of the implacable 'life cycle' of generation and decay proper to capitalist production itself.

> So long as there is semblance in history, it will find in nature its ultimate refuge. The commodity, which is the last burning-glass of historical semblance, *Schein*, celebrates its triumph in the fact that nature itself takes on a commodity character.[23]

Eric L. Santner gives an admirably clear elaboration of this:

> Natural history is born out of the dual possibilities that life can persist beyond the death of the symbolic forms that gave it meaning and that

symbolic forms can persist beyond the death of the form of life that gave them human vitality. [It] transpires against the background of this space between real and symbolic death, this space of the 'undead'.[24]

The nineteenth-century metropolis exists precisely in this realm. Here the phantasmagoric – history's own imaginary – doesn't merely summon up the horror of objects dead and decayed. In the uncertain half-light of the arcades it reawakens them with what Santner brilliantly analyses as the uncanny charisma of the undead. Compelled by a magical economy of 'deadness and excitation, stuckness and agitation',[25] the arcade's world of visual things – its waxworks, mannequins and replication of personae; its 'panoramas, dioramas, and cosmoramas'[26] – does more than mimic a semblance of aliveness, of *Schein*. With the inflation of a temporal model that knows only the (surplus) value of natural-historical repetition, objects divested of life become invested with the mania of heightened animation. They endure as signs but ones no longer capable of signifying, they survive as forms in which a phantasmal motility is congealed within the substance of matter itself. Hieroglyphs bearing no meaning, 'enigmatic signifiers', in Santner's phrase, un-decodable ciphers, in Adorno's version.[27] The arcades of the nineteenth century are the domicile of just such '[un]dead effects'.[28] Its *genius loci* – its guarding divinity of place – presides over that instant of dialectical in-distinction between life and death, its extravagant visibilities reside in the hollow of 'incoming and disappearing meaning'.[29] Or, as Benjamin writes in describing the souvenir as the necrotic waste of a now debased Idea:

> In the nineteenth-century, allegory withdrew from the world around us to settle in the inner world. The relic comes from the cadaver; the souvenir comes from the defunct experience [*Erfahrung*] which thinks of itself, euphemistically, as living [*Erlebnis*].[30]

The relic and cadaver refer, in the first instance, to Benjamin's 1925 study, *The Origin of German Tragic Drama*, the initial setting for the related conceptions of allegory and natural history as they describe the paradox of undead life central to his understanding of historicist process. While the arcana of seventeenth-century German theatre and Second Empire urbanism are clearly different – a distinction underscored, not least, by Benjamin's theological analysis of Counter-Reformation sovereignty in the former and his Marxist cultural analysis of sovereign capital in the latter – their untimely condensation (fragmentarily claimed in the *Arcades* but never systematically argued) is itself key to a methodology trained on temporal abbreviations and spatial abridgements.[31] It is not just that Baroque allegory and secular modernity both perform a fascination with the exorbitant, the apparitional and the dead. For Benjamin, the emptied excitations of the commodity – its endowment with no significance or, rather, bloated with too many significances – are already preformed in the vitiated objects of an earlier dramaturgy. 'Allegorical emblems return as commodities' is the key aphorism from the notes for 'Central Park' (1939).[32] Or, as he describes the Baroque devaluation of the object as it reappears with accelerated tempo:

> It should be kept in mind that, in the nineteenth-century, the number of 'hollowed out' things increases at a rate and scale that was previously unknown, for technical progress is continually withdrawing newly introduced objects from circulation.[33]

If we understand the commodity form as a recasting of life – 'recasting' understood in the sculptural sense of an aliveness shaped from the dried up, devitalized mould of things – then the arcades become the spatial occasion of the idol par excellence: the showcase of a modern golden calf, of the image 'put in its place'[34] or its modern corollary, a 'bourgeois allegory of shelter'.[35] Here, the object offered as a unity of visual being and visual meaning; here, history enlisted as the parade of this conceit. One of these conceits is the city itself. For beyond the interiorized space of the arcades (already, for Benjamin, a scaled-up version of the domestic *intérieur*), the Parisian city-plan spreads out as its own idolatorous expanse. It pledges an extended field of relations between the apparent and the absolute – 'what is the city but a vast monastery?' is Erasmus' famous question.[36] It confirms a secular eschatology in its vast projections of visually available space. 'As for the phantasmagoria of civilization itself, it found its champion in Haussmann and its manifest expression in his transformations of Paris,' Benjamin writes in his 'Exposé of 1939'.[37] The more the city is cleared out for improvement, the more its metaphysics multiply – cluttering Haussmann's emptied spaces with the profits of the 'big picture'.

3

In the 'Epistemo-Critical Prologue' to *The Origin of German Tragic Drama* that codifies his earlier insights into the relationship of truth and art, Benjamin describes the regime of vision in its 'intentional' relation to knowledge.[38] Here, as elsewhere, vision is defined by its temporality or by an eye that beholds a temporalized direction of space: foreseeing the future as the successive state, and thus ultimate sanction, of the present. The correspondence between sight and time, as Rebecca Comay notes, is shorthand for a whole retinue of idealisms and instrumentalisms that Benjamin will mark for their presumptive 'far-gaze into the blue'.[39] Thus, the 'chimerical pretention[s]'[40] of Saint-Simon's machinist reveries and the utopian socialism of Fourier's phalansteries, the vitalism (and incipient ultra-nationalism) of the Wandervogel of Benjamin's youth, the reforming optimisms of the Social Democrats and 'vulgar Marxists' of his contemporary Weimar – all 'will be convicted of a veritable "idolatory of Geist"', in Comay's words, reducing the present to a mere transition in their vertiginous schemes.[41]

A similar temporal-idolatory underpins the Haussmannian urban ideal. 'Long perspectives down broad straight avenues'[42] offer an image-prospect that is also a historical prognostic. A vast geometry of circulation routes and railroad networks intends an urban calculus in which each part wills the next without waste, remainder, respite and, under the expropriating zeal of Baron Haussmann, no matter what. 'These Parisian savannahs consisting of roofs levelled out to form a plain'[43] reiterate the basic point: vision as an unbreachable line of sight which elides the gaps in experience as time and history pass by way of the eyes. Thus, to the phantasmagoria of the commodity – its availability to sight, or the stasis of its natural-historical foresight – nineteenth-century Paris booms topographically. Its rectilinear organization shores up the urban subject's (frail, faltering) sense of emplacement. Its prolonged vistas expand an idolatrous – that is, evidential – relation to some future unfolding. If the laws of visual perspective given by so many avenues and boulevards seek a reconciliation of the finite and infinite, the phenomenal and noumenal, then the pedestrian street offers 'the monotonous, fascinating, constantly unrolling band of asphalt'.[44] 'Haussmann's urban works [have the] appearance of walling-in a massive eternity'.[45] With their surfaces 'smooth as glass',[46] they signal not only an ever-onward orientation but also the assimilation of time into its inexorable recurrence. Even the city's *Grand Projets* mime the idolatrous aesthetics of the Baroque stage:

> Opening of the Boulevard Sèbastopol like the unveiling of a monument. At 2:30 in the afternoon, at the moment of the [imperial] procession was approaching from the Boulevard Saint-Denis, an immense scrim, which had masked the entrance [...] was drawn like a curtain. This drapery had been hung between two Moorish columns, on the pedestals of which were figures representing the arts, the sciences, industry, and commerce.[47]

Thus the visibilities of the nineteenth-century city are not, or not only, an affair of spatial geometry, the affordance of view, or even a function of judgement.

In its 'equivocal illumination'[48] it is a space installed in the inscrutable course of natural-historical time. 'The [flaneur] takes the concept of marketability itself for a stroll',[49] writes Benjamin of the subject whose empathy with the commodity is its cryptic rapport with the excursions of undead life. Or we may say, if the commodity instantiates the 'moment of indifference between death and meaning',[50] then the city itself becomes a Baroque pageant – swelling out and discarding the voids over which it is mapped, rousing a space in which history, though abjected and abandoned, 'faithlessly leaps forward to the idea of resurrection'.[51]

4

Developed from his earliest metaphysical writings (1919–23), through the study of allegory and Baroque art and finally with *Theses on the Philosophy of History* (1940), it is of course Benjamin's task to rescue those moments where natural-historical life may be disrupted and a more authentic historical time (un-forcefully, temporarily) redeemed. And so: might there be another kind of vision and another kind of space interred within the 'modern lantern cast[ing]'[52] of Benjamin's city? In the face of the phantasies they exemplify, might his arcades return us to – or be the site of return for – the spectre of an alternative theology? To the mythic immanence of nineteenth-century urbanism, might we oppose a vision which again solicits a ghost? This time, to be sure, it is a ghost summoned not in the appearance of the image but precisely as its injunction, not as resurrected life but as its rupture – undoing the serial enthrallment of dead meanings or even, following Santner, as a 'de-animation of the undead'.[53] Thus, while Benjamin's urban study cannot be said to be driven by any theological impulse – unlike the declared messianism of Benjamin's early work and his final extant writing, the *Arcades* remains an explicitly materialist work[54] – might a Judaic dimension nonetheless be at stake? Along with this, might we stage another encounter between the secular and the theological: not a head-on collision and, still less, a seamless embrace but merely a small emendation in perspective, a 'slight adjustment'[55] in our angle of vision? Writing to Max Horkheimer in 1937 and informing him on progress of the *Arcades* manuscript, Benjamin alludes to something of this slim, susceptible, possibility:

> I will let my Christian Baudelaire be taken into heaven by nothing but Jewish angels. But arrangements have already been made to let him fall as if by chance in the last third part of the ascension shortly before the entrance into glory.[56]

Baudelaire, Benjamin's urban exemplar, is at once hoisted and high-jacked by 'Jewish angels'. Here, the setting – the space – of the city is crucial and it is to be distinguished as such. As we have seen, interpretations of *The Arcades Project* have long allied vision to a materialist critique of the commodity. And while Benjamin's many and varied treatments of modernist aesthetic production are specifically directed towards operations which defy idealization, my argument proceeds from a different point.[57] It is that a Judaic image-ban might be glimpsed in the chinks of Benjamin's city: that a 'small theology' inheres in the very space where modernity makes its most profane-historical case for visibility. The arcades, then, might not just be a scene of idolatrous phantasy or of a violated theological injunction, as this chapter has thus far presented. On the contrary, they might contain a theological pressure: throwing up a Judaic breach in the middle of the modern, avowing the presence of an older, occluded proscription – a 'ban' internal to the city, or a repudiation that returns precisely when no anticipation sees it coming.

Indeed, as he charts the cultural physiognomy of nineteenth-century Paris, Benjamin, like Georg Simmel before him, finds himself less the student of Haussmann than of a more errant (exilic) truth. To his famous remark on the status of futurity in Judaism – 'we know that Jews were prohibited from inquiring into the future'[58] – corresponds a space without that perception of depth able to be objectified by measurement or made legible by perspective. It is a space in which the future dissolves from view or, which amounts to the same thing, where the present itself is magnified and mobilized. As if there is no space outside the close, crammed corridors of the arcades, there is only an infinitely dilating 'now'. As if there is no time outside its clutter of objects, and the crises of their overproduced meaning, there is only an immediate space expanding to fill all time. Except for the street sign, the shop sign, the place name and – in this 'city of mirrors'[59] – those dazzling facades which replicate space but can never define it, there is nothing to align the eye or to help stake out the region one is in. Having no centralizing perspective – lacking any qualities to exact the Western aesthetic ideal of centration – there is nothing in this wildly circulating flux to enfranchise a 'point of view' or authorize the rules of visual and spatial cognition.

Part of what Benjamin's Paris retains from Edgar Allen Poe's *Man of the Crowd*, Baudelaire's flâneur, and from the literary anthropologies of Victor Hugo and Honoré de Balzac on which he also draws, is precisely the problem of framing the space of identity by means of the visual. 'He gains his image more quickly here than elsewhere and also sees himself more quickly merged with this, his image,'[60] writes Benjamin of a site in which the present intensity of the visual negates any self-subsistent identity. Here, the very exertion of the visual brings about its opposite: heightening the asymmetry between semblance and essence, exaggerating the altercation, stretching the dissensus, inciting another kind of attention. In a different register, here the image clashes with its own experience, generates its own interference, plunges 'into the depths which separate visual being from meaning'.[61] To 'liken [the city-dweller] to a mirror as vast as the crowd itself or to a kaleidoscope endowed with consciousness,'[62] then, isn't merely to describe the depleted existence of the urban body, the way in which sensory excess 'crowds' out the subject, producing and overwhelming the protective screen of which Simmel and Freud famously write.[63] Rather, on the level of perception, Benjamin's city misses or misdirects itself. With its endless multiplication of appearances and self-appearances it checks any fantasy of being in place, holding semblance apart from significance, undoing presence as the visual availability of the body to itself.[64] In the earliest preparatory essay for the *Arcades*, Benjamin addresses this inaccessibility, describing the city's spatial ambiguities in its 'collusion with nonbeing':

> The space that transforms itself does so in the bosom of nothingness. In its tarnished, dirty mirrors, things exchange a Kaspar-Hauser-look with the nothing [...] There is no thing here that does not, when one least expects it, open a fugitive eye, blinking it shut again; and should you look more closely, it is gone. To the whispering of these gazes, the space lends its echo: 'Now, what,' it blinks, 'can possibly have come over me?' We stop short in some surprise. 'What, indeed, can possibly have come over you?' Thus we bounce the question back to it.[65]

There is a kind of broken mimesis initiated at the height of visual relations. Or we might say that if an idolatrous regime intends a face (will it see? 'will it return [the] look?') and obsessively seeks a communicable form (will it listen? 'will it speak?'), then here the image deflects all accessibility along identificatory lines.[66] Pushed by the city to its most crazed, kaleidoscopic extreme, the image becomes subject to its own contravention. It prompts its own dispossession or disfigurement *within* appearance. If this approaches an iconoclasm it is not because the image concedes to the 'thou shall not' of any lawful obligation or divine command. It is because *in the city* the image begins to infract, to indict and to 'ban' itself.[67] Its crime, its scandal, is self-inflicted. Even the urban edifice modelled on an amplification of sight – the enlarging of optics into panoptics – effects its own 'unfulfilment'. The *ratio* and *extensio* of its visibilities twist into a counteractive visual sphere:[68]

> Let two mirrors reflect each other; then Satan plays his favourite trick and opens here in his way [...] the perspective on infinity [...] The Arc de Triomph, the Sacré Coeur, and even the Pantheon appear, from a distance, like images hovering about the ground and opening, architecturally, a fata morgana.[69]

A fata morgana is, of course, a wholly natural optical phenomenon – a mirage composed of layers of inverted and erect images which display alternations of compressed and stretched zones. Read as natural-historical allegory, however, it renders the city as perilous as that 'false land' created out of bent light to which the legendary name refers. In the very moment that the city's mirrors and architecture accede to greatest visibility, Benjamin shows them to be proscribed or overexposed from within: divulging a gap where visual presence decomposes, signalling an exclusion internal to representation, showing up the city's inadequacy to its own visions. Or we might recall Benjamin's study of Baroque and say that if time is not merely promised to death but makes *spectral remains*, then the city too contains, *beneath our gaze*, a space remaining. It is a space that precludes any captivation by optics and panoptics, or which operates below, or before, the intentional level at which visual mediation might begin. Like the distortions of the fata morgana or the psychic strata of a dream sequence (the analogy is, of course, fully Benjaminian), at issue is nothing less than the abeyance upon which the image sustains itself. It is a failure in the always present order of vision, an undecidablility, an invisibility in all that is given in plain sight.

That modernity and the city deform perceptual experience is, of course, a long-established theme, central to Benjamin's aesthetic theories as well as the large body of literature that engages it. My wager, however, is that the deformation in question has its origin in the Second Commandment. Crucially, as previously suggested, positing a Judaic remnant in the modern city does not mean summonsing another, superseded, separated world. Nor it is about discerning the application of an ancient prohibition in order to challenge the mythic visibilities of modernity. Rather, it means focusing the secular city in order to think about an absence within, or initial to, the structure of the image itself. In the manner of Benjamin's own 'weak' messianism, it is to affirm the double reference of the sacred and the secular, the theological and the modern, revealing the city's own unrealizability, its visual inaccessibility to itself. This doesn't diminish the mysteries of modernity. On the contrary, it discloses them. 'Truth,' as Benjamin writes in the Prologue to *The Origin*, 'is not a process of exposure which destroys the secret, but a revelation which does justice to it.'[70]

On the one hand, to invoke the theological secrets of the image is to convene, once again, that shadowy assembly of ghosts to which Benjamin's materialist account of the commodity form refers. On the other, as I have suggested, it is now a ghost invited not in the name of a phantasmal resurrection but as witness to a breach, a rent – a revelation? – in perceptual experience, turning what had served as the sponsor of idolatrous capture (the modern city) into a possibility for interception and inversion. What emerges is a visual field broken down in the primary site and, at the most acute point, of its unfolding. It is a break that arises at the very moment that the city arranges itself on a manifest plane as something visible, something settled. As Benjamin writes of Victor Hugo's topography:

> What had just taken place in this street would not have surprised a forest [...] This wild multitude sees there sudden apparitions of the invisible; there, what is below man distinguishes through the dark what is above man.[71]

5

If Benjamin's city entails a radical disruption of the visual, and if it is a disruption that relates to a Judaic notion of an image-ban, what critical force might be newly enabled? And how might we relate further the 'awakening' of this theological remnant within the uncertainties of the modern?

For, while the *Arcades* might well declare the persistence of idolatrous semblance – 'sculpture is found only in the city', reads one of its suggestive aphorisms[72] – and while so many reflections on reflection perform the very structure of representational practice, the city, as I've described it, contains its own anti-aesthetic interdiction. A heightened visibility reverses itself, splitting the image or exposing an incessant visual production to a blockage internal it. Furthermore, given in unabating mobility, the city produces a visual experience in defiance of all spatial accommodation: an urban eye that lives in the rhythm of place and displacement as they continuously depose, and rearrange, each other. To this erratic movement, Benjamin gives the elliptical phrase 'the colportage of space'[73] (a *colporteur* was originally the carrier or bearer of religious books), using it to invoke an impenetrable dimension shaped out of multiple and antithetical lineaments of space.

On the Colportage of Space: 'The sense of mystery [...] comes from remaining always in the equivocal, with double and triple perspectives, or inklings of perspective (images within images) [...] All things more suggestive just because they do appear.'[74]

If Benjamin's materialist critique concerns the way in which perspectival vision intends a prospective vision and so propels a falling away of actual experience, then any engagement with perspectives doubled, tripled or only vaguely intuited offers the possibility of a properly active visuality. With the 'colportage of space', vision detaches itself from the long view to become absorbed in the precipitous moment of the immediate. All the eye can do is to focus momentarily on a visual fragment and rapidly move on. In the split-second oscillations from one thing to another, all that is exhibited is the non-relation of things, the immediacy of their inconsistency in a purely presentational time.

'What is decisive,' Benjamin writes referring to the gnostic and occultist Alfred Schuler, 'is not the progression from one piece of knowledge to the next, but the leap [or crack] implicit in any one piece of knowledge.'[75] Put another way, in its version of the image-ban, the city produces an alternative where 'to see' means to dismantle the enchantments of both nostalgia and prediction. It means foreshortening a legible field in order to engage an eye that keeps low and close to the ground, that chances upon the contingent as it folds in and out of the path of observation.

If this suggests a distinctive visual and spatial practice it also, of course, produces a corresponding mode of thought. For, on a level as much experiential and epistemic, to see outside the time and space of the image is to arouse a present that the immensities of a distant gaze edit out. It is to revive the primacy of proximate contact over the mythical rigidities of depth and development. It is to permit the emergence of authentic cognitive difficulties or show that the authenticity of an object is, in principle, always liable to its failure as a concept. Furthermore, if the scrutiny of the smallest material thing is what enables its elevation to sustained analysis, then it is the rapid-fire refocus on another object that produces the explosive short circuits of Benjamin's dialectical imagination. This city, then, is not any specular space that, at its brightest, might announce a satisfaction – or even, a theophany. Nor does it assume any settlement within what is seen. What emerges, instead, is what Winfried Menninghaus in a different context terms an 'active production of imagelessness'.[76] If this refers to a withdrawal of semblance, or to the rushes and delays that in Benjamin dissolve it, then this is not just an anti-aesthetic. Taking the city as a space of an ancient Judaic remainder, it is an *ante-aesthetic* as well.

Thus, the image in Benjamin's nineteenth-century city incorporates its own 'ban'. Structured in mobility, it is divested of any intactness, submitted to all that is incompatible with the consummation of presence. If this is not an image on which one can, in fantasy or prayer, fixate it also produces the illuminative 'blindness' that corresponds to what I am describing as a Judaic mode of vision. The Benjaminian, and profoundly Judaic insight, is that with the loss of prospective sight, uncompleted possibilities – or, possibilities of incompleteness – shine forth anew. It is only when the intentional mediacy of the optical eye shuts that hidden lattices of meaning erupt to present time. Indeed, according to this contradiction, nothing is less transparent than when blindingly near; nothing becomes more foreign than when brought to extreme proximity or when, as Adorno says, 'thought presses up close to its object'.[77] Inaccessibility, impenetrability and immediation, then, do not merely challenge the priority given to the representational surface. They also insert into the chronology of a 'general view' the specificity of its event. They invest all systems of thought with the discomfort of what George Didi-Huberman calls the 'unthinkable of its unexpected'.[78] For Benjamin, it is only when one breaks with history-as-semblance that a truly immersive material practice can begin. Or, as Adorno's more austere version of the image-ban has it, 'It is only in the absence of images that the full object [can] be conceived.'[79]

6

Once again, the rejection of semblance has as much of a biblical and theological register as it does a secular and philosophical one. We might return to the scene with which this chapter began and recall that when in the aftermath of the Gold Calf episode, Moses takes possession of the second set of Tablets, the event is not only characterized by the fact that it occurs in the desert, in exile. The receiving of the Law on Mount Sinai also coincides with an act of non-appearance. In response to Moses' personal plea 'to see Your glory', God withdraws, disengages, he turns away. All Moses is allowed to see is his profile or his back. Exodus 33.18-23 note:

And he said, 'You cannot see My face, for man may not see Me and live.' And God said, 'See there is a place near Me. Station yourself on the rock and, as *My glory passes by, I will put you in a cleft of the rock and shield you with My hand until I have passed by.* Then I will take away My hand and you will see My back; but my face shall not be seen'. (emphasis added)[80]

Here the undead object of visual animation surrenders its claim. What we have, at most, is Moses' slanted, oblique, dubious revelation. Here, indeed, the intended object of knowledge not only retreats; it also literally 'passes [Moses] by'. In its place is a relation to the unknown, to the missings or 'passings' of visual experience and expression. What the revelation evinces, makes manifest, even discloses, is that which it excludes, keeps latent, sustains as unseen. For what is important is not merely that Moses' eyes are shielded and then unshielded by God's hand ('veiled' and 'unveiled' are the corollaries that Benjamin uses in his discussion of truth and beauty in Goethe's *Elective Affinities*)[81]. Such an opposition, Comay reminds us, would merely reify the desired object of sight: reducing the Judaic image-ban to a mythic esotericism or capricious sleight of signification,[82] to an 'enigmatic cruelty in actual meaning',[83] as Benjamin writes in *The Origins*. Rather than any play of visibility/invisibility, showing/hiding, light/absence – a duality that, like the logic of *fort da*, is a tempting of loss that is itself reassuring of presence – Moses is positioned at the limits of both domains. For while the God that reveals himself does not offer himself up to sight, nor does he retire into any positive or transcendent concealment. Rather, such a revealing bears the weight of a contradiction, one without remuneration.[84] It involves uncovering something by 'leaving it under cover',[85] as Maurice Blanchot has it; it 'implies that something shows that did not show itself'.[86] As in 'the way in dreams',[87] there is nothing that might follow on Moses' 'passing' sight or contract it out to an ultimate realization.[88] Rather, Exodus 33.18-23 are about a turning aside, a turning away, an obliquity in every demand of identity, visibility, presence. At stake is a truth that 'reveals by re-veiling'.[89] Neither affirmation nor negation, it is the exhibiting of peculiar non-presence; the estranging actuality of what, in his Goethe essay, Benjamin calls 'the object in its veil'.[90]

Revealing/re-veiling: if this is what characterizes Moses' vision on Mount Sinai then one of Benjamin's basic hypotheses comes down to situating the power of such perceptual indecision under the terms of time, which is to say, of history. Furthermore, if the city, as I've argued, is the space in which the image-ban returns to *re-veil* what modernity can neither hide nor give up to sight, then time necessarily has a part in these revelations. Time lives in the self-infractions of the image, in the suspension of the visible/invisible or, rather, within that movement of re-veiling which goes by the name of revelation. To locate time in the breach of visual being and meaning, then, also entails the reconfiguration of a sequential world filled, as it is, with the phantoms of historical intent. Better yet, the break or ambiguity in semblance enables a corresponding temporal gain. This is not a boon, the beneficial sustenance of supplementary or compensatory time. Like Rosenzweig's 'exilic middle', it is a *this-wordly* irruption, an un-commanded moment, a time come unstuck within the orders of time. It is an intensity charging within chronology, one that refocuses the question of presence as it quickens the actualities – that is, the anachronisms – of the present.[91] Thinking the visual and temporal together, then, Benjamin's central concept of *Jetztzeit* is not only a moment held here, held now for our palpable attention. We may also say that such a 'now-time' emerges only on the *near-side* or *this-side* of vision. Indeed, if such immediacy is the 'small gateway'[92] that Benjamin carves out for the entrance of the messianic, it corresponds to the image as it bears an interdiction in itself: not concealing or revealing but operating in the undecided manner of a 're-veiling'. What the Second Commandment prohibits, time can now remobilize. Here, the present comes to exist – and insist – only when vision, in both its fascinating and mediating functions, fails in its intention. Here, a kind of mismatched, *untoward time* is held alive precisely in the figure or face who *turns away*, severing the repetitions of mythic semblance or appearing only along with the risk of 'passing by': unsung, unremembered, missed, unnoticed.

Benjamin will always stress that nothing human or this-worldly directly equates to theological concepts – on the contrary, there lie the misrecognitions of both providential and pagan action. At the same time, it is the task of the Benjaminian method to mark out the constellatory arrangements of theology and a political paradigm of history, seeking the immemorial 'lodged in history' and taking 'the imprint of that hidden side of the seal'.[93] The concern of this chapter has been to find the Judaic law of the non-realizable installed within the visibilities of the modern city: attesting to the historical 'truth' of the city's lapses and ruinations, spotting a theological dimension which does not so much contest the production of an urban vision as impress, once again, its struggle to *take place*.

To argue for the imprint of the Second Commandment in the Second Empire, in other words, is not merely to find another language with which to rehearse a critique of the commodity form in the space of advanced capitalism. Instead, the Judaic prohibition constitutes the terms for thinking Benjamin's city as a space, a scene, which invites another kind of sight, and beckons another kind of ghostly presence: a presence that returns to expose the present and take a position in it. We might remember that it is not only the Judaic god who averts his face, refusing the visibility of direct frontal encounter. It is also Benjamin's most famous allegorical figure, the 'Angel of History', who faces away from its apparently irreversible direction of travel. Propelled backwards towards the future – mouth open, eyes like staring blindspots, outside of time but desperately flailing its wings within it – the Angel denounces an undeviating Progress in turning its back, in turning away. At issue is not any abstract rejection of the representational or the desire for its fulfilment – in any case, the Angel, unlike the Messiah, 'must fail in his task',[94] as Gershom Scholem reminds us. Rather, against any consummation of temporality and visibility – a model of which the seeing of God's face would be an analogy – is posed the perception of an emergent political space. It is the awareness, 'for a moment at least,' as Benjamin writes in his revaluation of 'The Destructive Character', of an 'empty space'. To be clear, this is not an 'empty space' of the kind into which the fetish might fall, plummeting into the cavity left by the expulsion of meaning and now bloated with the props and ciphers that proliferate around it. For Benjamin, it is 'the place where the thing stood or the victim lived'. 'Someone,' he adds, 'is sure to be found who needs this space without its being filled.'[95] Likewise, the 'someone' of such a space is not a nullified or unnameable subjectivity – historicism's fetishized disavowal of the 'victim' – and certainly 'no intangible *deus absconditus*'.[96] Its proper occupant is an activity: the consciousness of a new relationship to the objects and events of historical experience.

Fleetingly, passingly – and as 'little as it may be granted us to try write it with immediately theological concept'[97] – the city might be the site of such an occupancy. In this reading, it is an 'empty space' which contains, 'at least for a moment', the conditions of a radical incompletion: a vision which neither 'veiled' nor 'unveiled' forces a fundamental 're-veiling' of the visible itself. Indeed, if – and again, if only 'for a moment' – the city is no longer a site for the resurrections of the banned image but for its own self-indictment then it is not merely that a Judaic imprint returns to the present; it does so to make action a part of the present's temporal task. The Second Commandment, then, is not just written on the reverse side or underside of an urban phantasy. It is an ancient prohibition become a present potential. As Benjamin writes in a note to a letter to Scholem in 1934, 'Everything that Moses accomplished long ago would have to be re-accomplished in our world's age.'[98]

3

Liberalism pluralism and the mourning work of assimilation

Isaiah Berlin via Sigmund Freud

1

In 'The Origins of Israel' (1952), one in a series of essays on the history of the Zionist movement, Isaiah Berlin throws into relief what he sees as the persistent misalignment in Judaic identity: a privation of land supplemented by an oversupply of events:

> It was once said by the celebrated Russian revolutionary, Alexander Herzen, writing in the mid-nineteenth century, that Slavs had no history, only geography. The position of the Jews is the reverse of this. They have enjoyed rather too much history and too little geography.[1]

From the perspective of a nationalist imaginary, Berlin's point is clear: for the Jew, too much time but not enough space. This chapter sets out to reverse Berlin's own reversal. My suspicion is that it is not the 'too little' but the 'too much' of geography – and, mostly, the attempt to minimize this gratuity – that secretly partners Berlin's particular brand of liberal pluralism, supplying it not only with a spatial basis but with one whose language of loss bears upon the condition of the assimilated Jewish subject.

I begin with a single event and a single date: No. 44 Fontanny Dom (Fountain House), Leningrad, 26 November 1945. It was here in an unheated and barely furnished upper-floor apartment – the converted interior of the eighteenth-century Sheremetev Palace on the bank of the Fontanka River – where Anna Akhmatova first met Isaiah Berlin, then temporarily seconded by the British Foreign Office from Washington DC to its embassy in Moscow. First, the apartment's resident: one of the last remaining figures of the 'Silver Age' of Russia's pre- revolutionary artistic and literary life; along with her first husband, Nikolay Gumilyov, and fellow poet, Osip Mandelstam, a co-founder of the Acmeist circle of poets formed in 1911; a leading light of Leningrad's (then St Petersburg) cultural avant-garde and a presiding presence at its regular meeting place, the Stray Dog Café; a semi-fabled dissident who, while publicly celebrated, had been deemed politically problematic ever since the Cheka's secret trial and execution of Gumilyov in 1921.[2] And her visitor: a Latvian Jew born in 1909 who as a young boy had fled Riga for St Petersburg in 1917 and, following the Menshevik and Bolshevik Revolutions, emigrated to England in 1921; a Fellow of All Souls College, Oxford (the first Jew elected to that position), who was to become professor of social and political theory and founding president of Wolfson College; a lauded public intellectual and policy advisor beloved of the British political and cultural establishment. Berlin's award of a knighthood in 1957 and presidency of the British Academy from 1974 to 1978, his self-fashioned dominion over prominent academic appointments,[3] and invitations to the dining tables and drawing rooms of the Anglo-American elite (including those of Queen Elizabeth II, Winston Churchill, Presidents Kennedy and Thatcher) account for this most dutiful of foreigners ensconced at the heart of the cultural Cold War.

Thus visitor and resident. Seated on two wooden chairs, smoking, sharing a bowl of boiled potatoes, Akhmatova recalled the Black Sea coast and Odessa summers of her youth while Berlin recounted his early years in the old port city of Riga, where the blend of a haute-bourgeois Baltic German culture and a Russian imperial one set the stage of his distinctively a-typical *Ostjude* childhood. In their shared native tongue, they argued over his attraction to the refined ironies of Turgenev and epic breadths of Tolstoy while she defended her preference for the darker interiors of Dostoyevsky and Kafka. Akhmatova recited poetry (her own and Byron's *Don Juan*) and together they talked about the Great Terror: of the suicides of the poets Vladimir Mayakovsky and Marina Tsvetaeva; the murder of the theatre director Vsevolod Meyerhold; the persecution of Osip Mandelstam; the arrest of the art historian Nikolay Punin; and of the systematic purge, in Gulag transit and labour camps, of that whole generation of writers and artists who, for both of them, exemplified the last authentic Russian culture. As Berlin later recalled in his *Personal Impressions*:

> [Akhmatova] spoke of her loneliness and isolation, both personal and cultural. Leningrad after the war was for her nothing but a vast cemetery, the graveyard of her friends: it was like the aftermath of a forest fire – the few charred trees made the desolation still more desolate.[4]

That one night at No. 44 Fontanny Dom was to have enduring consequence. For Akhmatova, it is said, the encounter resulted in the 'Guest from the Future' – an image she was to include in a stanza of the then unfinished *Poem without a Hero*, the most intricately structured of elegies to a pre-Soviet past that also foretold her denunciation by Andrei Zhdanov at a meeting of the Writer's Union in August 1946 and the decades of internal isolation that followed. 'From the year nineteen forty/as if from a tower, I survey everything/ as if bidding farewell again,' as she wrote in an introductory section to the longer poem.[5] For Berlin, the month that followed was dedicated to writing

'A Note on Literature and the Arts in the Russian Soviet Federated Socialist Republic in the Closing Months of 1945' for the British Embassy, one of the first accounts of the Sovietization of Russian culture in the first half of the twentieth century. Less immediately, as his biographer Michael Ignatieff suggests, the late-night meeting with Akhmatova was encrypted into everything Berlin was later to write in defence of Western liberal pluralism and political freedom. 'His fierce polemic against historical determinism was animated by what he had learned from her, namely that history could be made to bow before the sheer stubbornness of human conscience.'[6]

On one level, this chapter is about the difference and distance between two spaces and two positions: that is, between Akhmatova's Leningrad apartment with all its encrusted memories of pre-revolutionary intellectual ferment and the many Oxford common rooms and London salons in which Berlin regularly held forth on revolutionary hope's betrayal by various militant and messianic illiberalisms. On another level, this chapter is about the delicate skein that weaves back and forth between them, entwining Leningrad with Oxford, connecting the displacements of the (internal) exile to the adaptations of the assimilated refugee. Crucially, it is a connection best understood as politically 'therapeutic'. I use the term experimentally but specifically. I suggest that Berlin's liberal pluralism not only shares structural similarities with the guiding terms of the psychoanalytic project; it also describes the hidden spatial premise of both. Thus although Berlin is the central protagonist in this chapter, I read him through another Jewish exile to London: Sigmund Freud. In so doing, I will be imagining a conversation between two projects that on the face of them have little in common: Berlin's liberal pluralism and a Freudian understanding of the structures of mourning.[7] The result, I hope, will be twofold. First, and against Berlin's assertion, that we understand what is constraining in living with *too much* geography; how its surplus of bonds, its excess of interior ties to space, paradoxically come to haunt the figure of the exile, the outsider, the dissident. Second, that we might identify the 'cure' for this excess in the very formation of Berlin's liberalism; or rather, in what I conceive as the liberal therapeutics of spatial assimilation itself.[8]

2

It is perhaps inevitable that any argument drawing on the shared terrain of psychoanalysis and political theory comes with a battalion of (symptomatic) caveats. The first is that there is nothing new in posing this relation. If Freud's *Civilization and Its Discontents* (1930) stands as the seminal theorization of the psychic repressions necessary to social life, then much subsequent analysis can be read as an assault on the essential stoicism of the Freudian argument, at once contesting the inherently destructive nature of the instincts and refusing a view of society opposed to human desire. Together with the study of the 'authoritarian personality' led by the Frankfurt School in the 1930s, it was the reception of Herbert Marcuse and Wilhelm Reich in the 1960s that consummated the 'unnatural marriage'[9] of class and the unconscious. Understanding the administrations of late capitalism to be coded into the structures of the individual psyche – eviscerating the creative energies of Eros and depleting the pleasure of its subversive potentials – any stress on the adaptive relations between the self and society, it was argued, could only enfeeble psychoanalysis as an agent of social critique.[10]

Where the anti-humanist strains of such Freudian-Marxism came to frame the revolutionary spirit of the 1960s, it was in this post-war period of political stalemate and reassessment that Berlin came to prominence as a spokesman for moderation, modulation, restraint.[11] Casting doubt on the assumptions of intellectual certitude, he was to declaim the aggression – and essential defensiveness – of all comprehensive explanatory systems, whether Marxist, Freudian or any of their unruly offspring. In a letter dated 1969 written from

America to the British sociologist, Jean Floud, and upbraiding what he took to be the moral and philosophical nihilism of the age, Berlin clearly punctures the stature of German-Jewish 'alienists' and 'pariahs' as well as the milieu of Weimar radicalism that had produced them. The 'intrusion' of Marcuse and Hannah Arendt into the mainstream of Anglo-American political discourse is, for him, a particular irritant:

> The terrible twisted *Mitteleuropa* in which nothing is straight, simple, truthful, all human relations and all political attitudes are twisted into ghastly shapes by these awful casualties who, because *they* are crippled, recognize nothing pure and firm in the world.[12]

Although himself an exile from Bolshevik Russia, not for Berlin the rhetorical virtues of a misshapen identity or any concept of estrangement that might be raised to a critical standard; not, for Berlin, any *excess* in thought or action; specifically, not for him that traumatized overabundance that had moved into the vacuum left by the recent failure of modern democratic reason, an overabundance implicated in the traumas wrought by fascism and totalitarianism in *Mitteleuropa* itself. For Berlin, as Stephen Aschheim puts it, 'damaged people ... produced damaged ideas.'[13] For Berlin, any notion that injury might itself be conceptually productive – to suffer from neurosis, Freud insists, means to suffer less from any event than from certain *ideas* – is not only politically untenable but essentially unintelligible.

And yet, even as Freud and Freudian interpretation held little interest for him, might the balanced – and tragic – poise of Berlin's philosophy be seen as the application of a basic psychoanalytic ethic? Might the abstinence of his sober realism speak less of a liberal-conservative reluctance to engage with more radically imagined scenarios than a refusal to fill out or inflate a given void? Might we read his equivocations not so much as the amelioration of post-war uncertainties than as the best way to meet and manage them? For if Berlin's complaint against a 'terrible twisted *Mitteleuropa*' signals a hostility to the neurotic symptom, his definition of liberalism also avoids any simple retreat from struggle. Whatever else it may be, Berlin's liberalism recoils from the assumption of any solution. At its centre is the exemplary fact of tragedy: unavoidable, unalloyed, abiding. So understood, it appears as an empirically and psychically proportionate realism. What it courts is neither an alleviation of damage nor a remission of its symptoms but a frugal and judicious way of surviving crisis itself: in this case, a qualified acceptance of Cold War exigencies and a less sentimental – that is, far more frustrated, thwarted – prognosis of the sheer 'givenness' of that situation.

In focusing on Berlin and refracting him through some key Freudian concepts, what follows is arguably in keeping with the very political and psychic quietism that so much post-Freudianism – and so much Jewish thought of Berlin's own generation – sets itself against. For my argument not only shares little with those critiques that excoriate liberalism as the ideology of modern Western capitalism – liberal toleration, for Slavoj Žižek, being the post-political impasse, *par excellence*.[14] In pointedly embracing a sensibility that is more discreet in its critical impulses, it is also more capable of grasping the ambiguities and indecisions to which Berlin's liberalism aspires. On the one hand, then, my aim is to affirm an authentic core to a particular political model or 'to recall liberalism to its first essential imagination of variousness and possibility', as Lionel Trilling famously puts it.[15] On the other hand, it is to reveal what is most fragile and, at the same time, most determined in Berlin's political philosophy, taking his characteristic restraint less as a prompt for critique than one whose very critical composure might give us pause. Thus, even as we don't usually think of Berlin as a historian of his own inner life – on the contrary, his posture of elegant high-mindedness, a kind of peremptory modesty, often seems like the fuss of sublimation, of deflection – we can read the positions and processes he rejected, as much as those he defended, as the surrogate of deeper psychological concerns. Most importantly, they are concerns that bear upon a specific spatial experience: that is, the spatiality of the assimilated subject as it underwrites the commitment to all that is precarious and ungrounded in Berlin's liberal form of life.

3

While the category of space offers us an unexpected route into Berlin's political philosophy, it is history *as such* which sets the apparent scene. Writing through the 1950s, 1960s and 1970s, in the middle of that 'broken-backed century',[16] in Osip Mandelstam's memorable phrase, Berlin's world was one in which Stalinism still raged, the murderousness of German fascism had not long passed, and parts of the socialist Left, old Trotskyists in particular, fought over the remains of the dismembered body. Moreover, the dilemma that Berlin saw at the heart of a modern history of ideas is still one of the most recondite of all: How did the moral and political liberties of the eighteenth and nineteenth centuries give way to the tyrannies of the twentieth century? How did their rich and dextrous textures dilute into thin and credulous dogma? 'How,' in Mark Lilla's words, 'did the Europe that produced Goethe and Kant, Voltaire and Rousseau, Tolstoy and Chekov also produce the *Lager* and the *Gulag*?'[17]

For Berlin, the question entails identifying a differentiated modernity, one in which reason and unreason, universalism and particularism, pluralism and singularity confront each other and in which freedom is determined by how one protects the field of tension between them. In such a precarious zone there is, for Berlin, no alternative but to nurture a practical reason grounded in an inescapable uncertainty, and no other way of easing the ideological strangleholds characteristic not only of modern totalitarianism but contained within the Enlightenment's best impulses as well. But if Berlin's political sensibilities are historically contingent, they are also implicitly spatial. Or, as we will see, they are given by a certain relation of subjectivity to space: a relation in which assimilation is in some sense structured by a Freudian therapeutics and liberal pluralism functions as a foundation for the maintenance of a (assimilated) self.

Like so many analyses of liberalism, the central criticisms of Isaiah Berlin often rest on the presuppositions – and sometimes presuppose the presuppositions – of his discursive mode or mood itself. It is not just that Berlin makes no creative leaps and breaks no bold ground – he is, at bottom, a borrower and generalist; 'the ideas and arguments about which [he] writes are', as Bernard Williams notes, 'always *someone else's*'[18] – but the abstractive stretch is precisely the move he refuses. If his prudence seems 'uncritical' or, at least, domesticating in its effects – Berlin's ideas 'partake of a basic Anglo-American mental household', is Russell Jacoby's charge[19] – it is because he is a writer whose cautious empiricism appears so hostile to speculative thought, whose principled hesitations can read as an anodyne pulling of punches, whose first task is always to check the strenuousness of anything maximal, magical, immoderate.

But if herein lies the dusty and stolid conservatism of which Berlin is often accused, it is also the result of an intellectual content indissociable from its form. 'Berlin's essays in the history of ideas,' as Lilla notes, 'are not only *about* liberalism. They are also displays of a liberal temperament [...], an existential matter, a certain way of carrying oneself in the world and in the company of others.'[20] Indeed, while his conceptual modesties – the assertion, for example, that 'there *is no* a priori reason for supposing that truth, when it is discovered, *will* necessarily prove interesting'[21] – might well be the (im)modest disguise of the urbane self-ironist, it is also apiece with Berlin's central case against the European Enlightenment. Specifically, it relates to his sustained critique of the monism of the eighteenth-century French *philosophes* and their followers in the German *Aukflärung* whose laws of universality Berlin condemns as the deadly prologue to modern technocratic power.

And the tracing of ancestry is key. For if the immediate context of Berlin's arguments is the recent memory of European fascism and the still ascending scourge of Sovietism, his essays – especially those written at the height of the Cold War – interpret their threat less as a repudiation of human freedoms than as the siren call of a perennial utopianism, both scientific and romantic, lodged deep in the strata of Western intellectual history. In this, however, the point of Berlin's project is not to dismiss the Enlightenment *tout court*. On the contrary, in his sympathetic presentation of certain humanist traditions, the intent is to preserve the principles of human emancipation and rational inquiry precisely by chronicling the impact of their exaggerated expression. 'The unparalleled services of the Enlightenment,' he insists, 'in its battle against obscurantism, oppression, injustice and irrationality of every kind are not in question.'[22] The wide sweep of Berlin's genealogies, then, concerns the ways in which innate tendencies come to be deformed, and theoretical orientations duplicated or distended, in obverse directions. Although never a consequentialist, his is an intellectual history that investigates the origins of things in light of their subsequent echoes. In *Freedom and Its Betrayals: Six Enemies of Human Liberty*, a collection of essays based on a series of BBC broadcasts in 1952, Berlin sets out to identify the precursors and 'early preacher[s]'[23] of modern totalitarianism, recognizing the 'earliest thinkers [who] speak a language which is directly familiar to us'[24] and locating the remote source of later routes. Focusing on figures who all wrote within a fifty-year period of the French Revolution, Berlin's critiques are acute even if unsurprising, featuring a cast of characters who, while foundational, are also broadly drawn. On this account, the eighteenth-century utilitarianism of Helvétius, like the utopian socialism of Saint-Simon, might well represent some of the earliest formulations of liberty. In turning ethics into a type of technology, however, they come to reduce it in an instrumental sense: freedom, qualified by the vision of social perfectibility, is inevitably 'dehumanized',[25] its inherent radicalism diluted and then betrayed by a new scientific logic of social and state efficiencies. Yet more grievous, for Berlin, are the rationalist *philosophes*: holding liberty to an absolute they effectively invert it, ultimately redefining liberty as its opposite.

Thus the paradox of Rousseau, as Berlin's Romantic Counter-Enlightenment story has it, emerges at the fateful point at which liberty, taken as the essence of the human self, faces off the equally absolute value of the general will and the adherence to moral law – a contradiction solvable only by redefining freedom *as* social obedience itself. If such an inversion could eventually cast state oppression in the guise of freedom – 'there is not a dictatorship in the West who in the years after Rousseau did not use this monstrous paradox'[26] – then German idealism, for Berlin, performs analogous betrayals. Thus, in Fichte – particularly, the later Fichte – the precondition for a free-willing and self-conscious individual is that it recognizes its limits and responds to the call of an external, social world. Berlin's concern lies with the nature of such a directive. If self-positing, in Fichte's sense, depends on the ability of the subject to answer to an objective or outside 'other', then for Berlin such a relation opens the way to a dangerously collectivist definition. It makes the essence of self-creation repose on its encounter with a higher, super-personal self and ultimately a nationalist one. 'The individual, [Fichte] begins to suspect, does not exist, he must vanish. The group – *Gattung* – alone exists, is alone real.'[27] For Berlin, the aggrandizement of metaphysical idea into historical action always threatens:

> Then the great paean begins, the great nationalist, chauvinist cry. Individual self-determination now becomes collective self-determination, and the nation a community of unified wills in pursuit of moral truth.[28]

Unsurprisingly for a history of ideas begun in the early 1950s, it is Hegel's apparent providentialism that slings the widest and deepest net. On Berlin's view, structures built on Hegelian foundations are not only unattainable but conceptually incoherent. If the first too easily thickens into impossible unities (Utopia, for Berlin, is paradoxically a pinched, fixed, phobic space), the second mistakes human society for a branch of the natural sciences. And so, freedom becomes compliant with the monism of world process, and rationality means accepting the theodicy of historical necessity.

For Berlin, in clean contrast, human liberty is non-equivalent: 'Liberty is liberty, not equality or fairness or justice or culture, or human happiness or a quiet conscience.'[29] Its validity and sufficiency depend on it being an end in itself, neither reducible to the reaches of knowledge nor submissive to the 'symmetrical fantasies'[30] of history. Nailing his progenitive colours firmly to the mast, Berlin is thus able to steer an unwavering course from Hegel through Marx to Stalin, locating modern totalitarianism within the inherent weaknesses of Enlightenment thought and inveighing against the human freedoms sacrificed on the royal road to ideality.

But if Berlin's search for the inborn defects of a Western philosophical tradition tends to smother its many variables, either stylizing its selected figures or inclining them to celebrity – for many, Berlin's reading of his central hero, Alexander Herzen, is particularly proprietorial[31] – his task, as Lilla insists, is 'simply pedagogical'.[32] From a range of historical and theoretical arguments brought into likely and unlikely association – from Machiavelli to Giambattista Vico and Johan Gottfried Herder; from Benjamin Constant and Joseph de Maistre to Karl Marx; from French and German Romanticism to the nineteenth-century revolutionary Russia of Herzen, Vissarion Belinsky and Mikhail Bakunin – Berlin's lesson is synthetic and salutary. It is that history 'has no libretto'.[33] That no metaphysics of the straight line can be hewn 'out of the crooked timber of humanity'.[34] And that only the permanence of uncertainty avoids the fallacy that 'all fundamental questions are in principle answerable and that life formed according to the true answers would constitute the ideal society'.[35]

Bringing the goal much closer, any genuine political morality, for Berlin, comes from an intensely immanent conception of reality. It means existing – in practice and principle – in the circumspect middle of things, within the contingent and contextual, and without the lure of a systematic solution. Distinguished from the rigid energies of the rationalized optimists and 'system-builders',[36] it entails living and 'suffering through'[37] the infinite textures of the day to day: remaining *in situ* and seeing how restrictive is the far-off horizon when it annexes the imagination.

Although often a rhetorical pose rather than the result of specific argumentation – Sphinx-like, he asks but doesn't always answer his own questions – Berlin prioritizes the tactic of the present over the strategy of the next step. The principal value of this resides not in the present's ideas – its plans, its predictions – but in the deeper rhythms of experience and action that plot its moral course. If the political solution hides a monstrous dimension then, for Berlin, it is transience that must take up our time. In his introductory essay to Herzen's *Childhood, Youth and Exile*, Berlin chooses his citations with this in mind:

> What is the purpose of the song the singer sings? [...] If you look beyond your pleasure in it for something else, for some other goal, the moment will come when the singer stops and then you will only have memories and vain regrets [...] because, instead of listening, you are waiting for something else [...] I would rather think of life, and therefore of history, as a goal attained, not as a means to something else.[38]

Again, in a longer essay Berlin re-describes the social and moral questions of Herzen and the revolutionary anarchist Mikhail Bakunin:

> Everything in nature, in history, is what it is; and its own end. The present is its own fulfilment, it does not exist for the sake of some unknown future. If everything existed for the sake of something else, every fact, every event, creature would be a means to something beyond itself in some cosmic

plan [...] Is the culmination of a process *eo ipso* its purpose? Is old age the purpose of youth [...] ? Is the purpose of life death?[39]

Thus limitation, Berlin implies, curbs nothing. On the contrary, it is the very reality of the limit that, in nature as in history, bestows value and accounts for inspiration. As though existing 'for the sake of an unknown future'[40] is itself, paradoxically, an assault on fulfilment, it is the limit that distinguishes the urgent from the merely determined, or confers the pleasure of what is actually possible and actionable.

4

With this in mind, one might understand Berlin's delimited present as a version of that middle space we encountered in the previous chapters: an interruption in the unrestricted continuum of time, a presentness we are not so much *constrained by* as *released* or *expelled into*. Dislodging first principles and final ends, then, is not simply an argument against origins and culminations. It becomes a case for slackening the line that connects them, unleashing to the present what had been dictated by direction. Furthermore, in taking up Herzen's precept that 'if we merely look to the end of the process, the purpose of all life is death',[41] Berlin not only identifies a peculiar fatality – or, at least, a fateful inertia – at the core of progressivist projects. He condemns as reactionary, as an enemy of life, all that aspires to immortality. On this account, political idealism's craving for certainty and duration is also what accounts for its fundamental conservativism: an essential aversion to incompletion ruins its creativity and, finally, makes it indistinguishable from death or the changelessness which insures it.

Although their languages and conceptual contexts are very different, Berlin comes close to re-describing what in Freud goes by the name of the 'death-instinct'. If the pursuit of 'something else'[42] detaches from the present or exempts it, what Berlin is pointing to in this detachment is rather something like a re-attachment: fastening onto an end that, to the unconscious, is the impulse to regain an original state of quiescence, an end that ultimately refers to the purity of a beginning – indeed, refers to that inorganic, intransigent time even before the beginning. In its first formulation in *Beyond the Pleasure Principle* (1920), Freud's terms are curiously akin to Herzen's articulations of which Berlin so approves.

> If we are to take it as a truth that knows no exception that everything living dies for *internal* reasons – becomes inorganic once again – then we shall be compelled to say that '*the aim of all life is death*' and, looking backwards, that *inanimate things existed before living ones.*[43]

Putting aside the idioms of Freudian naturalism – the death-instinct, as first conceived, belongs to the conserving nature of biological existence – both Freud and Herzen, and by extension Berlin, seem to share common ground. What connects them is not just a fundamental scepticism about striving towards social or individual perfectibility. It is a concern with the consequences of its application: of how we come to suffer from our loyalty to (inanimate, transcendent or 'terminal') ideals and of how we misconstrue such loyalty as a kind of freedom. For at its most basic level, Freud's 'pressure towards death'[44] is not just an urge to shore up resistance to the empirical, assuaging the final (biological) fact of death by sustaining an ideal of it. Like Berlin's attack on political dogma as it denies the essentially unformulatable logic of things, the death-instinct is a kind of historical erasure: the desire to be independent of life and the terrors of it, to be free of its conflicts, its inventions, its choices. It is a refusal to live in the world as it is, or a wanting it to be other than it is, either by supposing that an end – a death, an ideal – could be coherent with the idiosyncrasies of one's history or by hoping it might make one's efforts and forfeits bearable, intelligible. Thus Berlin's Herzen, writing as eyewitness to the

1848 Revolutions in Rome and Paris and recounting the high promise and defeat of the mid-century's radical political movements:

> If progress is the goal, for whom are we working? Who is this Moloch who, as the toilers approach him, instead of rewarding them, draws back; and as a consolation to the exhausted and doomed multitudes, shouting '*morituri te salutant*', can only give the [...] mocking answer that after their death all will be beautiful on earth [...] A goal which is infinitely remote is no goal, only [...] a deception; a goal must be closer – at the very least the labourer's wage, or pleasure in work performed.[45]

If *'morituri te salutant'* (*those who are about to die, salute you*) is Herzen's lament for a failed revolution – he will, however, continue to defend the 'integrity of the Russian masses' and support the capacities of communal peasant organization [46]– in Berlin's account it refers, above all, to the assumed moral profits of such suffering: the compensatory pay offs of posthumous existence, death as a substitute and extended generation, the spiritual remunerations of sacrifice. For Berlin, these are the life-denying safeguards of all sacramental and moralizing politics, even – or, especially – those conscripted to the cause of human freedom. In surrendering the indeterminate to a coming purpose, it is a kind of theodicy with God left out or a faith replaced with an anticipatory politics. In both cases, it is not merely a desire for immortality – the secondary gain of an afterlife parodied by Herzen's Moloch. It is a matter of a life somehow opposed to itself, an inability or unwillingness to tolerate the anxieties of its transience. Indeed if, for Freud, the refusal of life is also the expression of desire – the death-instinct as an obscure resolution of life, the unconscious need to be saved or excused from it – then, for Berlin, safety is similarly menacing. Its threat is not quite the danger of nihilism. It is the threat of proposing a solution that pre-empts the experience of the living problem, of a tenacity that valorizes what it most revokes: the acknowledgement of loss. In this, the risk is an existence in which we fail to exercise our skills in answering to moral demands and so entertain the 'deepest of modern disasters': living proleptically, deflecting the present and overleaping the hour, 'reject[ing] fulfilment today, because [one] must own the future', also.[47]

That Berlin's liberalism takes moralities to be un-generalizable and ideals to be intensely finite and not flatly futural means that he places the present at the centre of his social and political thesis. 'Principles are not less sacred because their duration cannot be guaranteed,' he writes in *Two Concepts of Liberty*,[48] which means that transience, far from being a withdrawal from political or moral alignment, is precisely what makes such commitment possible. Insisting that the 'concrete situation is almost everything,'[49] it is the acceptance that each historical moment is its own complete reality and so already its own 'goal attained',[50] that moral responsibilities are not transferable and the contingencies of every situation too detailed and contradictory ever to be refined into rule. Crucially, this is not a simple passivism, an acquiescence to the extant and unavoidable. It is an engagement with the conditions of limitation itself. In short, scaling down our thought and action not only creates that 'human-horizon'[51] without which morality and inventiveness cannot survive. Such diminutions also converge with the pluralism that lies at the heart of Berlin's sensibilities. Moreover, as I come to argue, it is within such pluralism that we might locate the therapeutic work implicated in the spatial content of an assimilated subjectivity. Thus, Berlin's liberalism is not merely a valuing of the political in immediate reality. It also describes the subject riven between incompatible spaces or its submission to the losses it suffers but must somehow survive.

5

Let me be clear, what pluralism involves here is not any flat-footed moral relativism – or its ultra-individualist variant – according to which particular cultures have particular values whose moral authority cannot therefore be judged by any external or common metric. Berlin insists on this distinction. As he puts it when discussing the supposed relativism of Herder's defence of national cultural particularity against the claims of Enlightenment universalism:

> I repeat, pluralism – the incommensurability and, at times, incompatibility of objective ends – is *not* relativism; nor, *a fortiori*, subjectivism, nor the allegedly unbridgeable difference of emotional attitude on which some modern positivist, emotivists, existentialists, nationalists and, indeed, relativistic sociologists and anthropologists found their accounts.[52]

But if value-conflict is enduringly human and if agonism is endemic, it would also be incorrect to see Berlin's pluralism as concomitant with that supposed acceptance of difference that goes by the name of liberalist multiculturalism. More precisely, insofar as Berlin insists on a field of inescapable tensions and un-consoled ends, this is not a pluralism compatible with the repressive tolerance of those brands of liberal coexistence – what Žižek calls liberalism's 'tolerant intolerance'[53] – which, nonetheless, allow only the adjustable parts of foreign thought in and ensure that its unwanted content stays outside. Finally, it is only the most ahistorical of arguments that would confuse Berlin's pluralism with the 'culturalization of politics'[54] in which social inequalities, named and neutralized as cultural difference, become the basis of a contemporary liberal ideology.

But it isn't just that Berlin comes from a different time and place. Nor is it merely that his empiricism sets a limit to theoretical ambitions in political and ideological terms. Rather, with a humanism at once realist and radical, Berlin's pluralism entails a world in which essential difference and dividedness – both private and public – mean that we cannot escape the permanence of conflict: a conflict that persists without the interference of consensus or arbitration. Contrary to the monists who would fashion a culmination the better to evade incompatibility and opposed, too, to a traditional liberalism, which holds to an agreed commonwealth generated out of a clash of interests, Berlin takes the conflict between equally compelling values to be ineliminable. Neither a derivative nor a multiplication of a singular good but precisely a *pluralism*, as Steven Lukes notes, a space in which all human values might assemble is, for Berlin, not only practically impossible but formally incoherent.[55] Here the choice between 'ends equally ultimate, and claims equally absolute' makes conflict – 'and tragedy' – immanent and ineradicable.[56] Here, too, irreducible difference not only occurs between opposing value systems; it names the dividedness internal to human subjectivity itself.

And so, the familiar liberal dilemma: 'How are we to choose between possibilities'?[57] What and how much must be weighed against what? Which goods should be emphasized at the expense of which others? Or, if 'the first public obligation is to avoid extremes of suffering',[58] as Berlin phrases it in distinctly Freudian terms, how does this task sit with the inescapability of conflict? When the realization of one value is only gained with the loss of another, what of the irresolutions and remains inevitably incurred? In sum, if the price of liberty is permanent uncertainty, how do we entrust to what Berlin calls an 'unstable equilibrium'[59]: lurching between the threat of achieved satisfaction on the one hand and the threat of frustration on the other?

To the extent that Berlin's liberalism involves a certain comportment towards conflict rather than any normative model for a liberal polity, such questions remain open. Their remit, however, extends beyond the ethics of value pluralism. For Berlin's sensibility not only bears on his distinctive political philosophy. It engages a particular experience of space; and we cannot, I suggest, approach Berlin's pluralism without also thinking what it means to be an *assimilated* subject. Which is to say, a subject not only split across two geographic spaces and two incompatible states but who might inhabit what Berlin calls the 'flow of life'[60] in between: keeping to the disorientations of this 'middle', putting the freeze on consolatory desires, refusing both native predicates and the voyage to 'dim ... and distant ends'.[61] 'Assimilation-as-liberalism', then, secures neither existence nor pleasure: it coincides with the undoings of spatial displacement, and with the disorders in 'any and every space we [might wish to] call home'.[62]

6

Assimilation-as-liberalism: while the analogy I have in mind is a structural one, it is by no means a direct or simply substitutive move. It consists not in how a departure from a native place for life in another calls on the powers of self-creation and subjective volition that are, of course, part of a general liberal lexicon. Nor is assimilation merely another word for cultural 'adoption' and 'adaptation' where it becomes the means towards some ultimate singularity or indistinguishability in identity. Here, assimilation is its own form of radical incompletion: the depleting of one scene in order to live (perilously but inventively) in an alternative one. Indeed, as a kind of pragmatic meditation on Berlin's politics, assimilation might be thought as a process in which the obstruction proves to be the opening: cooperating with contradiction, self-severing, living with thoughts and 'forms of life that are [properly] not one's own'.[63] Neither the stranger's outsiderness, nor the exile's distress – not any *extremity in either detachment or re-attachment* that would deny Berlin's present flows – assimilation thus rests on turning lost things to new account. It sponsors a condition where incompatibility is not the paralysis of crisis but signals what Freud calls a certain 'preparedness for anxiety'.[64] It aspires to the thin line where critique functions within compromise and to a life in which difference lives in the company of some important damage. So conceived, assimilation cannot be confused with any political or psychic 'non-position' in the manner of an evasive or resigned 'making-do'. It is, rather, about possessing, though never mastering, the breach of a formative dis-possession. We can describe it as a non-violent dividedness, a kind of pro-social conciliation with conflict. What it signifies is not any final overcoming of incompletion but the readiness to dismantle our metaphysical and political occlusions of it.

Importantly, this understanding of assimilation is very different from Berlin's own rendition of the term. In fact, it is direct contrast with it. In the first instance, Berlin never uses it as a self-description – his comfortable relocation in London and entrée into the narrow circle of the British establishment perhaps discount that as a possibility. More importantly, assimilation is a formation of identity Berlin explicitly rejects, especially as a descriptor of the history of modern European Jewry. Thus in 'Jewish Slavery and Emancipation', first published in a series of articles in *The Jewish Chronicle* in 1951, he regrets those who had 'to make themselves familiar with the habits and modes of behaviour' of other people and warns against the fawning propriety to 'get this right' and 'not miscalculate'.[65] Here, as elsewhere, Berlin's enunciates a version of cultural solidarity, which is often taken to be the disquieting aspect of his Counter-Enlightenment story: a certain advocacy of opaque irrationalities, an insistence on the ethical importance of inherited cultural membership, even an implicit hostility to the idea of cosmopolitanism. Berlin's life-long investment in Romanticism, we remember, is integral to his critique of universalist reason; without it, he insists, neither political liberalism nor modern individualism could have emerged.

Part of what informs Berlin's rejection of assimilation is his appeal to a nineteenth-century tradition of liberal thought; an inheritance that, against its eighteenth-century progenitors and twentieth-century inheritors, championed cultural specificity as a source of social stability legitimately anchored in the formation of the modern nation-state. For John Gray, this is the role that Benjamin Constant, Alexis de Tocqueville and John Stuart Mill play in Berlin's work, positing a liberalism able to reconcile individual freedom with broader participations on the one hand while refraining from abstract combinatory principles on the other.[66] Moreover, in understanding common cultural forms, and their modes of adherence, as inherently plural, Berlin is able to retain them within his guiding principle of incommensurability. Individuality is carried over into a national collectivity – and, for Berlin, might even thrive there – precisely because its creative origin is itself constituted by a variety of allegiances and across a diversity of communities.

But in his continuation of an older Romantic liberalism, it is Berlin's rehabilitation of Johann Gottfried Herder that remains most problematic. For while Berlin's Herder might be the theorist of an expressive *Volkism* capable of countering a nationless universalism, it is the Herder who helped produce the violent identitarianism of Berlin's own time that exposes him at his most vulnerable.[67] That there are striking tensions in Berlin's repertoire is not in doubt: whence the imputing of intellectual inconsistency, of the ineffective or overstuffed synthesis of some of his more turbulent contradictions, of the fact that his moral references and rhetorical finesse often do duty for the logic of consistent enquiry. Confining Herder's nationalism to the terms of a benign culturalism – 'Herder', Berlin asserts, 'does not use the criterion of blood or of race',[68] 'nationality for him is strictly a cultural attribute'[69] – and doing at a moment when *volkism* had been redirected towards an avenging ethno-nationalism, is arguably one such impasse.[70] At the same time, all this contributes to the essential disfiguring that I identify at the core of an assimilated subjectivity, a traversal between spaces and states that is also a commitment to conflict, one that – by the logic of Berlin's own pluralism – never settles.

In 'Benjamin Disraeli, Karl Marx, and the Search for Identity',[71] Berlin gives an account of nineteenth-century Jewish life in England and Germany in which assimilation happens amid the pervasiveness of nationalist assertion. Like his disdain for religious conversion as it purchases a convenient 'entry ticket to European culture', as Heinrich Heine famously describes the first-generation of emancipated Jews associated with the Young Germany

Movement in the 1830s–50s, the verdict that Berlin returns on Benjamin Disraeli and Karl Marx is equally dismissive. Assimilation, when it implies an abnegation of origin is, for Berlin, a wholly 'grotesque distortion':[72] less a predicament one has to bear than a sickness which savagely dictates. On Berlin's account, Heine's acquired Protestantism, as much as his later status as an exile in Paris, renders him a 'Mr Nothing': '*M. Henri Heine: Un rein, vous êtes Monsieur un rien*' (Nothing, you are Mr Nothing) is the title of a poem that an adolescent Berlin writes in 1928 as a parody of assimilation's deformations.[73] His Disraeli and Marx are similarly voided by the feints of their post-emancipation self-fashioning. While their 'new persona' might 'shed the emblems of servitude and inferiority',[74] the evasion of the 'Jewish question' – in Marx's case, diverting the national question in the direction of an internationalist proletarian movement and in Disraeli's transposing racial anxiety into an 'over-dressed'[75] extravagance of Jewish self-display – is nothing less than a 'neurotic distortion'.[76] Diagnosing assimilation as a moral pathology – an illness, on Berlin's account, for which the case histories of Heine's irony, Marx's theoretical abstractions and Disraeli's theatricality are attempted rectifications – also turns their politics into acts of reprisal. These become acts of bad-faith, of self-deceptive error. As Berlin's most recent biographer Arie Dubnov sketches it:

> [Disraeli] was an astute defender of modern conservativism and a strong believer in Jewish racial superiority, while [Marx], his mirror opposite, attempted to radically emancipate Jews from their primitive particularism; but what was their politics, Berlin argues, if not an expression of their 'Search for Identity' as converted Jews?[77]

Not much in Berlin's diptych convinces. While his descriptions are compelling –Disraeli becomes the flamboyant 'Pied Piper leading a bemused collection of dukes, earls, solid country gentlemen, and burly farmers';[78]

Marx's conversion reduces his thought to a lifeless prophesy, vacant like so many 'blank leaves between the Old and New Testament'[79] – the argument on which they hinge is one-dimensional in a way that Berlin seldom is. For, to be Jewish in truth and assimilated in *ressentiment* – an indictment of intellectual inauthenticity akin to those made against Marcuse and Arendt, the 'crippled' *Mitteleuropeans*[80] – not only diminishes the self-dispossessions internal to the formation of identity. But it also minimizes Berlin's signal concept of pluralism, thinning-out the agency of indeterminacy and invention in moral and political life that he otherwise so passionately endorses.

Paradoxically, then, Berlin's reading of Jewish assimilation – its dubious seductions and the absurdity of some if its outcomes – placates much of the tension at the heart of value-pluralism: the dissonance between an individual's needs and losses, their mutual and continual interruption of each other. He comes to sequester conflict, restricting it to a field of *external* discontinuities where competing values, beliefs and contents are born full-fledged, already ripened enough to participate in the opposing pressures of a shared world. Framed in this way, Berlin not only disregards the tensions constitutive of, rather than external to, the propositions of subjects and cultures. He also covers over the unpredictable gaps in which intervention becomes possible, bypassing the ways in which incommensurables do not resolve themselves rationally – the very life-denying posture he so abhors – but persist as an always present force.

How might we make different sense of Berlin's understanding of Jewish assimilation? How might we take it not as an attack or denial of identity, as his treatment of Disraeli and Marx suggests, but as the inverse? Can we read assimilation not as the defensive cover of some repressed inner world, but as a practice that dis-assembles those very defences? Relatedly, can we see the identificatory 'truth' to which Berlin alludes not as a connectedness to an original site of affiliation, but as an affirmation of its dislocations and displacements? The interpretation of assimilation I will be proposing here is thus the very opposite of Berlin's diagnosis. Far from being a pathology of self-evasion, it bears on what I want to thematize as the process of 'becoming-liberal': on what might be gained in loss, in the transience it permits, the relinquishments it demands, the incompletions it must entertain. If this means we have to bracket Berlin's portraiture – his discrediting of Heine, Disraeli and Marx – it also means we can do no better than attend to the central term of his political philosophy itself. Indeed, my suggestion is that Jewish assimilation catches something of a liberal pluralist model, involving less the rejection of identity or origin than a delimited view of their possibility, their actuality. Recalling Berlin's assessment of Herzen's politics, we may see it as a 'minimal area'[81] – at once most essential and least presumed – in which ideality and adjustment coexist: a small, unstable preserve; a little place for the living-along with collisions and in the shadow of their cost. In this, assimilation denotes neither similarity in identity nor any surrender of the self; it is the clarification of difference itself. *Contra* Berlin, it need not entail the psychic work of renunciation or repression. Instead, assimilation describes what I want to call a *self-limiting labour*, and one that is 'liberal' and 'plural' in just this sense. Its task is not merely to give up one place and identity in order to regain another. It is the (liberal) capacity of *bearing to be lost* or of incorporating loss as *a spatial bearing itself*.

7

To secure the analogy between assimilation and liberal pluralism we cannot rely on Berlin's appraisals of various assimilated Jewish intellectuals. We also cannot simply look at how his own spatial biography maps onto his political philosophy. It is not enough to be reminded of Berlin who, as a young boy traumatized by the violence of the Revolutions of 1917, fled St Petersburg for the newly independent Lithuania in 1920 and, confronting anti-Semitism from the authorities there, left for England in 1921. And nor is it enough to focus on the encounter in November 1945 when Berlin travelled back to Leningrad and met with Anna Akhmatova, finding, during one fugitive night, the seeds of a position that informed his later political philosophy. Instead, we might splice Berlin's liberal pluralism and assimilated subjectivity together, positing the relation not only in spatial terms but with an awareness of its hidden Freudian dimension. Here the assimilated subject is not only given by its successful crossing of 'homes'; it is a definition of assimilation as a liberal-therapeutic itself.

True, Berlin rarely mentions Freud. And when he does, it is largely to characterize the psychoanalytic project as yet another closed explanatory system. Although both Jewish refugees forced to find shelter in London, Freud's *fin-de-siècle* Vienna and Berlin's post-revolutionary Russia signal two canonical but distinct political and intellectual nativities. Yet, Freud's psychoanalysis and Berlin's liberalism not only share similarity as structural and historical models – the very coherence excoriated by Freudian Marxists for their political and psychic repose. Beyond this well-known contention, the partnering of psychoanalysis and political liberalism has another lineage. In a brilliant argument, Michael P. Steinberg demonstrates how Freud's early association with John Stuart Mill transforms classic liberal philosophy into the primal scene of the family and the treacheries of filial relations.[82] The salient event that Steinberg identifies is Freud's German language translations of four of Mill's essays undertaken on the recommendation of Franz Brentano in 1879 and 1880. While not alone in speculating on an early Mill-Freud connection – the presence of Mill in Freud's pre-psychoanalytic work has been often engaged[83] – Steinberg's far-reaching suggestion is that the literal project of linguistic translation be read as Freud's personal and theoretical investment in English liberalism's most celebrated 'family romance'.[84] On this account, the story of English liberalism – the passage from first- to second-generation Utilitarianism – accords with the psychoanalytic architecture of the family itself. Thus J.S. Mill's paternal legacy (of James Mill, the real father, and Jeremy Bentham, the 'theoretical' one) is simultaneously unseated and substituted; the fathers' laws of social good repudiated yet repeated by the son's/student's move away from raw utilitarian measurement towards the 'lived' interiority of the liberal self. 'With the essay, "Utilitarianism" of 1861,' Steinberg writes, 'Mills declares at once the replacement and displacement of his father's position.'[85]

Importantly, while Freud's 'family romance' is premised on loss, it is also geared towards a certain attainment. At its core is the harsh but valiant struggle of subjectivity, and of thought. Who am I? Where do I stand? How do I disinherit, detach, divest and *still* stand? – questions which involve the effort of regaining a place in the world, of relocating oneself in history or finding alternate ideas about authority and its sourcing. 'Who am I?', in other words, is not just a sign of insufficiency; it becomes a form of achievement. It allows for the ability to depose, deform, intervene and newly enable. It works via partial burials and strange retrievals; via renunciations that, curiously, become new resources. On this reading, the psychic drama of fathers and sons not only 'deliver[s] a strong epistemology to the basic principles of English liberalism'.[86] For Steinberg, Freud's own German language translation of Mill's essays doubles as a 'translation of political theory into psychology'.[87]

That Mill's *On Liberty* (1859) was to become central to Berlin's own formulations of the necessity of fallibility to a free society and subjectivity will not detain us here.[88] With Steinberg's literal and psychoanalytic 'translations' in mind, however, I offer an analogous one. That the relationship of liberal pluralism to assimilation is not only given by Berlin's lifelong indictment of monism; it might, most meaningfully, be described in terms of what in a Freudian paradigm we know as the 'reality principle'.

The phrase is, of course, only one in a series of terms that Freud uses to characterize that most crucial and difficult of tasks: How do we give up instinctual life for the sake of a rational one under abstract law? How do we regulate our internal energies so that they accord with what the external world can tolerate? For Freud, such questions are alive to one over-riding obligation: to avoid extremes of pain, to protect the ego whose role it is to manage the unconscious and its chronicle of lost objects. So it is that 'reality' becomes a viable term for Freud. It does not so much impede the aim of satisfaction as escort it: raising its value and affording it protection, precisely by saving it from its uninhibited excess. Taking up the question in *Civilization and Its Discontents*, Freud writes of the importance of suffering that, once acknowledged, allows us to reconsider the hopes for happiness we have for ourselves:

> We shall never wholly control nature; our constitution, itself part of this nature, will always remain a transient structure, with a limited capacity for adaptation and achievement. Recognition of this fact does not have a paralyzing effect on us; on the contrary it gives direction to our activity. Even if we cannot put an end to all suffering, we can remove or alleviate some of it; the experience of thousands of years has convinced us of this.[89]

Thus the 'realistic' confirmation of suffering – not its moralizing or negation – sets the terms of the human happiness, marking the boundary between what is desirable and realizable, and living the discrepancies between them. The problem of what Berlin calls the 'One and the Many', which forms the final section of *Two Concepts of Liberty*, shares the basic coordinates of these tensions. Like the reality principle that attunes instinctive drives to the checks of the social, the need to choose between ultimate goods is the very basis of pluralism's perpetual rivalries. 'That we cannot have everything,' says Berlin, 'is a necessary, not a contingent, truth.'[90] To wish for more is fundamentally regressive: an allure that, in terms reminiscent of Freud, Berlin understands as both a desire and a fear.

> It may be that the ideal of freedom to choose ends without claiming eternal validity for them, and the pluralism of values connected with this, is only

the late fruit of our declining capitalist civilization [...] This may be so; but no skeptical conclusions seem to me to follow. Principles are no less sacred because their duration cannot be guaranteed. *Indeed, the very desire for guarantees that our values are eternal and secure [...] is perhaps only a craving for the certainties of childhood or the absolute values of our primitive past.*[91] (emphasis added)

At best a return to an 'ancient faith'[92] and at worst an infantile wish for omnipotence – in his Enlightenment genealogies Berlin's warning is that these become one and the same – what such principles precipitate is not merely a hardening or rigidity in practice. They disown the conflicts they register; they fly from themselves. Whether a vision aims towards future fulfilment (as with Berlin's eighteenth-century *philosophes* and their twentieth-century successors) or involves a reversal (as with his critique of Fichte and German historicism) thus do monist philosophies simultaneously enfeeble and fortify themselves: desiring that all needs be satisfied, and all ends compatible. In contrast, the task of Berlin's pluralism is not the elimination of social or individual conflict. It is to break down our aversions to it. Like the reality principle, its work lies in accommodating the sacrifices endemic to all relations between self and world, living with – and *being alive to* – their insufficiencies and afflictions.

For Freud, of course, there is no right degree of suffering in any conventional moral sense – he neither condones masochism nor is indifferent to the fact of human pain. What is required, as his famous formulation has it, is a 'certain amount of suffering'.[93] Its plausibility is not simply apiece with life; it underwrites and endorses life as a vital requirement. Being answerable to the plurality of human values, for Berlin, demands a similarly painful economy. The point is not to harmonize, much less eradicate, significant loss but to understand it differently. The task, as George Crowder suggests, is to translate 'lost value' as a 'rational regret',[94] to secure it as a necessary precondition for 'manag[ing]' social conflict so as to prevent it from becoming damaging to

[that] same precondition'.[95] Thus, Berlin's pluralism, like the Freudian 'real', not only defines individual and social lives on the 'less pleasurable' grounds of difference, distance and restless dissatisfaction. Their analogous 'therapies' involve the struggle of tolerating the incomprehension between self and world and, with this, compose what Aileen Kelly calls 'the imperfect, unfinished prose of daily existence'.[96] It is not that loss is serviceable or can be turned to profit – there would lie the false deaths and flaccid compensations of idealism. Loss does, however, involve its own sort of boon: a non-abstracted liveliness (and fear), a certain quality of attention. But if Berlin, like Freud, insists that all analysis proceeds by concrete example, how might we argue the connection further?

8

This chapter began with a description of a single night in November of 1945, a night spent in a Leningrad apartment where a poet in internal Soviet exile met an assimilated Jewish political philosopher. As briefly noted, the meeting between Anna Akhmatova and Berlin inspired the haunting formulation of the 'Guest from the Future' – a line from her monumental *Poem without a Hero* which, begun in 1940, Akhmatova continued to work on until her death in a sanatorium near Moscow in 1966. Of her many interpreters and biographers, no one has yet decided who that ghostly, futural figure might be. Emma Gerstein, a close friend and literary critic, claimed that the imagined 'guest' was Akhmatova's current lover, and the 'future' was the life they planned together. Others, like György Dalos, suggest that the addressee was Berlin himself, or at least a summation of what this visitor from the West meant to her. Still others suggest that the spectral companion was a summons to an ideal reader or to virtual worlds and words: a plea to a not yet existing community, or back to a past one for which there are no longer any speakers. Certainly, as Dalos reminds us, the image of some coming cryptic country was central to those Cubo-Futurist poets, like Vladimir Mayakovsky and Velimir Klebnikov, who in the first decade of the twentieth century had called themselves 'citizens of the future', the *budetlyane* (from the Russian *budet*, 'will be').

For a poet persecuted by Zhdanovite diktat, however, Akhmatova's prospective phantom is less a matter of aspiration than of restriction: a guest who for structural and historical reasons can never arrive; a captivation, in the present, with a missing past and a future foreclosed. A call with no respondent, an appeal with no addressee, a dead letter to absence as such, the 'Guest from the Future' has the paradoxical quality of an unmarked excitation, a driven pointlessness. As a phrase it twists on the stress between immobility and agitation, between the boredom of stasis and the conjuring of some temporal occasion. In this, Akhmatova's 'Guest from the Future' has the status of what Eric Santner, in a different context, describes as a 'designified signifier'.[97] What Santner intends by this is a certain paralyzed content or hindered revelation. Repetitive, inexpressive, but endlessly fascinating, it is about a 'peculiar surplus of address'[98] or an 'excess of validity over significance',[99] which points up a fundamental uselessness in meaning. The psychoanalytic name for this is, of course, *trauma*. Trauma is a superfluity, a fastening and an impelling persistence. As an occluded event it can never be properly located or temporalized. As an experience it thwarts translation, symbolization and signification. In Santner's words, trauma involves the 'torsion'[100] of being coerced by an 'uncanny sort of surplus animation'. It is about bearing the weight of a '"too much" of pressure'; an elaboration, a magnification 'unable to be assumed'.[101]

If the validity of 'force without significance'[102] relates to trauma as it stations the subject 'outside of life',[103] it is also a phenomenon that, in Berlin's political terms, is not just phantasmatic but, properly, illiberal. As an ideation,

Akhmatova's 'Guest' hails from a time outside of time and from a place strangely untethered to an extant present one. That such an outlying time and place emerge out of the most urgent political coordinates does not, of course, mean that we cannot describe it in such terms – to do otherwise would be to separate Akhmatova's yearning for a hyper- or a-historical experience from its inherent historicity. For all her elegiac distancing, as Hélène Cixous writes, Akhmatova is a 'date-giving poet'.[104] Her anonymous 'Guest' from the far side of time is nonetheless given by the particularities of a specific present.

But if I've staged the association between liberal pluralism and psychoanalysis plausibly, Akhmatova's future caller does not embody a utopian will or any other genre of political or psychic need, which imagines an emancipation, a redemption, a coming action. In its traumatized aspects, it is a cementing to something missing; an over-identification with loss that is, simultaneously, an embalming of the present world or a flight from its conflicts. In this sense, Akhmatova's 'Guest' is not really a figuration of the future at all – not even an aspiration to have one. It culls its energy from an anachronism, from the excesses of that temporal knot.

Arrested, uninflected, at once restive and held fast – Akhmatova's 'Guest' might go by the Freudian name of melancholy. For whereas the labour of mourning, as Freud explains in his 1917 paper on *Mourning and Melancholia*, involves the 'working through' of loss and so demands its gradual abandonment, melancholy retards any such surrender.[105] In a pathological misdirection of desire, melancholy binds itself *to* loss. Faithfully cathected and failing to mourn, it refuses to modulate attachment or relinquish defence. So understood, melancholy resists the structured sacrifices that govern the reality principle. It resists the gradual decathexis of energies that, in confirming loss, enables the subject to reconstitute itself and ensure its future life. Indeed, if the aim of mourning is, as Freud says, to '[declare] the object to be dead', and so '[offers] the ego the inducement of continuing to live'[106] it is, in effect, distance and dislocation that make more life possible. It 're-homes' the subject precisely by making it itinerant, by moving it on.

Freud is explicit that the lost object may not be only a loved person, but also 'an abstraction [...] such as one's country, liberty, an ideal, and so on'.[107] In Berlin's recollections of his meeting with Akhmatova in Leningrad in 1945, her enthrallment is explicitly marked as such:

> Her sustenance came not from [people] but from literature and images of the past: Pushkin's St Petersburg; Byron's, Pushkin's, Mozart's, Molière's Don Juan; and of the great panorama of the Italian Renaissance [...] I asked whether the Renaissance was a real historical past to her, inhabited by imperfect human beings, or an idealized image of an imaginary world. She replied that it was of course the latter; all poetry and art, was to her [...] a form of nostalgia, a longing for a universal culture, as Goethe and Schlegel had conceived it, [...] of *a reality which had no history, nothing outside itself.* Again she spoke of pre-revolutionary St Petersburg [...] and of the long dark night which had covered her henceforth. She spoke without the slightest trace of self-pity, *like a princess in exile, proud, unhappy, unapproachable.* (emphases added)[108]

Impervious to intervening history, Berlin's Akhmatova stands apart or against the present, and is melancholic in just this sense. What Berlin calls her 'historico-metaphysical vision'[109] looks for its clarity to older, now inexistent, social models. Her inability to mourn straps her to them.

But even as melancholia is consecrated to stability and stasis, Akhmatova's refusal to divest from loss is not incompatible with the constitution of another kind of politics. For in pulling back from the present, or declaring a position before or beyond it, melancholy not only recedes from the conflictual 'flow of life' in Berlin's Freudian sense.[110] As a phantasy – and phantasmatic – attachment, to sustain a melancholic immersion means to insist on a substitute world, another reality, one that would not demand such losses. From this perspective, we may say that melancholy is also what marks the 'Guest from the Future' as the work of a radical political dissident. It is a defence against a loss that is also a distant, durational – strictly, death-driven – stretch, a prolonging of desire by locating it always and forever elsewhere. It is a dissidence whose loyal protest consists precisely in not relenting on the ardency of that desire.

Thus, Akhmatova, as Berlin describes her, is not merely excluded from a historical present. Her unyielding opposition to Sovietism also implies that most contradictory of political positions: a resistance to oppression that is also a resistant (because self-sustaining) investment in it, a refusal to comply that depends on the energy of its own consistency. Resistance, Rebecca Comay argues, is 'both intriguing and awkward as a political resource'.[111] At once 'impediment and impetus':

> [It] can either disrupt or sustain the equilibrium and steadiness of every state of affairs [...] It is] either a force for transformation or a bulwark against innovation, either conservative or transformative – and at times, disconcertingly both.[112]

If Akhmatova's melancholy means that she both resists and remains resistant, we may also say that melancholy is way of naming exile, otherwise. Reading Berlin via Freud, this would be the spatiality of a subject who refuses to relinquish a lost home because she spurns the work of its sunderings and re-settlements, who positions herself beyond the enlivening 'flow of things' for fear of conceding to their claims. In this, the concept of exile takes on very different structure to the versions explored in previous chapters of this study. Here, exile is stative; its movements are riveted, captivated; its upheavals are dead-locked, air-locked, devitalized. Absorbed in the indistinctions of resistance, in Comay's terms, or retaining the tendencies of the psyche before its reorganization by separation, this is exile understood as a dissension from the present, an adherence to a 'better time' that is also an exemption from the world of active transformation. Thus, even as Akhmatova's failure to mourn and 'move' makes her an advocate of fearless refusal – 'she behaved with heroism', Berlin admiringly notes, 'her entire life was [...] one uninterrupted indictment of Russian reality'[113] – the political register of her position, in the terms given by Berlin's own, is ultimately reactionary. Not giving way on the desire for a lost home makes her exile, like her melancholy, an 'unworked' plenitude, a derealization of reality. We might call it an illiberal rejection of insufficiency itself.[114]

Akhmatova, herself, is in no doubt about the redeeming values of her *idèe fixes*. Even in 1922, in the wake of Gumilyov's execution when supporters and fellow poets pleaded with her to leave the Soviet Union, Akhmatova was immovable. 'I am not one of those who left the land to the mercy of its enemies' reads the title of poem devoted to those who survive by denunciating the 'half-dead' life of the 'exile's lot': the 'darks paths' opened by 'the wanderer's' moral compromises, the blight of their disengagement, the giving of ground, which like 'wormwood infects [their] "foreign bread"'. In her stiff-necked austerity – 'we are people without tears', 'straighter than you', 'more proud' – every inaction, especially her own, becomes an exertion of self-fulfilment; even the failure to cry becomes an agent of self-retention and its own dry solace.[115]

And so, in the clearness of the vacated past to which she vehemently cleaves, Akhmatova is unaltered, her loss is intransigent and its metaphysical protections are untouched. In this, her melancholy is not merely a defeat of reality, in the language given by Freud and, implicitly, by the key themes of Berlin's political philosophy. It inflects exile with an unexpected meaning: an immovable distance from daily life, a steadfast apartness from its extant requirements, a rootedness, a sedentarization. In this version of exile lurk both the intact and the illiberal: the subject's refusal to be displaced from a place *fantasized* as being rightful and proper to it.

9

Might there be a corollary to all this? If we conceive melancholy as a form of exilic adhesion, or point up the escapist effects paradoxically produced by static attachments, is mourning traceable in the liberal drama of assimilation? And if exile-as-melancholia is the desire to be cemented in a rightful and proper place, can assimilation be thought as its 'liberal' redress? Or, to formulate the question in the terms offered by a Freudian reading of Berlin: Might assimilation signify an unsafe egress from states that are no longer? Might it initiate a break in the obdurate identification with a lost object and an accession to what this brokenness might cost? Furthermore, might the abandonment of an 'original' home, and the idea of it, turn into the (ambivalent) opportunity of something else?

The question, then, is whether an assimilated subjectivity embodies Berlin's model of liberal pluralism – actioning a history of loosened attachments, moving from monist commitments to a politics of everyday displacements, and so to the conflicts that constitute and sustain it. At issue, to repeat, is not the subject's detachment from one world and its re- absorption elsewhere. Nor, as with Berlin's own diagnoses of Heine, Marx, and Disraeli, is it an approach to assimilation in which performing a new identity means the forgetting of an originally given one. To the contrary, here the assimilated subject always joined to an object – a past, a place, a value – might nevertheless not be overtaken and subsumed by it. Here too, division and self-dispossession are what account for the struggle – and capacity – *to* assimilate. Despite his declared opposition to assimilation, I take the politics of Berlin's liberal pluralism as precisely this 'mournful' activity: a politics not merely riven between incommensurables but one in which the rift, the crack, is itself generative.

In *The Ego and the Id* (1923) Freud re-evaluates his earlier account of bereavement to argue for a theory of mourning as a predicament: not a trapping of affect but a redistribution of it, allocating it an opening beyond the empty excesses of melancholia.[116] Reconceived as a *labour* rather than a relinquishment, mourning now entails not a conclusive grief process but an interminable one, less a liberation from a lost object than sustaining the subject's ambivalence to it. On this view, we may say that mourning finds its analogy in the work of assimilation: that is, unsealing the past or putting a brake on its perseverance, traversing a displacement no longer perceived – *and preserved* – as exilic. Thus, in place of melancholia (phantasmatic, traumatized, resistant), mourning (arduous, laborious, achieved in *and* beyond attachment) inaugurates a form of credible grief. Like an assimilated subjectivity, it involves no decisive invalidating or consolatory revaluing in spatial and cultural bonds. As with Berlin's liberalism, it demands only the agility of living incompletely, in a kind of tragic state without hopeful suspensions or driving precipitations. It is, in short, living in the light of losing, of being unshielded amid, in the 'middle' of, plurality.

Alternatively, we might say that assimilation is not the absence or negation of exile; it is its re-description. It is 'exile *with a difference*',[117] to borrow a phrase from Michael Steinberg. In this lies the qualifying work that, for Freud, might limit the pathological symptom: bringing it into representation and circulation, reiterating something *with a difference* in order to re-route the authority of its pure, compulsive repetition.[118] As such, if the clinical process seeks to declare trauma but casts its expression in an alternative form, then assimilation as 'exile-with-a-difference' implies a similar shift: confirming the bereavement of one homeland without re-tethering the self to another, registering a kind of dual citizenship in a world of interminable dispossession, exposing a space of unending mourning.

Exile-as-melancholy and mourning-as-assimilation: two different, but interrelated, responses to being out-of-place. So understood, Akhmatova's Leningrad apartment and Berlin's Oxford common room no longer stand as two discrete sites, separated as much by personal biography and historical trajectory as by geographic distance. Rather, to put Leningrad and Oxford into conversation is to find the spatial basis of a political philosophy that, extracting the subject from its excessive passions, posits a small space, a 'minimal area'[119] for thought and action. What Berlin's liberalism entails, then, is not just the clash between ultimate claims and mutually exclusive values. It is an avowal of conflict which properly rids it of its exorbitance, reinvigorating dividedness as the basis of living plurally – mournfully, incompatibly, tragically – with others. Or, if Berlin's pluralism can be seen to answer Akhmatova's lament, then assimilation is the name of this rejoinder: converting the exile's excess of geography into a just-about manageable mobility, countering the extremities in spatial attachment with a political philosophy which always doubts which term to call home. Thus Berlin's visit with Akhmatova in 1945 becomes more than the meeting of an assimilated Russian Jew and a dissident Russian poet. In the incompletions it uncovers and inflicts, mourning chaperones the labour of becoming-liberal: the wrangle of its displacements and the measure of its loss.

4

'Wherever you go you will be a *polis*'*
Hannah Arendt via Rahel Varnhagen

1

In his essay 'The non-Jewish Jew,' based on a lecture delivered to the World Jewish Congress in February 1958, Isaac Deutscher recounts his childhood fascination with the story of Rabbi Meir. A second-century 'saint, sage, the pillar of Mosaic orthodoxy and co-author of the *Mishnah*', Meir took lessons in Judaic theology from Elisha ben Abiyuh (also Abuyah), the heretic known as 'Akher (The Stranger)' or, more derisively, as *davar akher* (literally, another or an 'other' thing).

> Once on a Sabbath, Rabbi Meir was with his teacher, and as usual they became engaged in deep conversation. The heretic was riding a donkey, and Rabbi Meir, as he could not ride on a Sabbath, walked by his side and listened so intently to the words of wisdom falling from his heretical lips, that he failed to notice that he and his teacher had reached the ritual

---

* Pericles' declaration to the Athenians in Hannah Arendt, *The Human Condition*, 2nd Edition (Chicago, IL: University of Chicago Press, 1998), 198.

boundary which Jews were not allowed to cross on a Sabbath. At that moment the great heretic turned to his orthodox pupil and said: 'Look, we have reached the boundary – we must part now; you must not accompany me any further – go back!' Rabbi Meir went back to the community while the heretic rode on – beyond the boundaries of Jewry.[1]

Like various scholars of the Mishnaic period, Deutscher worries over the origins of Akher's character. 'Who was he? [...] What made him transcend Judaism? Was he a Gnostic? Was he an adherent of some other school of Greek or Roman philosophy?'[2] For the Marxist historian and political biographer such queries do not, of course, bear on the narrative of rabbinical Judaism – either on the relationship of its orthodoxies to their esoteric variants or on its possible affiliations to the Classical canon. They set the frame for Deutscher's interpretations of Spinoza, Heine, Marx, Luxemburg, Trotsky and Freud – all those 'great revolutionaries of modern thought'[3] for whom the heretic, Akher, is a prototype of the figure whose rejection of Judaic tradition is also the sign of their participation in it.

> They were *a priori* exceptional in that as Jews they dwelt on the borderlines of various civilisations, religions, and national cultures. They were born and brought up on the borderlines of various epochs [...] They lived on the margins or in the nooks and crannies of their respective nations. Each of them was in society and yet not in it, of it and yet not of it.[4]

A year before Deutscher composed his parable of the defector-as-conformer, Hannah Arendt – who herself might have been included among his exemplars – published an intellectual portrait that in its own way celebrates the rogue Jewish subject, both as a corrective to the hide-bound particulars of early modernity and as an antidote to the homogenizing effects of subsequent emancipatory and assimilationist reforms. In *Rahel Varnhagen: The Life of a Jewess* (1957), her study of the late eighteenth- and early nineteenth-century

Berlin salonnière, Arendt sketches the Jewish *pariah*: a sociological type born of a distinct cultural or historical milieu on the one hand, and a personification which becomes something other than, or more than, its subjective dispositions, on the other.[5] In this, Rahel Varnhagen (1771–1833) fulfils the status of what Deleuze and Guattari describe as the 'conceptual persona'.[6] As we shall see, Rahel not only carries a representative function in the formation and mutation of Arendt's later political theory. She functions as a heteronym:[7] a proper name – *Rahel*[8] – that is no longer just as a historical referent, and still less a free-floating container, but the 'real subject of [Arendt's] philosophy'.[9] As both agent and intercessor, Rahel is also part of the dialogue with which the writer addresses herself.

In a letter to her former dissertation supervisor, Karl Jaspers, written in March 1930, Arendt describes her aims in terms similar to Deleuze and Guattari's formulation. Responding to Jaspers' concern that embedding a philosophical fundament in a particular historical circumstance means 'objectify[ing] "Jewish existence", existentially'[10] – and so undermining the basis of her method – she suggests the ways that the existential and experiential might retain their peculiarity even as they are enjoined to abstraction. Rahel's 'concrete, sensuous specificity'[11] is not merely the outward or accidental characteristic of being. Nor is it subsumed into what, for Jaspers' *Existenzphilosophie*, would be the dispassion of an inauthentic generality. On the contrary, here the contingencies of empirical life embrace 'the intensive features of concepts' and indeed, co-originate with them.[12] As she answers Jaspers:

> An objectification is in fact there in a certain sense, but not an objectification of Jewish existence (as a gestalt, for example) but of the historical conditions of life which can, I think, mean something (though not an objective idea or anything like that). It seems as if certain people are so exposed in their own lives (and only in their lives, not as persons!) that they become, as it were, junction points and concrete objectifications of 'life'.[13]

For all the folds and referrals between the author and her principal 'conceptual persona' – 'for all my life I have considered myself Rahel and nothing else'[14] – their two voicings are never collapsed.[15] Together with Arendt's finely tuned commitment to historical exactness, the nature of the 'Jewish question' for Rahel's generation of Enlightenment Prussian Jewry and its cataclysmic end in the Nazi anti-Semitism of the author's own time disallow any clean equivalence. 'Nowadays not only the history of the German Jews, but also their specific complex of problems, are a matter of the past,' Arendt declares in her preface from 1956.[16] At the same time, Rahel – and the concepts she carries – ranges along with the movements of her biographer's thought: changing its problems, constituting a point of view in which certain ideas and histories are distinguished from one another, slide together or are replayed on a new stage. It is precisely in this differential or relational sense that Rahel and Arendt – late eighteenth-century subject and mid-twentieth-century interlocutor, private individual and 'public' speaker – converse and, through this, exercise that self-opposed, agonal, vigour, which itself becomes pivotal in Arendt's later political and philosophical writings. In short, the dialogue between Rahel's German Jewishness and its tenor in the political emergencies of the early 1930s is not only the central hermeneutic of the Varnhagen biography. What will also concern us is how Rahel's idiosyncrasies enter Arendt's conceptual territory, claiming the Jewish pariah as a specific spatial figure, performing the central Arendtian dialectic of the subject's necessary insertion within the world, on the one hand, and its forceful deviations, on the other.

Or, we might reformulate things by emphasizing that, while largely finished by 1933, Arendt was to complete the final two chapters of the biography from her exile in Paris, in 1938. To wit: How does the early Rahel undo and redo Arendt's later concerns? What is the relationship of the Jewish pariah to the Arendtian *polis*? How do the exile-like properties of the former relate to the political community of the latter? Can we see exile as a counter-veiling – even contradictory – public space or another site of its exposition? Indeed, against the Arendtian formulation in which exile amounts to an unworldly existence – disappearing 'into the invisibility of thinking and feeling' is how she describes the position of the Jew in the early years of Third Reich[17] – might exile not inaugurate its own spatial significance? One whose subject, though publically anomalous, might best assert its political presence.

While such questions exercise key Arendtian concepts, they also adapt their problems. To be sure, more than any other figure in this study, Arendt's critical appropriation of the metaphor of the Greek city-state establishes her as a champion of enclosures and dividing lines as they map the relations of private and public interest. One of her starting points is that most material of conceptual derivations: the significance of the law etymologically drawn from the spatiality of the wall.[18] For a characteristic of Greek antiquity, Arendt reminds us in *The Human Condition* (1958), is that it did not 'count legislating among the political activities'[19] or see it as the outcome of a prior authority or decision. Legislators, like wall-builders, belonged to the category of the craftsman or architect. Both were designers and makers of structures: producers of things 'who had to do and finish [their] work before political activity could begin', fabricators of a definitive place 'where all subsequent action could take place'.[20] On this account, legislation and civic administration exist only by means of the wall itself. A divided, bounded field provides what it premises.

> The law of the city-state [...] was neither the content of political action [...] nor was it a catalogue of prohibitions, resting, as all modern laws still do, upon the Thou Shalt Nots of the Decalogue. It was quite literally a wall, without which there might have been an agglomeration of houses, a town (*asty*), but not a city, a political community. This wall-like law was sacred, but only the inclosure was political. Without it a public realm could no more exist than a piece of property without a fence to hedge it in; the one harboured and inclosed [*sic*] political life as the other sheltered and protected the biological life process of the family.[21]

To look at Arendt from the perspective of her Classical – and relatedly Heidegerrian – geographies is to see the politically productive qualities of location and the limit: the ways in which a line, a distinction, simultaneously separates and initiates, founds and joins, restricts and allows, 'hedges in' and clears room.[22] Here the wall not only designates a space but frees it for public activity. Here, in fact, the convening of political community – assembling the world according to a dimension of the 'in-common' – proceeds from a space, a location, itself. On this most basic of claims, to be outside the city walls is not just to be unsheltered, unguarded, susceptible. It is to be inadmissible to its infrastructures and thus irrelevant to the precinct of its concerns – extramural. Accordingly, dislocation is not merely the deprivation of a creating and preserving space. To be dislocated is, by definition, to be publicly untenable – non-political or, perhaps, pre-political as well.

What then of the outcast and the exile? And of the pariah, Rahel? What of Arendt's Jewish subject who, like Deutscher's Akher, moves beyond the boundary less to refuse its law-like walls than to reorient them: reconfiguring the *polis* in such a way that the outside becomes another form of the public and pariahdom means a new and unbounded capacity to act. In short, how might the pariah, though 'un-walled', initiate a political process of its own? The point is not to set Arendt's early and relatively minor study of an eighteenth-century German Jewish salonnière against those major works, *The Origins of Totalitarianism* (1951) *The Human Condition* (1958) and *The Life of the Mind* (1978), which constitute her chief philosophical achievements. And, *contra* Deutscher, the query isn't 'What made [Arendt] transcend Judaism?' 'Was [she] an adherent of some other school of Greek or Roman philosophy?' What I am after is a mode of thought bound by neither side of a wall but which, nonetheless, asserts the 'publicity' of unfortified life, or the political potential of being unprotected. While never an enclosing and disclosing *polis*, this is a version of exile made valid as a home; a space where the pariah might exercise a weak, even fugitive, collectivity or a kind of erroneous (because foundation-less) power.²³ For if a revitalized public world is not to submit to the powers of the nation-state or be dulled by its management – the very hypostatized community that in *The Origins of Totalitarianism* Arendt warns against – then how might this best be supported if not by reconceiving the pariah as a political agent and exile as its own form of action?

Conceived on the eve of her exile from Berlin in 1933 and written out of the recognition of her own pariah status, Arendt's study of Rahel is more than a double-portrait. And it is something other than a reflection backwards or prediction forwards of an escalating crisis of self-relating: Rahel's nineteenth-century German Jewishness defined by its cultural and religious distinction, on the one hand, and its twentieth-century mutation into a racialized – ultimately, biologized – difference, on the other. By means of the conceptual persona, Rahel Varnhagen exposes the actions exercised by the pariah itself and the kinds of political possibility founded by a spatial dimension that might be called exilic. Indeed, in the immediate post-war period, throughout the 1950s and early 1960s, one of Arendt's central questions – what is the meaning of political community in an era defined by sovereignty and foundation? – increasingly invokes a tradition of Jewish pariahdom first formulated in her early biography. Although 'still a stateless person', she writes to Jaspers in January 1946,

> I am more than ever of the opinion that decent human existence is possible today only on the fringes of society, where one still runs the risk of starving or being stoned to death.²⁴

Here, Arendt's fidelity to the derided pariah is the obverse to the usual terms of national belonging – or, is the recognition and final proof of its failures. Expulsion to the margins hints at its own form of public affirmation: no longer a barrier to action and association, but an attuning to them. In a wry dialectical twist, in other words, the post-war situation brings the limitations of the pariah to a head, transforming its illegitimacy into an unlikely licence. The very history that had always excluded Jews from participation in a collectively constituted commons now grants them unexpected admittance. Although still subtracted from any formal or substantial space, their exceptionality no longer renders them singular, unhistorical. While disaffiliated, they are not disbarred from a newly shared repertoire of what disaffiliation might itself produce. Thus is the Jewish pariah delivered over to a new public possibility. 'They get in exchange for their unpopularity one priceless advantage,' Arendt writes in her 1943 essay 'We Refugees':

> History is no longer a closed book to them and politics is no longer the privilege of gentiles. They know that the outlawing of the Jewish people in Europe has been followed closely by the outlawing of most European nations. Refugees driven from one country to another represent the vanguard of their peoples – if they keep their [pariah] identity. For the first time Jewish history is not separate but tied up with that of all nations.[25]

In what follows, I explore the connection by following a theme first thought through Arendt's Rahel: exile as an alternative kind of 'worldliness', incompletion as another scene of collective human engagement or what Jacques Rancière, in a different context, describes as 'the part of those without part'.[26] The point, as elsewhere in this book, is not to define exile as the primordial fate of the Jew or follow that determinative time which turns fatefulness into the rhythms of natural becoming: organic, inexorable, tautological, unremitting. Instead, it means seeing exile in terms similar to those with which Arendt defends her biography of Rahel against the initial reservations of Jaspers[27] – not as an objectified condition of Jewish uprootedness but as mode of engagement that 'arises from the very fact of foundationlessness'.[28] If Jaspers' fear of an objectified uprootedness is similar to the problem of assuming an originally wounded Judaism – one that, in its most destinal and disconsolate form, merges with a certain Zionist conception of an eternal anti-Semitism and, conversely, proved uncomfortably serviceable to a Nazi ontology[29] – Arendt reopens the wound itself. Hers is an uprootedness in which political authenticity occurs as a contusion, or only in the detachment from ethnicity, religion and territory.

The question, then, is what can be achieved outside the presuppositions of the *polis*: living unpredictably, episodically, temporarily; redrawing the topography of the city wall and the boundary line between citizen and refugee; refiguring what links and separates them or 'defining the latter as constitutive of the former'.[30]

2

It was Max Weber who first borrowed the term *pariah* from the Indian caste system and applied it to his sociology of ancient Judaism whose peculiarities, he attributes to a 'guest people' (*Gastvolk*), characterized by their voluntary ritual segregation and failure of autonomous political organization.[31] Arendt's more deliberative pariah, however, takes its cue from the French anarchist, Symbolist poet and early Dreyfussard, Bernard Lazare (1865–1903).[32] This pariah generates the very malfunction it is accused of. The accusation of anomaly becomes its self-identification, raised to the second power. It brings the play of approval and excoriation to a maximal pitch; this pariah enacts its ill-fitting capacities and installs these amid difference itself. In Arendt's 1944 essay, 'The Jew as Pariah: A Hidden Tradition',[33] Heinrich Heine, Sholem Aleichem, Franz Kafka, Rosa Luxemburg, Charlie Chaplin and Lazare himself are all assigned to the ranks of those whose social unviability is indistinguishable from their potentiality: irregularities become visible and audible, outsiderness is performed in public and submitted to the 'web of human relations'[34] found there. In the exclusions that drive them, Arendt's Jewish pariahs are incipient, if ambiguous, public beings: thus the social discomfiture of Heine's poetic scorn and Lazare's efforts to 'translate the same basic fact into terms of political significance;'[35] Chaplin's portrayal of the suspect's arbitrary relation to law (the 'innocent cunning of [the] perpetually harassed little man'[36] who is entrancingly brazen in the face of the law 'because he sees in it neither order nor justice for himself'[37]); Kafka's understanding of the unreality of Jewish existence (as with K., 'You are not of the Castle and you are not of the village, you are nothing at all'[38]) or its affordance only by a minor administrative mistake (K's 'status as a citizen was a paper one, buried "in piles of documents forever rising and crashing around him"'[39]). Arendt's Jewish pariahs assume the difficult burden of community as they expose the cracks and miscounts of which it is composed. Neither fully active nor fully passive – 'in society and yet not in it, of it and yet not of it', as Deutscher says of Akher – they nonetheless assert a certain inoperability as a form of authentic existence. They open up a sphere of common life, of a being in-common – and continue to keep it open – by opposing its stability, uniformity. At which point, the superfluity of the pariah is reversed; or rather, it is deployed in the direction of a politically marked thought:

> For Kafka only those things are real whose strength is not impaired but confirmed by thinking [...] [T]hinking is the new weapon – the only one with which [...] the pariah is endowed at birth in his vital struggle against society.[40]

But if Arendt's 1944 essay concerns the attributes of the Jewish pariah – its pathological symptoms, its existential dispositions and relational sensibilities – it is the earlier Varnhagen biography that traces its emergence out of the structural paradoxes of German-Jewish modernity. A product of that brief moment of Jewish emancipation between the decline of the ghetto under the enlightened absolutism of Friedrich II and the genesis of the bourgeois-Christian nation-state, Rahel animates a range of rival pressures: of fragmenting ethno-religious allegiances and mounting national patriotisms; of increasing schisms between traditionalist and secularized Judaism; and of more systemic divisions between 'Jews and other Germans'.[41] Arendt's closer focus is on that short intermezzo of 1790–1806, taking it as the exemplary moment in which Jewish entrance into German social life is optimistically prefigured – and its promise of political equality most resoundingly reproved.

Coinciding with Rahel's years as a celebrated Berlin salonnière,[42] the interlude crystallized what, for Arendt, was the essential fraudulence of Enlightenment assimilation: the degree to which resolving the 'Jewish question' at the formal level by legal emancipation and the extension of civil rights required the abrogation of historically conditioned difference – in fact, demanded the internalization of an invalidated, prohibited, subjectivity itself.[43] The perfidy of emancipation and social assimilation, Arendt makes clear, turns not only on depriving Jews of their specific properties (the very ones that shamed them and marked them out publicly) but on encrypting them deep in the chamber of the subject's inward and inmost self. This is the 'disgrace of unhappiness',[44] the 'madness of gloom'[45] and the 'slow bleeding to death'[46] which Rahel continually laments. This is 'the infamy of birth',[47] the 'special misfortune'[48] which, short of baptism, conversion or intermarriage, anticipates nothing except 'the clang of the murderous axe'.[49] For Arendt, then, the moment that the Jew is included in the 'public use of reason',[50] to use Kant's phrase, is the moment that its legitimacy is repudiated. Its distinctiveness becomes privatized, specialized; that is, depoliticized. Within the capacious accommodations of the Enlightenment, it becomes a subject which betrays itself in concealing itself. It is rendered indefinite and ineffective because 'no longer colliding with limits'; it becomes illusory, because 'no longer molested by anything exterior'.[51] Guarded in its autonomy and intimacy, Rahel's Jewishness is 'converted into a purely psychic factor'.[52] No longer visibly exposed – 'to be exposed means to be "posed" in exteriority', as Jean-Luc Nancy puts it[53] – it becomes fallacious, falsifying, because refusing or precluding relation. 'Thus the power of the soul [is] secured,' Arendt writes. But, it is

> secured at the price of truth, [...] for without reality shared with other human beings, truth loses all meaning. Introspection and its hybrids engender *mendacity*.[54]

Thus, in the sovereignty sealed by introspection, action is not only stripped of its shared social significance. Reality can gain no foothold. It 'merely impinges and rebounds',[55] and difference itself no longer carries any objective allowance. Sunken into 'self-thinking'[56] (a term that Rahel and Arendt borrow from Gotthold Ephraim Lessing) or feverishly 'dissolving into mood',[57] Jewishness becomes as limitless an internal perplexity as it is anonymized as a finite, worldly event.

In general terms, Arendt's target are those first generation of secular middle-class Jews, like Rahel, who eagerly sought admission into the so-called *Bürgertum* – as into those structures patronized by the salutary powers of German culture. Specifically, Arendt objects to Rahel's allegiance to the sentiments of Romantic individualism, which in the manner of Jean Jacques Rousseau's *Confessions* (1782) and Friedrich Schlegel's *Lucinde* (1799), provide her with a model of self-consciousness stopped short of action and consequence. Rahel's world is drawn as if by the hands of a self-portraitist or with the discreet tonal palette of the drawing room. It is the gratification of the aestheticized self, of 'living life as if it were a work of art'[58] but without the crucial quality of the artwork's *external representability*, without its appearance as difference on the 'stage-set'[59] of a publicized, political world. It is, then, Rahel's desire to be a self-willing subject that thwarts her claim to exposition and recognition. It reproduces the very occlusions it wants to overcome. Indeed, if such radical subjectivism nourishes her 'exceptional inner life',[60] it also turns Rahel into the figure of the 'exception Jew'[61] that Arendt so deplores:

not a differentially or disputationally articulated subject – a subject in community with a variety of other differentiated, disputational subjects – but a self-sufficient, unaccompanied, *uncommon* one. It is a subject who 'not defined from the outside'[62] cannot know itself outside itself, whose confidentiality closes down the reserves of openness constitutive of self-disclosure, and thus a subject of which the social need makes no accounting. 'Thinking amounted to an enlightened kind of magic which could substitute for, evoke and predict experience, the world, people and society,'[63] Arendt writes of the attempt to '[fend] off ungraspable actuality',[64] exchanging external impingements for the seemingly liberating capacities of boundless, anonymous, thought.

Against the background of eighteenth- and early nineteenth-century assimilation, Rahel not only compounds the solitary privacies – which are also, the social privations – of her German-Jewishness. On a political level, such 'inwardness' (*Innerlichkeit*) makes imaginary the very struggles of that identity, stripping it of the risks by which social struggle might be admitted and supported. The result is a kind of violent and self-violating solvency. This is not just a shrinking into the self – which is also, an enthroning of the self – as a bulwark against all contingencies, all exteriorities, all outside events. For Arendt, it is a refusal of the fundamentally non-identical nature of community; indeed, it is an aggressive dissembling of those separations – the multiple disruptions and differentiations, the exposing spaces *in-between* subjects[65] – which community draws out and communicates. Without such spacings there is no resistance to univocality, and no strategy except to acquiesce or concede to compulsion and necessity. 'In a society on the whole hostile to Jews', as Arendt puts it in the final pages of her biography,

> it is possible to assimilate only by assimilating to anti-Semitism also. If one wishes to be a normal person precisely like everybody else, there is scarcely any alternative to exchanging old prejudices for new ones.[66]

But if Arendt lays much of the blame of Rahel's privatized (in)difference on her Romantic leanings – its aggrandising introspections, its artful and collusive freedoms – it is the more robust abstractions of the Enlightenment which constitute the founding, and most dangerous, evasion of reality. Thus, Moses Mendelssohn, like other first-generation Jewish *Aufklärer*, whose legacy Rahel was to inherit, becomes emblematic of that perversion of freedom which takes reason as the essence of a generalized, unlimited humanity.

As long as it had been possible for Jews to assimilate to the Enlightenment, and to it alone, because it fully represented the intellectual life of Germany, a social rise for the Jews was not absolutely necessary. The possibility of acceptance, the chance for culture, existed, and was in fact easy as long as the potency of reason remained complete, because innocent of history. Thus Moses Mendelssohn was able to assimilate to his alien surroundings without abandoning his Judaism. He needed only to lay aside old 'prejudices' in a highly deceptive present, and learn thinking [...]. His lack of civil rights hardly troubled him [...] He was content with the enlightened absolutism of Frederick II under which 'the Jews enjoy the most honourable liberty in the exercise of their religion', under which 'the flourishing of arts and sciences and reasonable freedom to think has been made so general that the effects extend down to the least inhabitant of the state' (Mendelssohn). *He was satisfied to be that 'least inhabitant'* [...] Since he adhered to Judaism, since he did not recognize history, he maintained a dignified composure toward society which had banished him to the lowest steps of its ladder.[67] (emphasis added)

The problem, as Arendt sets it out in 'The Enlightenment and the Jewish Question' (1932), concerns the nature of Mendelssohn's minimal gratification: how satisfaction with being 'that "least inhabitant of the state"' effects a further diminution in expectation and desire, how such lessening itself assimilates to the emptied enforcements of self-preservation. For under the drive of a rational universality (as under a later Romantic variant of inner exceptionality), self-preservation not only amounts to a suppression of history or being innocent of historical limitations. For Arendt, self-preservation means replacing the political in favour of the benefactions of a 'virtual sameness',[68] plugging those difficult distances, the contradictory 'interspaces between men',[69] through which human plurality might pass into a public realm. Indeed, if remaining a Jew, for Mendelssohn, meant electing the 'potency of reason' (and the privacy of religion) over the contents of history, then the desires of a subsequent generation were further curtailed. To the social minimum of being 'that least inhabitant' or, conversely, to the illusory identification with a shared humanity – Lessing's placation of 'it suffices to be a man' to which Arendt later refers[70] – is added the final existential annulment: aiming to become equal by ceasing to be Jewish, and historical, at all.

> They felt themselves to be Jews only because as Jews they tried to throw off the Jewish religion. With dubious justification they considered their assimilation as already achieved because they had borrowed the blindness of the Enlightenment, for which the Jews were no more an oppressed people. They blamed whatever was alien in them upon their history; they saw whatever was peculiar to them as Jews merely as an obstacle to citizenship.[71]

The 'unhistorical argumentations'[72] of Mendelssohnian reason, like the mimicries of Romantic self-organization – the Jew who might become 'German by the grace of Goethe' as the sceptical rebuttal of *Bildung* glosses it[73] – are the central charges of Arendt's biography. And for much of her life, long before she is assigned the status of the pariah, Rahel is presented as the consummately worldless subject. She is the pictorial miniaturist, the quietist parvenu, the lamentable naïf, the easy concealer. She is Jew whose resentment of her own origins makes her incapable of disclosing herself in the public political scene of society or, better, who loses sight of the *political as the locus of self-disclosure itself*.

The theme of birth, what she theorizes as 'natality', is a key – although never systematically explored – theme of Arendt's political philosophy. First probed in her doctoral dissertation on 'The Concept of Love in St. Augustine', later addressed in fragmentary form in the final chapter of *The Origins of Totalitarianism* and scattered throughout *The Human Condition*, the biological fact of birth corresponds to the subject's introduction into political space: an insertion, an inception, that Arendt accordingly designates as a 'second birth'.[74] Closely connected to the category of action – one of the three terms that characterize Arendt's *vita activa* – natality, in this context, refers not to the determinants or necessities of bodily existence, but to the unique human capacity for newness, for initiation. Against the metabolic cycles – the relentless repetitions and reinforcements – of social processes, it is about the readiness to '[begin] something anew',[75] 'to set something in motion',[76] to interrupt the serried order of things so that the unanticipated, the spontaneous, the self-surprising might happen.[77] As Arendt will emphasize, birth as a beginning activity is not the same as the beginning of the world. It is not the gift 'of something but of somebody, who is a beginner himself'.[78] It rests on the actions of a nameable doer or speaker; it is achieved only through those words and deeds with which we reveal ourselves to the world and venture our distinctiveness in it.

The term 'natality' is never mentioned in the Rahel biography. Nevertheless, the idea of the natality of action, what François Collin calls 'birth-as-praxis',[79] is everywhere implicit. For if action as a mode of self-disclosure is one of the ways that we articulate a relationship to our birth – 'action without a name, a "who" attached to it is meaningless', Arendt writes in *The Human Condition*[80] – then Rahel's negation of her Jewishness, her refusal 'to consent to herself',[81] is not just a negation of ethnic identity. It also works against the life- and world-prompting resources that Arendt associates with the condition of natality. It impedes the generation of self-initiated action, shackling the unknowable potential – and uncertain effects – 'inherent in all beginnings and in all origins'.[82] Like the paradoxically atomized figure of the 'world-citizen' or the nameless 'upholder of the Rights of Man',[83] to nullify one's Jewishness is not merely a failure to confirm oneself outwardly: an undoing of the 'birthing' activity of intervening and altering, an inability to posit the unprecedented and allow the future to remain unnervingly open.[84] Rahel's self-denial amounts to an exanimate, un-enunciated mode of being. It is to be 'literally dead to the world', as Arendt puts it in *The Human Condition*. It is to exist but be unable to make one's appearance in the world, to be insignificant to those others whose presence and perception alone verify 'the reality of the world and ourselves'. It means living a life that 'has ceased to be a human life because it is no longer lived among men'.[85]

Arendt's Rahel is without action and the relations of *inter*-action in just this sense. The elimination of her Jewish birth, the extirpation of its stain or the forgeries of assimilation which accomplish it makes her 'stand face-to-face with nothing'.[86] This is the real 'blindness'[87] of Enlightenment humanism or the inactivity – perhaps even the stillbirth – that is its unacknowledged foundation. It not only bars Rahel's capacity to see and speak of herself as a Jew. It prevents her being visible and audible as one in the *vis-à-vis* of the plural or within those relations between separated selves on which publicness and the political depend. At this point, the paradoxes of German-Jewish assimilation take on added pathos. From the perspective of natality, the injuriousness of having been born a Jew turns out not to be a barrier to Rahel's entrance into a common world; it is the very means by which such entrance is actioned. The fact of ethnic distinctiveness does not block her from the site of community or constrain her to the semblance of an exclusive selfhood; the value of natality lies precisely in its *being-exposed*, that is, in *being-shared*.[88] It is from this inaugural perspective, too, that we might name the Jewish pariah as a particular kind of newcomer or beginner: not just a stranger defined by a fidelity to its difference but a subject able to initiate unexpected relations and realities because of it, recognizing that a common life consists only in the communication between plural equals, making life happen by virtue of one's birth and in originating links and separations on that basis.[89]

The human condition of natality, then, is neither accidental nor determining. It is about what is possible – and unpredictable – in that which is also actual. It has to do with what might newly be brought into the 'in-common', and so into a space already constituted by plurality. In short, the priority that Arendt gives to birth entails how we begin, and how we make our way politically as a process of beginning and constant re-beginnings. Given over to unpredictability, its task is not to resolve the question of identity or secure its enrolment within any 'common will' of a 'common nature'. On the contrary, the very *conditionality* of Arendt's 'human condition' means understanding natality as a battery of non-natural, non-biological, inorganic acts. It is the performance of a 'political fact'[90] open to the conceiving and seizing of something new in the world. Which is also to say, natality is identical with the exposition of plurality; its survival is limited to the actuality of that pluralized event.

3

It is only after a series of formal name changes (from Lewin, to Robert and finally to Varnhagen), her Christian baptism and marriage in 1814 to the Prussian diplomat and civil servant Karl August Varnhagen von Ense that Rahel exercises her natality. But opening lines are also a form of geniture; and the first words of Arendt's intellectual portrait, said to be Rahel's dying utterance, instigate a belated newness: an outstanding or overdue birth.

> What a history! – a fugitive from Egypt and Palestine [...] With real rapture I think of these origins of mine and this whole nexus of destiny, through

which the oldest memories of the human race stand side by side with the latest developments. The greatest distances in time and space are bridged. The thing which all my life seemed to me my greatest shame, which was the misery and misfortune of my life – having been born a Jew – this I should on no account now wished to be missed.[91]

Celebrated in life as a parvenu, Rahel departs it as a pariah; 'pushed out of the world'[92] by the forces of assimilation, she is finally pushed into it as a Jew. Holding to both conditions, she resumes writing in Yiddish, with Hebrew characters; she embraces the events of the July Revolution in 1832 by becoming a Saint-Simonist; she finds cause with the young Heinrich Heine – 'only galley slaves know one another'–[93] she became 'entirely interested only in what the *earth* can make for us: it and our actions upon it'.[94]

> The old, unreal, desperate existence suddenly seemed to Rahel far more real, more true [...] It turned out that the pariah was capable not only of preserving more feeling for the 'true realities', but that in some circumstances he also possessed more reality than the parvenu. For the latter, being condemned to lead a sham existence, could seize possession of all objects of the world not arranged for him only with the pseudo-reality of the masquerade ... [I]t became apparent that the fate of the Jews was not so accidental and out of the way, that on the contrary it limned the state of society, outlined the ugly reality of the gaps in the social structure. Consequently there was no escape, unless it were to the moon.[95]

Some hundred years separate the death of Rahel in 1833 from her biographer's flight into exile in 1933. Worldlessness has become statelessness – for Arendt, its logical extension, its ultimate end – as totalitarianism displaces politics and the active life of community is systematically destroyed. By the early 1930s, then, biography slides into autobiography as Arendt confronts the inescapability of her own besieged Jewishness. Or, as she later puts it, she confronts the 'simple principle [...] that one can resist only in terms of the identity that is under attack'.[96] But if the question in *Rahel Varnhagen* is one of social recognition, the problem now is how to translate an identity under assault into a viable collectivity but without invoking a model of nineteenth-century European nationalism or the self-serving miseries of an assimilationist alternative. It is with this understanding that Arendt distinguishes a sovereign Jewish state from the mobilization of a people in the form of a national homeland whose institutions might guard the commonality of all its citizens: that is, might guard the distinctions that obtain *between* them. Arendt's vociferous opposition to the vision of Herzlian Zionism rests on this crucial distinction.[97] At best, an inactive 'escape or deliverance'[98] from anti-Semitism and at worst a militant, because politically unviable, repression of difference, there is nothing in political Zionism that supplies the pluralities necessary to the sphere of political life.[99] Writing in 1948 amid the growing consensus of American and Palestinian Jewry, Arendt spells out the implication of unanimous support for partition and Jewish statehood:

> The land that would come into being would be something quite other than the dream of world Jewry, Zionist, and non-Zionist. The 'victorious' Jews would live surrounded by an entirely hostile Arab population, secluded inside ever-threatened borders, absorbed with physical self-defence to a degree that it would submerge all other interests and activities. The growth of a Jewish culture would cease to be a concern of the whole people; social experiments would have to be discarded as impractical luxuries; political thought would centre strategy; economic development would be determined exclusively by the needs of war [...] *Thus it becomes plain that at this moment and in present circumstances a Jewish state can only be erected at the price of a Jewish homeland.*[100] (emphasis added)

Arendt's attempt 'To Save a Jewish Homeland', then, is an attempt to save it from sovereignty. Once Palestinian Jewry and the Zionist movement had lost the qualities of (in-common) contestation which had once characterized their debates, any Jewish state would dematerialize into worldlessness, 'lead[ing] the Jews out of reality once more, and out of the sphere of political action'.[101] For, it is not simply the case, as Arendt presciently argues in 1944, that proposals for a Jewish state would 'effectively [reduce] Arab Palestinians to second-class citizenship, [force] them into voluntary migration' or lend further support to the militant terror of the Revisionist principle of displacing an indigenous population entirely.[102] Nor is it just that the feasibility of such a state would depend on the intervention of international superpowers: 'Nationalism is bad enough when it trusts in nothing but the rude force of the nation. A nationalism that necessarily and admittedly depends upon the force of a foreign nation is certainly worse.'[103] Rather, any division between Jew and Palestinian in the name of political survival is, at heart, an anti-political decision and, as such, a declaration of its own death. Jewish sovereignty (or pseudo-sovereignty as she also puts it) would amount to little more than 'the sovereign right [...] to commit suicide'[104] as actuality finds itself absorbed into an *a priori* end.

In contrast, any Jewish homeland would have to be a recognizably pluralized space.[105] It would be a world constructed in communication between its Palestinian-Arab majority and Jewish minority; a visibility of cohabiting citizens not ethnic claimants; a 'home' in which Jewishness might appear freely by virtue of what it can rationally share *with* nonidentical others – and simultaneously react *against* them – in a properly differentiated, not divided, sense. And it would have to be an intensely artificial space. Indeed, to the extent that Herzlian Zionism, in its resemblance to nineteenth-century European nationalisms, increasingly conjured the (pre-political) language of biological life – the nation as a blood unicity, an *ethnos*, a 'natural-historical' becoming – Arendt's homeland opposes it as fabrication, experimentation, declared denaturalization. Artificiality would be its initiative: the substance of its activity and the proper meaning of its natality.

Arendt's national home is artificial in at least two ways. First, much like the Greek *polis*, she argues for a made and produced site, a concrete location, a bound whose very act of enclosure might 'call something into being which did not exist before'.[106] Second – and in contrast to the reproach of Zionists and anti-Zionists alike – such a fabrication is to be explicitly avowed. Its non-organicity is the source and safeguard of the homeland's significance, and the uniqueness that gives it 'human and political value'.[107] Indeed, against that generation of Jewry 'brought up in the blind faith in necessity – of history or economy or society or nature',[108] the artifice of place is not only of a piece with the nativity, the initiatory activity, which for Arendt defines the realm of public, political life. Its 'natal', experimental accomplishments are all that stand between historical humanity and the mythic fatalities of nature, intervening in autochthonous attachment, questioning the ideological enlistment in such attachment. In short, artificiality not only dismantles the idea of a Jewish nation-state as the natural and necessary response to the extant problems of 'antisemitism, poverty and national homelessness'. It also upends that rational kind of magic which assumes such problems are rewarded with known solutions because of what they already and 'naturally' are; that such 'challenges by themselves […] had produced something'.[109]

Fashioned and fabricated, such a homeland is, however, never a fiction. Its very artificiality is what offers a route back to reality: back to a home that cannot homogenize those to whom it applies – the very lifeless 'unreality' that Rahel first exemplifies – and whose vitality, which is to say its political viability, survives only insofar as its artificiality remains recognizable. Likewise, it is not that Arendt ever refutes a Jewish right to place. On the contrary, the lesson of the *polis* is precisely of place as it occasions the terms of a non-natural political existence. It is only a 'place in the world which makes opinions significant and actions effective,' as she puts it in *The Origins of Totalitarianism*.[110] But it is in her *Jewish Writings* of the 1940s and 1950s, where place is submitted to it onto its own deflations, its attenuations, or onto a weakening and re-founding of its foundations. Resistable, amendable, 'unnaturally' in-common: it is an understanding of place as it discloses a space for the self as well as for the conceptual surprises of strangers and newcomers. Alternatively, we may say that in such a place the Jewish pariah appears. More insistently: here the pariah *must* appear if Arendt's Jewish homeland is to be defined and defended 'publicly', if a pariah people is not to give way to the ritual exclusions of a pariah state.[111]

4

Of all the late nineteenth-century figures who fulfil Arendt's typology of the 'conscious pariah',[112] it is the French revolutionary anarchist, Zionist and early Dreyfussard, Bernard Lazare, who best exemplifies the occupant of a Jewish homeland in its non-natural, non-sovereign collective capacities. Thus, in 'The Jew as Pariah: A Hidden Tradition' as well as in the short comparative study, 'Herzl and Lazare' written two years earlier,[113] Lazare emerges as a common actor, a political agent, who sees resistance to anti-Semitism in terms of the plurality on which articulated solidarity depends, and thus as a movement opposed to any unity in racial, ethnic or religious belonging. Lazare's life-long insistence on the conflicting class interests within European Jewry, his specific concern with the condition of East European Jews (the 'Russian hard-labour prisoners [...] the Romanian Jews whose human rights had been denied, the Galician Jewish proletarians starved by financial trusts'[114]), as well as his later advocacy of a confederated Jewish nation based on a cross-national and cross-class mobilization, is not only Arendtian in its politics.[115] Together with his aversion to the (bourgeois) circumspections of Herzlian diplomacy, Lazare's is also a Zionism suspicious of any claim to land. 'To Lazare the territorial question was secondary – a mere outcome of the demand that "the Jews should be emancipated as a people and in the form of a nation."'[116] In 'Le nationalisme juif', a lecture delivered in 1897 to the Association of Russian Jewish Students, he argues that only the most narrow of nationalisms would require an investment in territory. The Jew who proclaims,

> 'I am a nationalist', will not say in any special, specific or clear way that he is a man who wants to reconstruct a Jewish State in Palestine and dreams of conquering Jerusalem. He will say: 'I want to be a completely free man, I want to enjoy the sun, I want to have the right to human dignity [...] 'At certain times in history, nationalism, for groups of human beings, is the manifestation of the spirit of freedom.[117]

Lazare's Zionism, then, is one in which spatial dispersion is in some sense foundational, or where a principle of non-sovereignty ensures the freest forms of alliance and identification. Alternatively, we may say that this is a version of the Jewish pariah – his own term is 'fugitive'[118] – whose very impermanence enacts a public function. What Lazare presents is not an individuated figure positioned outside a common space – the pariah as unsociable, unapproachable alien. He is a subject re-positioned in and through the unpredictability of a pluralized people, a worldly pariah ex-posed – posed externally – in a space of shared concerted struggle.[119] That Lazare's Zionism was to be eclipsed by the Herzlian vision and, further, 'that [he] was passed over in silence by his Jewish contemporaries, to be recovered to us by Catholic writers'[120] is, for Arendt, not only one of the great omissions of nineteenth-century Jewish historiography. Lazare's forgotten pariahdom is a lost future and part of Zionism's political failure.

But there is another, much earlier, failure and one that draws on a more explicitly prophetic source. For if Lazare offers a nineteenth-century account of the freedoms lost when statehood supplants homeland, Arendt looks to an event two centuries before which she hails as the 'last great Jewish political activity':[121] the revolutionary mass movement that had engulfed the early modern Jewish world in the mid-seventeenth-century, centred on the quasi-divine figure of Sabbatai Sevi and his self-appointed prophet, Nathan of Gaza. In 'Jewish History, Revised', her 1948 assessment of Gershom Scholem's seminal work of revisionist Jewish historiography, *Major Trends in Jewish Mysticism* (1946), Arendt focuses on the eventual victory of rabbinic Judaism over Sabbatai, the Apostate Messiah. It was a 'debacle'[122] that not brought an end to emancipatory fervour but a loss which, for Arendt, lies at the origin of modern Jewish worldlessness in both its assimilationist and sovereign forms.[123]

Arendt is, of course, largely hostile to explicitly political forms of religious arcana[124] – and in the early 1960s was famously to engage in fierce debate with Scholem over her coverage of Adolf Eichmann's trial for *The New Yorker*, subsequently published as *Eichmann in Jerusalem: A Report on the Banality of Evil* in 1963. What constitutes her appreciation of Scholem in this instance, however, is his interpretation of Sabbateanism less as a heresy than as a mysticism itself constitutive of rationalist modernity. Key, for her, is Scholem's clarification of the doctrine of divine emanation as a counter to the legal and logistic exegeses of orthodox Judaism: replacing the social obligation to moral law with a 'discovery of a working knowledge of reality',[125] freeing up a sphere for human cognition and action within a higher, more infinite, domain.[126] What appeals to Arendt, in particular, are the ways in which emanationism's central idea of *En-Sof* – of a 'hidden God' everywhere distributed and discoverable within the tangible substance of things – not only lends the modern values of experimentation and investigation to the esoterica of Jewish mysticism. It also revokes the passivity of an *ex nihilo* creationism: endowing the human with the 'mystical-material power'[127] of participation, replacing its hapless victimhood with a new model of historical responsibility, recasting 'the religious Jew [as a] protagonist in the drama of the World'.[128] Searched by way of cognitive experience, tested and retested by it, it is precisely emanationism's earthly attentions, its proto-modern 'research into reality'[129] that, on Arendt's account, explain Sabbateanism's mass appeal. Its antinomian impulse to 'break with the mere interpretation of the Law'[130] is the basis of 'translat[ing] itself directly into real popular action'.[131]

More significant, however, is something that Arendt's references to Sabbatean theology and the doctrine of emanation invoke but do not fully develop: that is, how a messianic version of political action might itself depend on exilic existence. Following Scholem, she cites the Lurianic Kabbalah, specifically Isaac Luria's adaptation of the Myth of Exile on which Sabbatai Sevi was later to draw,[132] in a way that ties spatial dispersion to the conception of the Jew as a political participant. No longer a form of suspended life or an existence reduced to mere survival, exile corresponds now to a worldly vitality. Like emanationism, it returns 'redemption' to the order of experience and the everyday. Both provoke a probing of material space, which is another kind of historical engagement. Both are versions of freedom in the Arendtian sense: realizable exertions, actionable endeavours. As Scholem puts it:

Formerly [the Diaspora] had been regarded either as a punishment for Israel's sins or as a test of Israel's faith. Now it still is all this, but intrinsically it is a mission: its purpose is to uplift the fallen sparks from all their various locations. 'And this is the secret why Israel is enslaved by all the Gentiles of the world: In order that it may uplift those sparks which have also fallen among men [...] And therefore it was necessary that Israel should be scattered to the four winds in order to lift everything up.'[133]

If the messianic valorization of exile – 'its mystical interpretation [as] action instead of suffering'[134] – is part of what Arendt gets from Scholem, the question remains of how this speaks to her more secular concerns. How might exile be rethought as a politics of splinters, as a public of 'fallen sparks'? Is there a way to understand the riven and scattered not as a threat to worldliness but as another form of reality, or a means for its realization? Indeed, instead of repeating Arendt's gesture in *The Human Condition* where the *polis* is confined to a topographically designated place, might we consider her 'Jewish History, Revised' as its own form of displacement? For while the Kabbalist's image of 'fallen sparks' (Luria's *sephirot*) might presuppose the hope of their final in-gathering, the ultimate mending of fractured, diasporic parts, Arendt's reference to it underscores another reading. That the unpolitical is not what happens in dispersion but precisely in the attempt to surmount it. That what disengages the subject, or makes it uncommon, is not exile but rather its reparation: returning to all those inactive spaces – whether statist or assimilationist – that no longer generate the (emanative, emancipatory) condition of exposure. The victory of rabbinic Orthodoxy over Sabbatian mysticism is thus not only the neutralization of a 'great political movement'.[135] It is an event with a far-reaching legacy. 'From now on', Arendt declares towards the end of her review of Scholem's account,

> the Jewish body politic was dead and the people retired from the public scene of history.[136]

A reference to the same mid-seventeenth-century history concludes her 1946 essay, 'The Jewish State: Fifty Years after, Where Have Herzl's Politics Led?':

> I do not know – nor do I even want to know – what would happen to Jews all over the world and to Jewish history in the future should we meet with a catastrophe in Palestine. But the parallels with the Shabbetai Tzevi [sic] episode have become terribly close.[137]

Arendt's references to the traditions of Jewish mysticism are brief – more allusive than analytic – but they take us to the heart of this chapter's dual concerns. What it means to understand exile as a particular way of inhabiting this world: not of being out-of-place as much as stepping into an unpredictable outside, venturing into an unguarded realm in which plurality might publicly take place, experiencing those shared exposures which place makes possible. And what it means to understand the pariah as the persona proper to this conception: the subject who appears within a public placing, one defined by its shared separations, by its 'in-common' incompletions. Both exile and the pariah are *this* exposure, *this* incompletion. Or rather, they are a resistance to those violences – and sovereign securities – that fill up the 'interspaces'[138] constitutive of community and with this the distances and displacements necessary to worldly engagement itself.

5

By May 1947, on the eve of the establishment of the State of Israel, Arendt is plainly right to say: 'We Jews are not or not any longer exiles.'[139] Positioned as a potential citizen, however, she resists the summons by virtue of a recent history unable to be comprehended by established political categories. Not only had the customary content of 'national concepts and national membership'[140] been wholly invalidated by the distortions of Nazism. Any attempt at their revalidation would be similarly voided.

> In Auschwitz, the factual territory opened up an abyss into which everyone is drawn who attempts after the fact to stand on that territory. Here the reality of the politicians of *Realpolitik*, under whose spell the majority of the peoples always and naturally falls, has become a monster that could only urge us to perpetuate annihilation the way the Nazis continued to produce corpses in Auschwitz.[141]

Where the Final Solution so literalized the relation of de-nationalization to death – on a juridical level, as Agamben reminds us, it was non-citizenship that anticipated and accomplished life in the concentration and extermination camp[142] – Arendt will insist that all post-war exhortations to an older national culture could only reproduce that ultimate (deadly) ratio. No rehabilitation of what Nazism had destroyed could again inscribe nativity (life, action) in the exercise of the nation-state. Although articulated as a reclamation of the political, any attempt to reengage Germany with the ground of its own national genealogy, merely re-empties the vacuum, deepens the abyss. What has been lost – a foundation, a membership, certain 'elements of a reality within which one could live and move'[143] – has been lost irrevocably, without recourse and with no appeal. Any possibility of a coming political community necessarily begins here: on this verge, at this limit, marking the irremediable crisis of the 'factual territory' and living as closely as possible to the ragged edge of what it refuses and excludes. If this bears on the task of Arendt's 'humanity in dark times', it also describes the spatiality of the pariah: a condition given by displacement and a self-exposure that is the opposite of self-preservation; not so much a statelessness as a 'being-in-exodus of the citizen'.[144]

'Dwelling, in the proper sense, is now impossible', 'the house is past', Adorno famously declares in *Minima Moralia*, the journal he begun in 1944 while in exile in America, and completed in 1949.[145] While the larger fragment to which both aphorisms belong concerns the fate of intimate life and property under the conditions of a functionalizing modernist aesthetic, Adorno's broader judgement is of an economic and political order which has made a well-homed life unviable. Indeed, if *Minima Moralia* is Adorno's ironic inversion of the Aristotelian *Magna Moralia* – and thus an inversion of the commonly disclosed space of the *polis* – then now we are beholden to only the most meagre of moral requirements. 'The best of conduct [...] seems an uncommitted, suspended one: to lead a private life [...] but not to attach weight to it as something still socially substantial' or, alternatively, to tarry with the forces of a divested existence by 'not [being] at home in one's home'.[146] In the shadow of a totalitarian collective, Adorno's homelessness is an argument over what might remain of the private sphere even as its ethics have been evicted. In contrast, Arendt's homelessness – and its conceptual realizations – is adamantly public.[147] At issue is not just the loss of the preserving house (or the nostalgia that cleaves to it) but the more radical resolve of no longer 'wanting a house',[148] inhabiting homelessness collectively, making natal a future in which the *polis* might find a new political meaning. This place would neither correspond with a state or territory nor delineate those admissible or assimilable to it. It is a place where exile and citizen might publicly meet, where they might act upon to interrupt, to in-determine, each other. The pariah is its only thinkable inhabitant. Arendt's 1947 'Dedication to Karl Jaspers' carries the unnamed echo of Rahel Varnhagen. A spectre, a citation, she enters into a newly contingent history and a newly displaced space from which to speak:

> If the factual territory has become an abyss, then the space one occupies if one pulls back from it is, so to speak, an empty space where there are no longer nations or peoples but only individuals for whom it is now not of much consequence what the majority of peoples, or even the majority of one's own people, happen to think at a given moment. If these individuals who exist today in all the peoples and in all the nations of the world are to reach understanding among themselves, it is essential that they learn not to cling frantically any longer to their own national pasts – pasts that explain nothing anyhow – for Auschwitz can no more be explained from the perspective of German history than from Jewish history – that they don't forget that they are only chance survivors of a deluge that in one form or another can break over us again any day, and that they therefore may be like Noah and his ark; and finally that they must not yield to despair or scorn for humankind but be thankful that there are quite a few Noahs floating around out there on the world's seas trying to bring their arks as close together as they can.[149]

5

Posthumous place
W.G. Sebald and the displacement of landscape

1

Unlike the other figures in this study, the post-war German novelist W.G. Sebald was of course not a Jew. Unlike Rosenzweig, Benjamin, and Arendt, Sebald cannot be allied easily or consistently to the preoccupations of Jewish-European identity, or to the disaster of that encounter in the horrors of National Socialism and, above all, the Holocaust. Although himself an émigré – born in 1944, Sebald left the Alps of his native Bavaria for the flatlands of Norfolk, on the English east coast in 1966 – his spatial and historical trajectory is markedly different from the company of individuals with whom we have been concerned. Certainly, the often perplexing stylistics of Sebald's poetry and prose fiction – a conflation of peripatetic scrap, antiquarian essay, misshapen dream, the extraneous reference, the shrouded citation – not only capture a morass of formal discomforts but any amount of misaligned histories and identities.

Why include him? What role does Sebald play in an argument whose central proposition is a specific Judaic conception of exile as it bears on a particular disorientation and reorientation of thought? As the only figure in this study born on *this* side of the definitive gash in twentieth-century Jewish European history, how might he relate to an exilic consciousness, as this book understands it? The answer to these questions (or question-affirmations) is twofold. First, that if exile entails no necessary privation, this is because it entails no proprietary rights either; indeed, that its real force has little to do with any exclusivity in identity, geography or history but with the very displacement of their duties. Second, it is with Sebald's treatment of the aesthetic and spatial trope of *landscape* that this displacement is fully registered; that the obscurities of exile are best illuminated when, as with Sebald, it puts pressure on a concept usually born of the transparencies of space and sight, and challenges the particular drives of time we know as memory. The task of this chapter is thus to admit Sebald as an exemplary, if eccentric, exilic consciousness and to describe a conception of landscape that accords with it. If this perspective is to make sense, landscape itself has to be detached from the relations of place to human presence in favour of all that overflows their form. By which I mean an exilic existence: dis-identified, un-reserved, without duration; contingent but also excessive of the history and the geography that brings it about.

2

Vesania is the sickness of a deranged reason – but in this last kind of mental derangement there is not merely disorder and deviation from the rule of the use of reason, but also *positive unreason,* that is *another rule,* a totally different standpoint into which the soul is transferred, so to speak, from which it sees all objects differently. And from the *Sensorium communi* that is required for the unity of life, it finds itself transferred to a faraway place (hence the word derangement) – just as a mountainous landscape sketched from a bird's eye view prompts a completely different judgement about the region than when it is viewed from level ground.[1]

So writes Kant of *vesania* in his *Anthropology from a Pragmatic View*, a condition defined by a radical disorganization in the subject's cognitive structures. While Kant deems such a condition to be a 'craziness' or 'insanity' (*Aberwitz*) and locates it within his broader taxonomy of mental disorders, such an affliction is less a flaw or deficiency – 'a mere disorder or deviation from the rule' – than an altered form of judgement. It is '*another* rule, a totally different standpoint'; a perspective that, severed from the collective body of the '*sensorium communi*', furnishes the means to receive and interpret 'all objects differently'. In the derangement of reason, Kant finds the sort of contingencies in cognition that make the *a priori* truths of logic, at least to the afflicted person, invalid. The sufferer

> chases after principles that can be completely exempted from their touchstones, imagining that he conceives the inconceivable. – The invention of squaring the circle, of perpetual motion, the unveiling of the supersensible forces of nature.[2]

In his short essay 'Scapeland', Jean-François Lyotard takes a brief detour via Kant to argue the ways in which landscape outruns the sense perceptions navigated by signification or by any given system of knowledge or description.[3] Before being reprised as a literary or pictorial response to a spatial phenomenon, a landscape, in this reading, is met as a destabilizing force: a surfeit of raw matter 'beyond the realm of form' which defeats and 'leaves the mind DESOLATE'.[4] With 'scapeland' – an inversion of the two units which make up the aesthetic and geographical term – Lyotard unmoors the privileged relation of place and the inhabiting body, or cuts the intimacies in attachment between them. In contrast to an established phenomenology of landscape as a spatial frame, a modelling of perspective, a certain intelligibility of the gaze, Lyotard offers a sub- or counter-proposal. Landscape is not that which gives itself to be seen or to be read; it exposes excessively or slips away. Nor is landscape measurable or scalable – as by a visual line, a graphic trail, a progression of steps or a studied calculation of degrees. It rescinds every agreed benchmark of expressivity and evaluation. Illimitable and without horizon, it is a dimension 'without a destiny'[5] or, rather, it is a kind of spatial relation to non-destination. The distance in landscape, then, arises not as a 'before' or 'beyond' of a location imagined, inhabited, moved through. It is not any extension of space that might be overcome in an act of projection, possession, occupation. In this, distance makes landscape 'the opposite of a place'[6]; it effects 'a quite different judgement', as Kant suggests of the *Verrügung* (the derangement or displacement) of *vesania*.

In precipitating the very distance it would otherwise adjudicate, landscape, on Lyotard's account, voids any determination by topography (the mapping of an area, a locality, a terrain) or by chronography (the recording of past events in time). It no longer functions as a scene of geographical and historical inscription, whether such meanings are revealed to view or, if lost and concealed, may be reconstructed by it. Rather, it begins in the implosion of all such cognitive supports. Landscapes, Lyotard writes:

> do not come together to make up a history and a geography. They do not make up anything; they scarcely come together at all.[7]

Thus landscape revokes or deposes every symbolic context of a knowable place. For if to 'history' is conventionally ascribed the ambition of being faithful to a past, and if to 'geography' is attached the visible features and effects of a location, then here we are asked to think their alternative: to annul the disclosures of what Paul Ricoeur calls the 'bright region of memory',[8] to inhabit the blind underside of the claim that what has been remembered has *taken place*. At this point, which is also the estrangement from a point of view or, like Kant's *vesania*, is the *point of view of the estranged*, landscape becomes the opening in which such strangeness, or estranging, breaks in.[9] Indeed, if this kind of landscape arises outside the joint reciprocities of figure and ground, it also registers the consciousness of a certain failure. The structure of the defeat, as Lyotard makes clear, is a specific one. It is not a question of being thwarted with regard to an intentional state or propositional attitude (an object *sought* in the vagaries of a far-off distance); it concerns the dissolutions or 'disconcertment[s]'[10] *given in distance* itself. Here, one is no longer a cognitive and communicative subject able to take the measure of its surroundings, but a subject exposed to something like the demands of the immeasurable.

> If anything remains [in a landscape] it is an absence which stands as a sign of the horrifying presence in which the mind fails and misses its aim. It fails not because it was looking for itself and did not find itself, but [...] in the sense that one can say that *one missed one's footing or fell, or that one's legs gave way, as one sits on a bench, watching a window which is lit up but empty*.[11] (emphasis added)

Landscape – or its inversion as 'scapeland' – thus composes a certain discomposure: a disarrangement of sensibilities and standpoints that cannot be rearranged, an ungraspable object that yet cannot be let go, an experience unable to be modulated or assuaged in meaning. It is the appearance of a distancing to which other opacities attach. What should be added emphatically, however, is that this is a distance whose temporal vector is not a remembered past or a future to-come. Its action is neither retroactive nor projective. On the contrary, distance occurs on the plane of the extant and present. What is henceforth 'here' – implacable, impassable, *in place* – is obscurity and the indiscernible itself. As in *vesania*, such a distance permits no site or situation but absorbs us into the density and vacuity of the vanishing point itself. At issue is neither pursuit nor passage – and certainly never something that can be continuous with a panorama. In an early essay, 'Le lecture de Kafka', Maurice Blanchot describes this space as a mode of 'exile in the fullest sense'[12] or, in a later parsing, the neutralized 'point at which here coincides with nowhere'.[13]

3

One can find such a conception of landscape and of distance almost anywhere in the prose fiction of W.G. Sebald. It arises not only as the function of existential dislocation – what Kafka famously calls that 'old incapacity'[14] to belong to the world – and the separations and errors that inform it. It is assigned, too, by the vacuums in the author's own identity, torn between a post-war German predicament of a missing community, on the one hand, and a self-conscious appointment outside the spatial and temporal borders of that experience, on the other. In all of this, as we shall see, landscape-as-distance invades Sebald's writings, turning places inside out, cutting them adrift from perspective and position, opening onto an exile through which there is no passing and nothing to pass on. These are the grey, indifferent exhaustions that wash over Sebald, leaving the author – and his narrators – powerless to discern what they see or to posit a relation that would mediate it. This is also what imposes an immobility at the heart of their agitated itinerancies, binding them to an intransitivity, latching them to things incapable of address or connection.

Put another way, if it is true that Sebald's writing abounds with traditional landscape description – the careful detailing of topographic and geological structures; vivid evocations of colour, light and the phasing of seasons; the organic mutations in animal and botanical life[15] – it is also true that, with Sebald, one is never in place. Neither ordered by a clear administration of belonging – geographic, juridical or political – nor by the subject's organization of perspective, orientation or direction, these are landscapes presented only in the invisible announcement of what is not there: things evacuated, blanked-out or which remain irretrievable. What *is* grasped, however, is the 'totally different standpoint', the 'missed footing', the glaring nullity of a 'window which is lit up but empty' of which Kant and Lyotard respectively speak: continual positings of placeless places, temporal distancings which seem to withdraw, to disperse, to cancel, all presence into itself.

Waiting rooms, boarding houses and railway stations or dead-end corridors, underpasses, blind paths and blocked openings or the falsified 'day-for-night' world of Antwerp's Nocturama in *Austerlitz* (2001) or the crumbling city 'hollow to the core' and 'left now as a necropolis or mausoleum' that, in *The Emigrants* (1997), describes the post-industrial wastelands of 1960s England.[16] Sebald's places reverberate as so many modalities of remoteness – places that allow 'the unheard of force of distance' to be heard.[17] In the autobiographical 'Dark Night Sallies Forth', the last in a triptych of prose poems that make up *After Nature* (1988), the city of Manchester surfaces under just this kind of erasure. While searching for Strangeways Prison, with 'walls ... as high as Jericho's', the emigrant-author finds himself in 'a sort of no-man's land' of buildings 'due for demolition' or 'left vacant'.[18] The crisis – whatever it was – has already passed. The event – left unspecified – is detectable only in the stray inscriptions that are its aftermath: 'Goldblatt, Grünspan and Gottgetreu', 'Spiegelhalter, Solomon, Waislfish and Robinsohn'.[19] In what is an unmistakable, but silent, allusion to Kafka's *Amerika* whose young protagonist finds employment with the 'Nature Theatre of Oklahoma'[20] (and which features another character by the name of Robinson) Sebald comes across an entrance. 'Stuck to it was old placard for the musical *Oklahoma!*'[21] But erasure, not attestation, is at work here. Far from signalling any lines of relation or of legacy, it is the missed encounter – which is also an encounter of the missing – that shadows the scene: a caesura where history, even literary history, disappears under the weight of its own inconsequence.

So it is that the people of Sebald's fiction emerge in response to this loss. 'Solomon, Waislfish and Robinsohn', or Kafka with his own

Robinson: these are names of the dead which, while still faintly traceable, are indexes of the inadmissible, the unassimilable, the un-archivable.[22] Not so much robbed of history as bereft of it, they are no more than pallid apostrophes: signifiers of subjects whose biographies cannot be verified, whose voices cannot carry, whose memories cannot disclose and who, while brought tantalizingly close, remain indifferent as objects of identification. Exiles, orphans, suicides or the inmates of hospitals, sanatoria, asylums: these are the inhabitants of the *abgrund*, the abyss, within landscape; figures whose presence is nothing other than the endurance of ever-denser silences and separations. A mist-laden, dust-laden veil covers them. They are the people who have no place, who have lost their way or whose afflictions have, in some important sense, become chronic: the sickness is a sickness of time, a temporal mode in which nothing ever quite happens or comes to pass, and nothing ever quite passes away. The nature of their loss is as irretrievably distant as it is extravagantly present. It awakens absence as it accosts and dilates all that is now given.

Thus Sebald's subjects, like his landscapes, are without project or possibility. Or, we may call them 'posthumous people', to recall Nietzsche's memorable aphorism.[23] Here, however, being posthumous is not to be known only after death, or becoming recognizable and visible in some anticipated, ensuing time, as Nietzsche defines it. Rather, I want to say that Sebald's characters are posthumous insofar as they originate in estrangement – always missing from presence, just as they are always missing from place. At issue is less a recognition that arrives too late than an existence in which the future is unable to find its place in any present, and in any present to come. It is the future blankness of a 'now' which leaves nothing and points to nothing beyond itself. Even 'signposts at the forks or crossings of the tracks gave no direction to any place or its distance', writes Sebald in *The Rings of Saturn* (2002), as he journeys through the flatlands of rural Suffolk.

There was invariably, to my mounting [confusion] no more than a mute arrow facing pointlessly this way or that [...] Several times I was forced to retrace long stretches in that bewildering terrain [...] I cannot say how long I walked about in that state of mind, or how I found a way out.[24]

Thus place, deprived of its usual invitation to inhabitation and identification courts only the voids of its own implausibility, invisibility.[25] No longer capable of hosting a foundation for past recollection or future anticipation it becomes an exposure to an endless erosion, or falls away into what Sebald elsewhere calls a 'night-side vanishing point'.[26] It is an insensible place beyond all action, initiative, position; and it is an encrusted time which, while claiming the category of history, relays only the inabilities to meet it. The fortress of Breendonk, in Sebald's final novel *Austerlitz*, best amplifies this condition. Built by the Belgium army in 1906 as part of the strategic defence of Antwerp and requisitioned as a German prison and transit camp between 1940 and 1944, Sebald's Breendonk produces a very different form of entrapment. In it, history itself is what interns, incarcerates, and duration proves to be the stoniest means of confinement. As the narrator recounts the first of his two visits undertaken in the summer of 1967:

> My memory of the fourteen stations which the visitor to Breendonk passes between the entrance and the exit has clouded over the course of time, or perhaps I could say it was clouding over even on the day when I was in the fort, whether because I did not really want to see what it had now to show or because all the outlines seemed to merge in a world illuminated only by a few dim electric bulbs, and cut off for ever from the light of nature. Even now, when I try to remember them, when I look back at the crab-like plan of Breendonk and read the words of the captions – *Former Office, Printing Works, Huts, Jacques Ochs Hall, Solitary Confinement Cell, Mortuary, Relics Store* and *Museum* – the darkness does not lift but becomes yet heavier as

I think how little we can hold in mind, how everything is constantly lapsing into oblivion with every extinguished life, how the world is, as it were, draining itself, in that the history of countless places and objects which themselves is never heard, never described or passed on [...] I had to resist the feeling taking root in my heart [...] a sense that with every forward step that air was growing thinner and the weight above me heavier.[27]

These are the strange pressures of Sebald's terrain. Thus, even as his writings abound with topical histories – places worked over by human events and inscribed with specific dates – they take shape only with the present force of the unheard, the unreachable, the unbreathable, the unbearable. If this is landscape, or 'scapeland' in Lyotard's peculiar sense, it is also 'the undiscover'd country' – an allusion to Hamlet's soliloquy which Sebald uses as the title of his 1972 essay on Kafka's *The Castle*.[28] Here, the subject deprived of its own place (its situation, its shelter) is revealed only to its own anonymity. Here, the traveller covers huge distances only to beat the same path, turn at the same fork, stumble over the same 'posthumous present' over and over again. These are sites where time and territory are directed against their own ends or which precede and ruin the very possibility of having a *place in time*. As Adorno writes in his 1928 study of Schubert's *Winterreise*:

> The eccentric structure of this landscape, where each point is equidistant from the center, is revealed to the wanderer who traverses it without making headway: every development is its own perfect antithesis, the first step is as close to death as the last, and the dissociated points of the landscape are visited in a circle, without it ever being left far behind. [These landscapes] have no history but are merely viewed from different angles. The only change is a change of light.[29]

Cited in his reading of *The Castle* – the mysterious site of authority which K., the 'eternal Land-surveyor',[30] attempts but fails to reach – Adorno anticipates the many travellers who ply the landscapes of Sebald's own work. Estranged from the discourses of history – unable to assume the disassociations of their own condition *as* history – they are defined less by the conclusiveness of an event than by a surplus of time that simultaneously impedes and surrenders it. Or again, they are 'posthumous people' in my reuse of the phrase: animated by the lifelessness that attends their individual existence and, conversely, reviving the lifelessnesses that have gone before them. Indeed, they are subjects whose spectrality is the insignia of historicity *as such*. 'And so they are ever returning to us, the dead,' writes the narrator of the first story of *The Emigrants*. Gazing out of a train window *en route* to Lausanne, he scans the glaciers of the Bernese Oberland while contemplating the suicide of his interlocutor, Dr Henry Selwyn, and the recent discovery of the remains of Selwyn's alpine guide, missing, presumed dead, since 1914.

At times they come back from the ice more than seven decades later and are found at the edge of the moraine, a few polished bones and a pair of hobnailed boots.[31]

If these are landscapes which 'have no history',[32] it is not just because the past is ungraspable but because it is placeless: at once always elsewhere and posthumously still-here. Sebald's world is precisely this temporal derangement. Here, history becomes inoperable. Here, as Adorno writes in 1953 *Notes on Kafka*, 'the déjà vu' is declared permanent'.[33]

4

In spite of the equivocations of his approach, Sebald's work is often received as part of that generic and historical formulation we know as 'Holocaust literature'. More exactly, it is taken as a variant of the cultural, and specifically literary, sensibility of *Vergangenheitsbewältigung* – a coming to terms with, a disarming of the past – which from the early 1960s sought to register the complex culpabilities in Germany's Nazi past and the years of debt and denial that followed. Thus even as Sebald deals as frequently with the deep time of the Renaissance, the Enlightenment and the devastations of European colonization, it is nonetheless twentieth-century German history that is said to guide his reflections. This is not especially inaccurate. The comprehensive destruction of German cities in the closing years of the Second World War clearly informs Sebald's world: landscapes of undigested remnants and ruins, dust and ash, the material deposits of combustions, conflagrations, firestorms.[34] Certainly, the continuance of unexamined Nazi legacies – or the silence, shame and apologias that service them – is the declared content of the four essays collected in *On the Natural History of Destruction* (2003).[35]

But to take Sebald's writings to be about Germany's past or its active (if unacknowledged) post-war affinities still isn't quite right.[36] It not only flattens or straightens out the complex dissimilarities that are his distinctive literary style. It also obscures the extent to which Sebald's writing is less a thematization of German history than a question of what that history de-homes, 'de-shelters'[37] or releases us into. If the first is narratable, a connective tissue composed of revealing, even revelatory, actions and events, the second is not: whence, the temporal entanglements that prevent the succession of past into future; the inactive perpetuity of a posthumous present in which nothing ever quite happens and from which nothing ever quite follows – for Sebald, not even memory itself.

However, to say that he locates us in non-historical relations of time is not to suggest that Sebald's writing has no referent. Even as it eschews conventional historical and narratological form, it resonates with the undeniable fact of the Holocaust: the disfigurements of which cannot be held by language or cognition and a past unappeasable by any approach to it. Every experience and description arises from the grounds of its own oblivion, every speaker is witness to its own silence, just as every landscape is the depletion which disorientation demands. No defined place or presence can develop from this point, and no recounting can retrieve them either – except insufficiently, and except to clarify the mass of its sodden opacity. It is a strange form of historicization: the blank of the indelibly inscribed, things external to history but 'historically so'.[38]

There is a reason for this. Although Sebald only skirts the substance of the historical record, we know that the relation of place to presence, under National Socialism, was never just emblematic or symbolic. With an absolute internal logic, the one presupposed the other. 'One of the few rules the Nazis constantly adhered during the course of the "Final Solution", Agamben reminds us, 'was that Jews could be sent to extermination camps only after having been fully denationalized.'[39] Breaking the spatial relation between nativity and nationality was not merely an existential index, a token, of death. Displacement was preliminary to death, its pre-requisite. It was non-citizenship itself (the juridical relegation of those already transformed into second-class citizens) that anticipated and accomplished the status of 'sacred life' in Agamben's archaic usage: a 'life devoid of value', one 'unworthy of being lived'.[40] It is in this sense, too, that place enters Sebald's work where, like the in-distinction between law and life, it is irreparably reduced: not something to reclaim or get back to, but its own point of no return, the renunciation of a renunciation. Thus, in *Austerlitz*, as the eponymous protagonist, a child of the *Kindertransport*, traces his mother's deportation to Terezín (Theresienstadt), the journey delivers him to an unintelligible time with no border conceivable.

> It does not seem to me, Austerlitz added, that we understand the laws governing the return of the past, but I feel more and more as if time did not exist at all, only various spaces interlocking according to the rules of a higher form of stereometry, between which the living and the dead can move back and forth as they like [...] As far back as I can remember, said Austerlitz, I have always felt as if I had no place in reality, as if I were

not there at all [...] Even the next day, on my way to Terezín, I could not imagine who or what I was. I remember that I stood in a kind of trance on the platform of the bleak station at Holešovice, that the railway lines ran away into infinity on both sides, that I perceived everything indistinctly [...] When I got out of the train in Lovosice after about an hour, I felt as if I had been travelling for weeks, going further and further east and further and further back in time.[41]

5

In his *Reader for Those Who Live in Cities* (*Lesebuch für Städtebewohner*), written around 1927/8, Bertolt Brecht calls for the erasure of place and presence in a way that presages Sebald but for very different reasons.[42] Mordant, nihilist, savage, he offers pragmatic advice for a new social morality: retreat; be disaffected; don't acknowledge your friends; avoid determinate individuality; pull your hat low over your face; button up; never open the door; separate yourself from all solace. Above all, 'Cover your tracks!' and 'Once again: Cover your tracks!'[43] – be unmemorable, unremarkable, of no account; inscribe nothing and leave no trail lest someone identify and indict you. In the closing decade of the Weimar Republic, it is this very unmarking that will prove most portentous. What life requires is the eradication of every trace; existence relies on the irretrievable. Negate yourself before the inquisitors arrive, the battle begins and the expropriators take all.

In his 1939 'Commentary on Poems of Brecht' written on the eve of his imprisonment in the French internment camp near Nevers, Benjamin cites a letter in which the German-Jewish writer Arnold Zweig describes Brecht's prophesy. '[Zweig] has remarked that this sequence of poems has taken on a new meaning in the past few years'.[44]

It depicts the city as it is experienced by the émigré in a foreign country. This is correct. But we should not forget that he who fights for the exploited class is an emigrant in his own country [...] 'Erase the traces': A rule for those who are illegal. 'If you find your ideas in anyone else, disown them': A curious role for an intellectual in 1928, but crystal-clear for the illegal intellectual. 'Make sure, when you turn your thoughts to dying/That no gravestone divulges where you lie': This is the only rule that might be obsolete. Thanks to Hitler and his people, members of illegal parties have been relieved of this worry.[45]

Although it refers to a poem from the late 1920s which concerns the 'crypto-emigration'[46] of the class warrior, by 1939 Brecht's *Reader for Those Who Live in Cities* has become 'an object lesson in exile and living outside the law'.[47] It 'describes exile before exile',[48] as Zweig puts it, suggesting how clearly the political revolutionaries of Brecht's Weimar might prefigure the later subjects of Nazi expulsion. For our purposes, however, living a traceless life refers less to the tactics of Brecht's illegal city-dweller, than to place as it insubstantiates and anonymizes, in the Sebaldian sense referred to above. For whereas the fear, for Brecht, is that the mark might locate and so incriminate (the danger lies precisely in the certifications of legibility, in the evidentiary nature of the sign), with Sebald there is only the terrain of an ongoing insensibility. It is a move from one register of removal to another, from one zone of death to the next. Indeed if, as Benjamin suggests, National Socialism finally allayed the dangers of the trace, this is precisely because it had already made all references to identity obsolete: not merely obliterating names and places but effacing the obliteration itself.[49]

All of which is to say that Brecht's erasures stand in relation to Sebald's invisibilia as the 1930s do to the period of the post-war years. What for Brecht is the exile's first rule of self-deletion – do not divulge, sign nothing, say nothing twice, *do not commemorate* – is completed by the Sebaldian landscape: places not merely emptied of attribution but the realm in which the vacuum of disattribution transpires. If the first is an essential technique for survival, in the second the compounded debts of that imperative crash in: uninterpretable, untransmittable. 'Too many buildings have fallen down, too much rubble has heaped up, the moraines and deposits are insuperable', says the character of Michael Hamburger in *The Rings of Saturn*, as he attempts to recall his Berlin childhood before his forced emigration to England in November 1933.

> If I now look back to Berlin [...] all I see is a darkened background with a grey smudge in it, a slate pencil drawing, some unclear numbers and letters in gothic script, blurred and half wiped away with a damp rag. Perhaps this blind spot is also a vestigial image of the ruins through which I wandered in 1947 when I returned to my native city for the first time to search for traces of life I had lost. For a few days I went about like a sleepwalker, past houses of which only the facades were left standing, smoke-blackened brick walls and fields of rubble along the never-ending streets of Charlottenburg.[50]

Hamburger's words are about much more than the limits or failures of historical recovery. They are about the disorders of distance that, I am suggesting, is the true *point of view* of place – and which emerges as the secret ground of its historicity. Even on his daily walks through the well-defined centre of present-day Vienna, the author-narrator of the 'All'estro' section of *Vertigo* (1990) is given in relation to a nonevent, a no-place, a missing location. While an inveterate consultor of maps, his every stride is a going-back to the start; every advance is the repetition of an earlier failed movement; every recognition is the clouding that decomposes it.

> Early every morning I would set out to walk with no aim or purpose through the streets of the inner city, through the Leopoldstadt and the Josefstadt. Later, when I looked at the map, I saw to my astonishment that none of my journeys had taken me beyond a precisely defined sickle- or

crescent-shaped area, the outermost points of which were the Venediger Au by the Praterstern and the great hospital precincts of the Alsergrund. If the paths I had followed had been inked in, it would have seemed as though a man had kept trying out new tracks and connections over and over again, only to be thwarted each time by the limitations of his reason, imagination, or will-power, and obliged to turn back again [...] On one occasion, in Gonzagagasse, I even thought I recognized the poet Dante, banished from his home town on pain of being burned at the stake. For some considerable time he walked a short distance ahead of me, with the familiar cowl on his head, distinctly taller than the people in the street, yet he passed by them unnoticed. When I walked faster in order to catch him up he went down Heinrichsgasse, but when I reached the corner he was nowhere to be seen.[51]

And so we have: the posthumous presence of the exiled poet Dante, and the author coming around full circle to a beginning but without arriving anywhere. If this amounts to a historicity, it is not for any accounting of time but because of its perennial – essentially traumatic – incompletions: tracks that lead nowhere, encounters which do not happen, a space not so much intruded by a past but which presides over its absenting.

6

But it is not just that the Sebaldian landscape registers the presence of a posthumous place. Nor is it just that the spectre of the exiled Dante (like the ghosts of Kafka, Stendhal, Pisanello and Casanova who also stalk the pages of *Vertigo*) becomes, in its dream-like congruity, a companion to the narrator's un-identity. Here, as elsewhere, Sebald enacts another kind of posthumous survival, doubling, or *déjà vu* – this time, the author's own. It relates to the problem of *nachgeboren*, of being born-after, and to finding a form that might correspond to that implacable fact.

How does a German writer born in 1944, and so part of a generation for whom the catastrophe of mass death and exile was already on the cusp of passing, try to reconstruct the primary event or deal with the distancing that time has already produced? Where can one find an answer to the problem of distance if not in the dissipations of time and place that create it? Might distance be an attempt to translate a formative temporal disruption into a spatial one, rendering exile as the analogue of being 'born-after'?[52] In the revised version of his 1997 Zurich lectures which forms the basis of 'Air War and Literature' (1999) later included in *On the Natural History of Destruction*, Sebald implicitly describes the condition of the *nachgeboren* in these terms:

> I spent my childhood and youth on the northern outskirts of the Alps, in a region that was largely spared the immediate effects of the so-called hostilities. At the end of the war I was just one year old, so I can hardly have any impressions of that period of destruction based on personal experience. Yet to this day, when I see photographs or documentary films dating from the war I feel as if I were its child, so to speak, as if those horrors I did not experience cast a shadow over me, and one from which I shall never entirely emerge. A book on the history of the little market town of Sonthofen, published in 1963 to celebrate its civic status, contains a passage which runs: 'The war took much from us, but our beautiful native landscape was left untouched, as flourishing as ever.' Reading that sentence, I see pictures merging before my mind's eye – paths through the fields, river meadows, and mountain pastures mingling with images of destruction – and oddly enough, it is the latter, not the now entirely unreal idylls of my early childhood, that make me feel rather as if I were coming home [...] I know now that at that time, when I was lying in my bassinet [...] looking up at the pale blue sky, there was a pall of smoke in the air all over Europe, over the rearguard actions in East and West, over the ruins of the German cities, over the camps where untold numbers of people were burned.[53]

On one level, such autobiographical details describe the adoptive process that Mirianne Hirsch has famously termed 'post-memory';[54] that is to say, memory as it lives in the encounter of primary and inherited experience, a matter either of direct familial transmission or of broader affective affiliations that, in both cases, speak of the 'imaginative investments' of our historical lives, their 'projection[s] and creation[s]'.[55] On another level, post-memory is precisely not the Sebaldian condition. For all the periodization implied in being 'born-after', Sebald's landscapes do not imbue a place or a past with any identificatory content, or if they do it is only to confirm its superfluity, its insignificance, the undoing of history at the heart of memory. Distance is not bridged, not even in fantasy: there is no attempt to retrospectively represent or suture temporal disconnections in a gesture of intergenerational inheritance or compensation. Whether moving in the direction of remembering or its grey fading away, it is the namelessness of an event – its unredeemable distance, its indistinction – and not any recreation that erupts into presence.

Put otherwise: where the wealth of significance is gone there is no temporal endowment; no conveyance from past 'witness' to present 'heir'; no ending of an earlier life, or ending of an earlier death, implied in the state of being 'born-after'. There is only a cavity, a frayed point left hanging in the relations of events and recognitions that make up the work of remembrance. Being 'born-after', in this sense, is not any kind of inheritance; it is a certain divestiture, a deprivation, a disallowance. Unlike Hirsch's post-memory that carries, however imaginarily, a community of witnesses or the possibility, at least, of some temporal referentiality, being 'born-after' consists in a deeper disabling of time. This is the 'darkness [that] does not lift yet becomes even heavier' which assails the narrator of *Austerlitz* at Breendonk prison. This is the accumulated obliquities of 'countless places and objects which themselves have no power of memory' and so are 'never heard, never described, or passed on'.[56] It is also the 'moraines and deposits' that make the pre-war Berlin of Michael Hamburger's youth impossible to reimagine:

All that was required was a moment of concentration, piecing together the syllables of the word concealed in the riddle, and everything would be as it once was [...] Instead [...] I walked and walked, aimlessly and without being able to grasp even the simplest thought, well past the Westkreuz or the Halles Tor or the Tiergarten, I can no longer say where.[57]

But mostly, such a failure are those 'images of destruction [...] merging before [Sebald's] minds-eye' when he tries to recall his boyhood landscapes in Sonthofen: a site that offers no place from which to testify yet makes the *nachgeboren* 'feel rather as if [he] were coming home'.[58] Here, where memory fails, place succumbs to dissolution and dissolution, in turn, makes up the meaning, and the very materiality, of place. Here, where there is no past to which any return may be directed – and no name for what might be found there – 'coming home' means to incorporate the truth of a dissolution already in place.

This is the substance of Sebald's born-afterness – or, perhaps, born-'afterwardsness', to give it a Freudian inflection.[59] Indeed, if what characterizes Hamburger's wartime trauma is the inability to piece together the splinters of actual historical experience – to 'make the witness absent', in Shoshana Felman's memorable phrase[60] – then how much deeper the dispossession of experience for Sebald as a later, subsequent, subject? How much more clamorous the silence for those who, by virtue of their distance, are doubly muted, doubly deafened? Or those, like Sebald, concerned less with translating the past than holding to that which is non-communicable, non-commemorable: to 'keep watch over [its] absent sense',[61] in Blanchot's words? The point is less about the muteness of a previous generation than its amplification and magnification in an ensuing one: a vacancy both 'originary' and 'secondary'; a death that lives on posthumously in a present and whose central submission is silence – giving nothing up and refusing to pass anything on.

Thus Sebald not only modifies the logic of transition and transmission that underwrites the concept of 'post-memory'. He announces the problem of living outside available models of temporal and spatial reference, or in a state where the impassibility of historical inheritance is also the impossibility of expunging ghosts. If this is a dimension of what I have called a 'posthumous present', it is also a version of what Arendt intends when, in her Preface to *Between Past and Future*, she borrows an entry from René Char's *Leaves of Hypnos*, the notebook the poet kept while leader of a rural guerrilla unit of the French Resistance from 1943 to 1944. 'Our inheritance was left to us with no testament,' writes Char: a missing past, a bequest with no content. For Arendt, the predicament to which the poet alludes (in this case, the Nazi occupation of France and Vichy collaborationism) involves a kind of 'un-preserving', a break or block in the bestowals of time which leaves 'the mind of man wander[ing] in obscurity'.[62]

> Without testament or, to resolve the metaphor without tradition – which selects and names, which hands-down and preserves, which indicates where the treasures are and what their worth is – there seems no willed continuity in time and hence, humanly speaking, neither past nor future, only sempiternal change of the world and the biological cycle of living creatures in it. Thus the treasure was lost not because of historical circumstances and the adversity of reality but because no tradition had foreseen its appearance or its reality, because no testament had willed it for the future.[63]

Such a loss is not merely the failure of tradition; it lays bare our thought to the brutal departure of thought. If the unprecedented and unforeseen event no longer has a place in continuity, how can it be retrieved – even by thought? Without testament what is left but a wordlessness, a dismemberment, in Arendt's sense: an inheritance contracted to no-one and which no-one, no community, receives? For Blanchot, the question refers less to the limits of philosophy's moral capacities than of its technical possibilities. '*How can thought be made the keeper of the holocaust where all was lost, including guardian thought?*'[64] The question is also Arendt's:

> The tragedy began [...] when it turned out that there was no mind to inherit and question, to think about and to remember. The point of the matter is that the 'completion,' which indeed every enacted event must have in the minds of those who then are to tell the story and to convey its meaning, eluded them; and without this thinking completion after the act, without the articulation accomplished by remembrance, there simply was no story left that could be told.[65]

Thus, the past wills nothing and there is no present auditor. Its temporality is not of experiences delivered over and their meanings questioned or 'completed' by remembrance; it is loss itself lost: memories of an event we do not manage to conceive, a history not so much forgotten as 'consummated by oblivion'.[66] The traumatic burden that Arendt weighs in Char has it analogue in the Sebaldian condition of being 'born-after'. An inaudible distance resounds in both; the insensibility of the event remains. What kind of scene or story might be told by the *nachgeboren*? What kind of history is it that has already broken from relations of recognition, and whose 'main characteristic is not to bear witness'?[67] Alternatively, how to address such a silence but without stilling or normalizing its infinite injury and without evading our infinite responsibility? For Sebald, the answer, if there is one, involves identifying the point at which the past is simultaneously invoked and extinguished. It is less a matter of finding the means of which to speak of a German history than of being freed of a historical frame precisely to disorient it, to expose it, at every moment and again and again. If this is the dimension of what I have called a posthumous present, it is also the extent to which place, were it to hold to this temporality, would be uninhabitable, exiled, infinitely (even patiently) estranged. Indeed, insofar as the 'miracle' of post-war German reconstruction might be seen as redemptive, it is because place has smoothed over such estrangements: been recouped by history's project, anaesthetized by its transitions, atoned by its time. This is not just the caricature of recovery but one which lays waste to the wastes of which it needs to speak: a 'second liquidation',[68] Sebald calls it. On his return to his home village of Sonthofen, bombed by allied aircraft in February and April 1946, he recalls one site, in particular – a turn-of-the-century villa:

> Nothing was left of it now but its cast-iron garden railings and the cellars. By the 1950s the plot of land, where a few handsome trees had survived the catastrophe, was entirely overgrown, and as children we often spent whole afternoons in this wilderness created by the middle of town by war [...] A few years later a self-service shop opened on the site of the Herz-Schloss, an ugly, windowless single-storey building, and the once beautiful garden of the villa finally disappeared under the tarmac of a car park. That, reduced to its lowest common denominator, is the main theme of the history of post-war Germany.[69]

Sebald's writing is of course a literary project and not a philosophical or political one in any emphatic way. Even within this framework of expectation there is, nonetheless, the question of how fiction relates to our capacities to imagine a new 'ethos of place',[70] a mode of dwelling that might exile and detach the very foundations that the word 'place' seems to indicate. The guidance that Sebald offers can only be minimal: less a demand to acknowledge what has happened, or *taken place*, than to attend to living on in the absence of an event, and *on its site*. For all his painstaking geographic descriptions, in other words, Sebald returns us to the distance of the world, to a displacement, which we – perhaps 'born-afters' all – are called to inhabit. Moreover, to the extent that it is transparency that makes us disappear – clarity's 'second liquidation' – it is at the height (or depths) of opacity that Sebald sustains a fidelity to time in its most secreted fragments: to *another tense* that might do justice to the out-of-reach and listen to the discordant strains of its posthumous presence. Walking from site to site as he does (obsessively, repetitively, belatedly, abortively) requires, above all, a detour or derangement in our relation to history. In a landscape which no longer knows or wants *its place in time*.

Epilogue
Placeholding

In 'Refugee Conversation' (*Flüchtlingsgespräche*), a collection of prose dialogues begun in his Finnish exile in the autumn of 1940 while awaiting his visa to the United States, Brecht declares:

> Exile is the best possible school for dialectics. Refugees are the sharpest dialecticians. They've become refugees as a result of changes, and they spend all their time studying changes. They see the smallest signals as harbingers of the most significant events – if they've got any sense, that is. When their opponents are victorious, they calculate the cost of the victory, and they have a keen eye for contradictions. Long live dialectics![1]

Set in the café of Helsinki's central railway station, Brecht's dialogue is as succinct as any a formulation of thought proper to exilic space: reflexive, discordant, concerned with change (or freed from the stability of inherited belief) and attuned to the most meagre and unlikely of possibilities.[2] But if, according to one version of the dialectic, the contradictions which Brecht's exile (inadvertently) illuminates might be surmounted ultimately by the accumulation of their difficulties, then this study is perhaps bested by its own difficulty: the difficulty of enjoining exile to Judaism today at all. It is not just that the contemporary Jewish state revokes, invalidates, overrules the theological and philosophical principles of an exilic tradition; it instrumentalizes – directs, organizes, rigidifies – a specific history of spatial dispossession, enlisting it as licence and exculpation for its own territorial violations.

These closing pages will not address the raging ironies of Zionist militancy, illegal land occupation and Palestinian expulsion. But I want to suggest that if Israel cancels exile as a key resource in Judaism's own theological and intellectual tradition, this is not because its politics of place so brutally divides Jews from Palestinians, citizens from strangers, fully legalized subjects from those 'outside' (which is, of course, also 'inside') its law. It is because it expels place's own misconducts, evicts the constitutive rifts and rents that a Judaic understanding of exile has always committed itself to: the work of the non-identical and the incomplete, the uneven and infirm ground that territory repetitively checks and that displacement critically releases. This is why our concern is not with exile as a space set apart from the terms of identity but the inverse. It is an abandonment of those protective borders that preserve us in place and keep us from dwelling in the breach of what I have called a *non-national middle*: within an original of loss of boundaries and, therefore, within those untimely breaks and dismemberments on which all coherences (and idolatries) anxiously hinge.

For Eric Santner who looks to the Freudian or 'psychotheological' dimensions of Judaism, the question is less any exile 'out of Egypt' than an 'exodus out of [...] Egyptomania':[3] that is, out of that fatal fusion of energy and impairment which quarantines our duress, passionately invests in it, and limits our access to an interruptive terrain. Egyptomania is perhaps what the Jewish state presently enacts: not just a negation of Judaism's 'anoriginal' exile but the compulsive need to master its internal strains, overwriting its founding insufficiencies – indeed, its insufficient foundations – in the preservation of various kinds of sovereignty.

Part of what Freud tells us is that excess, like expulsion, is the best clue we have to our fear; that one is imperiled less by this or that primary wound than by the freneticism of our attempts at a self-cure and the immunizations of a history defined by them. If this is so, then Santner's 'exodus of out of Egyptomania' offers at least two possible routes. The first allows us to examine the paradoxes of traumatic identification: of a wounded subject, or people, as it turns cruel in the struggle to tolerate and survive itself; an internal dislocation so unbearable or uncontainable, it has to be denied but is preserved in another form. This is the route that Jacqueline Rose takes, unravelling the unconscious biography of modern Jewish statehood from its founding vision by secular intellectuals in the late nineteenth century to its revisions after the genocide of European Jewry. 'Why or how', she asks, 'did this movement – inspired, fervent, driven by the disasters that had befallen its people – succeed, so miraculously but also so tragically, in fulfilling itself?'[4] In the adamantine fit of psychic violation to political violence, it is the cumulative wreckage of shame, disavowal and humiliation which, for Rose, sustains the wild constraints (Santner's 'Egyptomania') of Israeli policy: oscillating between privation and acquisition, converting abjection into omnipotence and the collapse of identity into the coercions of the state. The persistence of the self-cure, the militancy of the attempted solution, in this way inevitably assumes a managerial or ideological cast. It not only comes to hoard the trauma which occasioned it; it arms and incessantly re-arms it. The second route, suggested by Santner but perhaps most clearly elaborated by Judith Butler,[5] returns us to the wound less to reveal the repetitions which recycle and ensconce it – the essential index of traumatic enslavement – than to renew or recharge the wound itself. It is a small adjustment in approach that suspends the reparative cure: mobilizing the injury into its own site of possibility, exercising its excesses and asking that we respond – and correspond – to the unnerving openings it unloosens. For Butler, this does not mean imagining what Judaism might yet become but accentuating what it already is: a founding scattering or ceding of the self that makes any language of security and containment redundant, an original expulsion drawn into its own borders, a displacement that must itself be 'brought home'[6] – not to assimilate or absorb it but precisely to re-issue, we may say, re-inflict it.

This book has followed a variant of this route. Like Santner's call for an 'exodus out of Egyptomania', the point has been to reactivate the 'wound' of exile or agitate it in a new way: unsettling those locations *forced* or *fantasized* as being properly one's own, avowing historical existence in the production of its disorientations, in the very liveliness of 'losing and being lost'.[7] Far from the psychic constrictions of the self-cure (the organization of borders, defences, the remedial forces of territory and its reiterations), the possibility of exile is granted on the basis of an infirmity: a certain 'unhealing', an unshielding. It is a spatiality that posits nothing and positions no-one but vouches for that which is urgent, emergent, endangered. Indeed if, as often suggested, what is so injurious about the contemporary Jewish state is that it tends to its own injuries so assiduously, so extensively – 'Israeli legislation countervenes, represses and even cancels Freud', writes Edward Said[8] – then the demand is to live the injury generatively, to bare the abrasion emphatically.

From different perspectives, and in very different languages, all the figures gathered here take the exilic source of Judaic tradition as this kind of conceptual resource. Sebald, who in the logic of these matters, though not in his own identity, speaks the final impossibility of place; a fundamental dislocation that, with Benjamin, appeared as a biblical injunction in the field of visual and spatial aesthetics. While their affinities are well established – Sebald as Benjamin's *doppelgänger* is by now familiar shorthand for the archive of modern European literature – what links them here is less any network of equivalence with respect to critical disposition, compositional method or biographical personae. It is the impress of a certain Judaic understanding of space and sight. By this I mean a perceptual capacity that arises not in the appearance of anything or any passage from the unknown to the known, but is given in the depletions of dispersion: oblique or over-exposures, journeys without respite or recuperation, temporal lapses and misdirections into which phenomena slip the moment they are glimpsed.

If in Benjamin I related this to theological understandings of time and the image that render urban modernity inoperative – visions of the city defamed, indicted or 'banned' *from within* – then with Sebald place itself becomes posthumous. In both cases, the fate of place and presence is to remain inaccessible, untenable, anachronistic. In both, the mythic drama of the Wandering Jew or its modern kin, the 'rootless cosmopolitan', is itself dismantled as soon as place detaches from its own presuppositions, revealing its history only to who see it from the allegorized – which is also to say, exiled – ruins of time or, at least, outside the unfolding locales of chronology. Like Benjamin's city, Sebald's landscapes describe something like a negative phenomenology: falling short of any intentional horizon (anticipatory or re-collective), renouncing the purview of a *horizon* itself, or bound only to the opacities of disinherited, divested, in-determining time.[9] Whereas, in Benjamin, a Judaic approach to the image is won back for profane attention – an ancient theological command returned as a struggle of and within secularity – Sebald's landscapes awaken those temporal abridgments of exile in which past and present contract into each other yet never coincide or whose historical submission is its refusal to bear witness: leaving nothing behind but also unable to hand down or move on. Born-after, given in distance and outside the composures of a composing frame, they relinquish all that pertains to the representational conditions of belonging. 'I know that what oppresses me is no neurosis, but rather precisely reflected reality',[10] writes the camp survivor and essayist, Jean Améry, with the same kind of iconoclastic or, in temporal terms, *ante*-aesthetic pressures which Benjamin's and Sebald's spaces variously register.

On the face of things there is little reason to think Arendt and Berlin together; their personal antipathy aside, they stand as opposing Cold War Jewish thinkers occupying two different geographies and two mutually exclusive political philosophies. And yet, in their shared preoccupation with the dilemmas of assimilation – or, 'exile-with-a-difference'[11] in its therapeutic re-description – both formulate the condition of 'being-plural' as co-originary and coextensive to 'being-without-place'. In this, the divergent figures of Berlin's Anna Akhmatova and Arendt's Rahel Varnhagen meet at an angle, forming something of a breached encounter in which the antimonies between exile and assimilation come undone, their identifying qualities unsettled at the point that they stumble over their internal indecisions. Thus read together, the exilic condition that defines the public political world in Arendt loses its force with Berlin's Akhmatova where it marks a melancholic resistance, a kind of deadly or 'stative' attraction to loss in which exile, paradoxically, hovers on the edge of an autochthony. Likewise, the assimilative model which in Berlin secures the terms of a liberal political pluralism is inverted – or better, incompleted – by Arendt's Rahel where assimilation acquires the diagnosis of a private malfunction, shrouding the exposures of worldly existence, its actions and actualities.

What appears as a straightforward identitarian division – exile or assimilation, the pariah or adaptor, Arendt or Berlin – loses its coherence as neither option can assume stability. The point, however, is not that exile and assimilation share some sort of affinity if one pushes beyond their distinctions, either reducing one to another or looking to surpass them. Rather, both introduce something in the order of a remnant or remainder: a certain disassembled or decomposing domain in identity and belonging that, in Arendt and Berlin, describes the contestations of the in-common as it bears on the contingencies of the out-of-place.[12] We might say that with Arendt and Berlin we revisit the idea of the middle (a middle 'rended not mended'[13]) as it repositions the political subject: a spatiality that allows for a new sort of action and agonism, one no longer constituted by membership to a bounded place or an enrolment in the usual part/whole accounting of its social relations. Here, provisionality, even perishability, becomes a politics. Something exorbitant has been unstopped; an incompletion stands out; a break has occurred. Indeed, here, the place of the political might better be thought as a *placeholder*: a gap or blank that signifies, may even be significant, yet which carries no determinate meaning; a mark of the interruptive and impermanent, but also, subtly, of a receptivity, a jeopardy and a future. As placeholder, it becomes undecidedly poised between void and affirmation, between emptiness and inauguration: a desert, a desertion, its own form of a 'broken middle'.

In this study, the first figure that occupies the place of this holding is Rosenzweig for whom exile transforms chronological time into redemptive time – not to adjourn the future or outshine the chiaroscuros of the present but to intensify, quicken and rouse us to them.[14] Judaic exile, in this sense, is not the subject's lack of a world; it is the vitality of its disorientations. And it is the metahistorical vocation of this disorientation that Rosenzweig wanted to describe in the *Star of Redemption*. At the same time, as Benjamin and Arendt also insist, an idea or essence only exists if it is embodied in empirical, experiential reality. Indeed, it was precisely idealism's *Volksgeist* – so concretely realized in the events of the First World War – that underwrote Rosenzweig's refusal of all modern nationalisms, and countered this with the old exilic call of Judaism. That said, while exile might describe the spatial fundament of Judaic existence, it cannot negate the fact that, in the Europe of the early twentieth century, no type of society allowed for a form of life based on it.

> Inasmuch as we want to live, our participation one way or another in the life of Nations is unavoidable, even if it is only a passive manner.[15]

To what extent then might Rosenzweig's theologically derived exile be translated into a profane or political one? For if he propounds a model of redemption which, by definition, cannot be accomplished in historical time, it is equally true that the conditions of the day offered no basis or measure to test its validity. Does this mean that the *Star of Redemption*, as Rosenzweig was later to warn, could only lay down a theoretical guide – circumventing any historical and political application or, worse, secretly consoling the existent, a mere 'pretext for our need for comfort'?[16] In short, what is the claim of Rosenzweig's theology on political practice save to provide a running critique or point up 'the limit imposed on all politics'?[17] And if so, is the purity of a theory, its practical inapplicability, sufficient proof against it? In a letter to Hans Ehrenberg in 1927, Rosenzweig defends the theory which the *Star* intends:

> Theory is invariably only a line. The roads of life deviate more or less, to right or left, from the beeline of theory. That line indicates only the general direction; anyone who insisted on walking the straight line could not move from the spot. Nevertheless, the beeline is the right one; the road to the left and the road to the right (to which small scale maps reduce the network of roads shown by General Staff maps) are in reality as little negotiable as the beeline, and are moreover theoretically false simply because there are two of them [...] It would be a good thing if at least the leaders [of the Diaspora and present-day Palestine] could see the beeline. Only a very few do [...] Nevertheless it works; the awareness is not so important as that.[18]

What we find in Rosenzweig, then, is not just a fidelity to the values of theory. As with Benjamin, Arendt and, in their own ways, Berlin and Sebald, it is a faith in the irresolutions between knowledge and its object and in a temporality that might thwart the onward march of things: suspending the power of chronic confirmations, unhinging the crusted rivets of origin and end. Put otherwise: if there is merit to the impracticality of theology, it resides in the fact that it cannot be verified – naturalized, reified – and cannot service a history defined by the bleached stretches of successive time, spatialized by the geographical governance of totalities and separations, protected by precedence or what Rosenzweig calls the 'specialization and fortification' of all foundational assertions.[19] As such, if a theological 'beeline' can only be a guide to our mobilities, then it is precisely a guide out of secularity's false divisions – and the need for their policing – towards an uninsured openness: an exodus, an expulsion, from the ensnarements of territorial time and back to the immersion in an 'anoriginal' middle. Only under the aspect of detachment might we bind ourselves, but without being tethered, to the unknown. Only from such a space can we recognize when it is no longer possible, or fundamentally impossible, to cleave to (profane) imaginaries of arrival or completion.[20] At the very least, it is a guide that allows things and forms of life to deflect – however briefly – from their stated direction, avowing the densities and out-of-joint-ness that exceed any normative spatial organization, not integrating the diversity of possible detours or mediating between them but keeping their internal dispersals always on the move.

If exile corresponds to this zone, then, it is not only incorrect to say that Judaic theology is divorced from a politics; rather, it arises on the side of the political and for the surprise of its unhealed openings: its inter-spaces and passings, its 'in-common' estrangements and in-determinations. And we might add, it belongs to the side of an 'eternal' – at once, timely and untimely – justice.[21] In a world that allots little room for it, exile makes it thinkable to suspend a chronic (even if reasonable) despair over what is bordered, barricaded, walled-in, kept-out. One can have no faith – in redemptive graces or theological guides – and yet, if the moment arises, recognize the eruption of a middle, a 'sudden meantime', in social and spatial being. Exile is *this* anachrony and *this* misplacing. That no current historical or geopolitical situation can promise or plan for its appearance does not exclude its proximity, its hidden contiguity. The anoriginality of Judaic thought, its original relation to a non-location, renewed even when, especially when, we encounter a commonality of people struggling and unable to find their way home.

NOTES

Introduction

1. Borrowed from a different context, the Lacanian phrase is Eric L. Santer's. See Santner, 'Miracles Happen: Benjamin, Rosenzweig, Freud, and the Matter of the Neighbour', *The Neighbour: Three Inquiries in Political Theology*, ed. Slavoj Žižek, Eric L. Santner and Kenneth Reinhard (Chicago, IL, and London: University of Chicago Press, 2005), 100.

2. Aviva Gottlieb Zornberg, *The Particulars of Rapture* (New York: Schocken Books, 2002), 200.

3. Rashi in Zornberg, *Particulars of Rapture*, 200.

4. On this, see Michael Walser, *Exodus and Revolution* (New York: Basic Books, 1985), 53. For an extended interpretation of the Exodus story as it frames the history of modern political radicalism, see also Walser, *In God's Shadow: Politics in the Hebrew Bible* (New Haven, CT, and London: Yale University Press 2012).

5. Maimonides, *The Guide for the Perplexed*, trans. Shlomo Pines (Chicago, IL: University of Chicago Press, 1963), 1:526–8.

6. Ibid.

7. On the Fabian motto of the 'inevitability of gradualness' implicit in Maimonides' argument, see Nehama Leibowitz, *New Studies in Shemot, Exodus*, trans. Areh Newman (Jerusalem: World Zionist Organisation, 1976), 55–6.

8. On this theme which links his series of essays on the significance of Judaism and Jewish mysticism to the development of European philosophy, see Levinas, *Difficult Freedom: Essays in Judaism*, trans. Seán Hand (Baltimore, MD: The Johns Hopkins University Press, 1997).

9. Zornberg, *Particulars of Rapture*, 202.

10. Ibid.

11. In the second part of his last major work *Moses and Monotheism* (1937), Freud retells the story of liberation as an experience of traumatic repression with the Israelite's murder of Moses – an idea also suggested by Goethe in his ironic retelling of the Moses story – forming part of his analysis of the patterns of denial and atonement at the compulsive core of religious belief. For the principal engagements with

Freud's analysis, see Yosef Hayim Yerushalmi, *Freud's Moses: Judaism Terminable and Interminable* (New Haven, CT, and London: Yale University Press, 1991); Jan Assmann, *Moses the Egyptian: The Memory of Egypt in Western Monotheism* (Cambridge, MA: Harvard University Press, 1997); Jacques Derrida, *Archive Fever: A Freudian Impression* (Chicago, IL, and London: The University of Chicago Press, 1995); Richard J. Bernstein, *Freud and the Legacy of Moses* (Cambridge: Cambridge University Press, 1998); Edward Said, *Freud and the Non-European* (London: Verso, 2003).

12 On anxiety as a relation to a *non*, passing or unfixed object, see Lacan, *Anxiety: The Seminar of Jacques Lacan, Book X*, ed. Jacques Alain Miller, trans. A. R. Price (Cambridge: Polity Press, 2014), 89–100.

13 Deployed in various contexts and with different emphases, Benjamin's phrase refers to approaching the origin not as singular beginning but as the site of ontological difference itself. See Andrew Benjamin, *The Plural Event* (London and New York: Routledge, 1994).

14 Gillian Rose, *The Broken Middle* (Oxford: Blackwell, 1992), 247–96. For Rose, the deficit of both thinkers lies in what she sees as their principled opposition to modernity. In particular, she calls out Strauss' *Philosophy and Law: Essays toward the Understanding of Maimonides and His Predecessors* (1935) and *Natural Right and History* (1953) for overlooking the pre-Olympian strata of Greek religion in classical political philosophy and misrepresenting the rationalism of modern Judaism. Rose's more complex assessments of Levinas, from his *Existence to Existents* (1947) and *Totality and Infinity: An Essay on Exteriority* (1961) to *Otherwise than Being or beyond Essence* (1974), involve the ways in which the primacy he attributes to ethics supposedly leads to a dismissal of modern political history, and of the historical as such.

15 See also Rose, *Judaism and Modernity: Philosophical Essays* (Oxford: Blackwell, 1993), 1–10 and Rose, *Mourning Becomes Law: Philosophy and Representation* (Cambridge: Cambridge University Press, 1996), 15–40.

16 Rose, *Mourning Becomes Law*, 81.

17 Rose, *Judaism and Modernity*, 18.

18 Rose, *Mourning Becomes Law*, 79.

19 Ibid., 37.

20 Ibid., 83. The honorific – a response to Derrida's ludic word play when signing off as 'Reb Derissa' in the final essay of *Writing and Difference* – is Susan Handelman's. See Handleman, *The Slayers of Moses: The Emergence of Rabbinic Interpretation in Modern Literary Theory* (Albany: State University of New York Press, 1982), 163.

21 Rose, *Judaism and Modernity*, 10.

22 Rose, *Mourning Becomes Law*, 10.

23 Rose, *Broken Middle*, 308.

24 Ibid., 310.

25 Discussions of Krauss' maxim most often relate to its use by Walter Benjamin. Among others, see Richard Wolin, *Walter Benjamin: An Aesthetic of Redemption* (Berkeley: University of California Press, 1994), 37–43 and Anson Rabinbach's discussion of Benjamin's theory of origins in 'Critique and Commentary/Alchemy and Chemistry', *New German Critique* 17 (Spring 1979): 7–9.

26 For a different, but related, formulation, see Judith Butler, *Parting Ways: Jewishness and the Critique of Zionism* (New York: Columbia University Press, 2012), 4–8.

27 W. R. Bion, *Cogitations* (New York: Routledge, 1994), 304.

28 Rose, *Broken Middle*, 308.

29 The phrase is Michael P. Steinberg's, see Steinberg, *Judaism Musical and Unmusical* (Chicago, IL: Chicago University Press, 2007), 56.

30 Isaiah Berlin, *Freedom and Its Betrayal: Six Enemies of Human Liberty*, ed. Henry Hardy (London: Pimlico, 2003), 18.

Chapter 1

1 Rosenzweig, *Franz Rosenzweig: His Life and Work*, ed. Nahum N. Glatzer (Indianapolis, IN and Cambridge: Hackett Publishing, 1998), 54–5.

2 For the full account of this 'young German-Jewish "generation of 1914"', see Anson Rabinbach, 'Between Enlightenment and Apocalypse: Benjamin, Bloch and Modern German Messianicism', *New German Critique* 34 (Winter, 1985): 78–124.

3 Rosenzweig, *Philosophical and Theological Writings*, ed. and trans. Paul W. Franks and Michael L. Morgan (Indianapolis, IN and Cambridge: Hackett Publishing, 2000), 13.

4 Ibid., 17.

5 Rosenzweig, 'Concluding Remark', *Franz Rosenzweig: Philosophical and Theological Writings*, trans. Paul W. Franks and Michael L. Morgan (Indianapolis, IN and Cambridge: Hackett Publishing, 2000), 82.

6 G. W. F. Hegel, *The Philosophy of Right*, trans. T. M. Knox (Oxford: Oxford University Press, 1952), 222.

7 Rosenzweig, '"Germ-Cell" of *The Star*', *Franz Rosenzweig's 'The New Thinking'*, ed. and trans. Alan Udoff and Barbara E. Galli (Syracuse, NY: Syracuse University Press, 1999), 63.

8   For the seminal and enduring analysis of Jewish messianic radicalism as it emerged in the immediate aftermaths of the First and Second World Wars, see Rabinbach, *In the Shadow of Catastrophe: German Intellectuals between Apocalypse and Enlightenment* (Berkeley, CA: University of California Press, 1997).

9   For the full text of 'The New Thinking', the explanatory essay written to clarify the main themes of *The Star* published in the October 1925 issue of *Der Morgen*, see Rosenzweig, '"The New Thinking": A Few Supplementary Remarks to *The Star*', in *Franz Rosenzweig's New Thinking*, 67–102. On the (profound and, at times, troubling) resemblances between Rosenzweig's philosophical transformations and similar departures made by Martin Heidegger (evident especially in Heidegger's 1964 essay 'The End of Philosophy and the Task of Thought') see Peter Eli Gordon's major study, *Rosenzweig and Heidegger: Between Judaism and German Philosophy* (Berkeley, CA: University of California Press, 2005).

10 Gordon, *Rosenzweig and Heidegger*, 192.

11 See Rosenzweig's 'Glauben und Wissen', based on lecture notes on the subject in 1926 in *Zweistromland: Kleine Schriften zur Religion und Philosophie*, ed. R. and A. Mayer (Dortrecht, 1985), 581–95. The coinage 'absolute empiricism' – one of the few slogans or 'Isms' that Rosenzweig allows himself – appears at the end of 'The New Thinking', *Franz Rosenzweig's 'The New Thinking'*, 101.

12 The original form of the 'Germ Cell', the preparatory essay of the *Star*, is Rosenzweig's letter to Rudolf Ehrenberg dated 18 November 1917. See 'The New Thinking', 45–66.

13 Ibid., 57.

14 Franz Rosenzweig, *The Star of Redemption*, trans. Barbara E. Galli (Madison, WI: University of Wisconsin Press, 2005), 427.

15 Rosenzweig, 'Globus: Studien zur wetlgeschichtlichen Raumlehre' (A Study of World Historical Space) cited in Paul Mendes-Flohr, 'Rosenzweig and the Crisis of Historicism', in *The Philosophy of Franz Rosenzweig*, ed. Mendes-Flohr (Hanover and London: University Press of New England, 1988), 155.

16 Ibid. For a discussion of *Ökumene* and *Thalatta* as the geopolitical principles that Rosenzweig uses to allegorically map the distinction between historical time and an extra-historical eschatology, see Mendes-Flohr 'Rosenzweig and the Crisis of Historicism', 138–61.

17 Jacques Derrida, 'Force of Law: The "Mystical Foundation of Authority"', trans. Mary Quaintance, *Cardozo Law Review* 11 (1990): 987.

18 Ibid., 997.

19 On the extent to which Rosenzweig aims less to disprove Hegelianism than to 'take [Hegel] literally' by following the inner workings of his thought into concrete historical reality, see Stéphane Mosès, *The Angel of History: Rosenzweig, Benjamin,*

Scholem, trans. Barbara Harshav (Stanford, CA: Stanford University Press, 2009), 35–48. For his extended exposition and interpretation of Rosenzweig, see Mosès, *System and Revelation: The Philosophy of Franz Rosenzweig*, trans. Catherine Tihanyi (Detrioit: Wayne State University Press, 1992).

20 Rosenzweig, *Star*, 323.

21 Ibid., 319.

22 Ibid., 318–19.

23 Ibid., 352.

24 Ibid., 354.

25 Ibid., 354.

26 Ibid., 352.

27 Ibid.

28 Ibid., 354.

29 Ibid., 353.

30 Ibid., 352.

31 Rosenzweig, *Star*, 353.

32 Eric L. Santner, *On the Psychotheology of Everyday Life: Reflections on Freud and Rosenzweig* (Chicago, IL and London: University of Chicago Press, 2001), 62. For further elaborations on the idea of 'sovereign temporalisation', see Santner, *On Creaturely Life: Rilke, Benjamin, Sebald* (Chicago, IL and London: University of Chicago Press, 2006), 66–9.

33 Rosenzweig, *Star*, 359.

34 Ibid., 352.

35 Ibid., 354.

36 Ibid., 334.

37 Walter Benjamin, 'Critique of Violence', *Reflections: Essays, Aphorisms, Autobiographical Writings*, trans. Edmund Jephcott (New York: Schocken, 1989), 277–300.

38 Rosenzweig, *Star*, 353–4. Here.

39 Rosenzweig, *Star*, 354.

40 Derrida, 'Force of Law', 1009.

41 Rosenzweig, *Franz Rosenzweig's 'The New Thinking'*, 87.

42 Rosenzweig, *Star*, 177.

43 Rosenzweig, *Star*, 319.

44 Ibid.

45 Ibid., 306.

46 This conception of time is of course also consonant with Benjamin's concept of 'weak messianic hope' that runs through his writings on the dialectical image. By Benjamin's own admission, the theological content of *Theses on a Philosophy of History* (also *On the Concept of History*) owes much to the earlier *Star*. Other similarities between Benjamin and Rosenzweig involving theories of language and translation, specifically as they relate to the metaphysics of a 'pure' or holy language, further deepen the connection.

47 Rosenzweig, *Franz Rosenzweig's 'The New Thinking'*, 87.

48 Rosenzweig, *Star*, 358.

49 Rosenzweig's 'metahistorical' Judaism carries some surprising, even idiosyncratic, implications for the notion of Jewish 'chosenness' or election. As Mosès, Gordon and others point out, it is not just that the realisation of 'national spirit', in Hegel's sense, is unavailable to a Jewish people. Rather, Rosenzweig's argument, as it develops in correspondence with and against the leading Protestant theologian, Eugen Rosenstock-Huessy, shows how the conception of election comes to belong to the Hegelian and Christianizing logic of modern political formation itself. From this perspective, biblical election is no longer the preserve of Judaism; it is a formulation from which the 'metahistorical vocation' of Judaism is necessarily distanced. On this, see Mosès *The Angel of History*, 29–34 and 46–8 as well as his *System and Revelation*, 210–12. For a wide-ranging analysis of Rosenzweig's understanding of exemplarity and election in relation to the ambitions of universalism, see Dana Hollander, *Exemplarity and Chosenness: Rosenzweig and Derrida on the Nation of Philosophy* (Stanford, CA: Stanford University Press, 2008).

50 Rosenzweig, *Star*, 318.

51 See *The Spirit of Judaism*, which forms the first part of *The Spirit of Christianity and its Fate* in G. W. F. Hegel, *Early Theological Writings*, ed. T. M. Knox (Philadelphia, PA: University of Pennsylvania Press, 1975), 182–204. While never intended for publication, the text interprets most of the central debates within Judaism – e.g., the un-representable essence of the Judaic God, Judaic election, the separation from nature, the structural incompleteness of its Law, the meaning of sacrifice. To the extent that it is turned against Judaism, and towards infinite or 'Absolute Life,' the text forms the basis of numerous studies of Hegel's ostensible anti-Judaism. Together with Jacques Derrida's 'side-notes' in *Glas* (Paris, Galilée, 1973), see also Joseph Cohen, *Le Spectre Juif de Hegel* (Paris: Galilée, 2005); Yirmiyahu Yovel, *Dark Riddle: Hegel,*

Nietzsche and the Jews (Philadelphia, PA: Pennsylvania University Press, 1988); Emil L. Fackenheim, *The Religious Dimension in Hegel's Thought* (Bloomington, IN: Indiana University Press, 1971).

52 Rosenzweig, 'A Note to a Poem by Judah ha-Levi', in Glatzer, *Franz Rosenzweig: His Life and Thought*, 335.

53 Slavoj Žižek, 'Neighbours and Other Monsters: A Plea for Ethical Violence' *The Neighbour: Three Inquiries in Political Theology*, ed. Slavoj Žižek, Eric L. Santner and Kenneth Reinhard (Chicago, IL: University of Chicago Press, 2005), 155.

54 Rosenzweig, 'The Nations and Their States' in Glatzer, *Franz Rosenzweig*, 337.

55 Ibid.

56 Rosenzweig, *Star*, 323.

57 Rosenzweig, 'The Nations and Their States', 339.

58 Rosenzweig, 'Four Letters' in Glatzer, *Franz Rosenzweig*, 354.

59 Writing to the German Zionist newspaper *Jüdische Rundschau* in 1928, Rosenzweig refers to the internal contradictions of a Jewish *Volk*: 'That we are a *Volk* is not to us what it is to Herzl […] the end of the theoretical problematic and the liberating breakthrough into the realm of the practical; No on the contrary, it is here that the theoretical problem first begins for us. We are a *Volk*: this does not mean for us what it means to the Zionists: because or insofar as we are not a religious denomination but precisely insofar as we are a religious denomination […] ' On this, see Leora Batnitzky, *Idolatry and Representation* (New Jersey: Princeton University Press, 2000), 170–2. For a related analysis of how Rosenzweig's complication of a Jewish *Volk* relates to the 'nation-defining' role of language, see Dana Hollander, 'Franz Rosenzweig on Nation, Translation and Judaism', *Philosophy Today* 38:4 (1994): 380–9.

60 Hermann Cohen, 'The German and Jewish Ethos II', *Reason and Hope: Selections from the Jewish Writings of Hermann Cohen*, ed. and trans. Eva Jospe (New York: W. W. Norton, 1971), 188. For an extended analysis of Cohen's account of Kantian rationalism and the ethical precepts of Judaic faith, with specific reference to the difference between Rosenzweig and Cohen, see Derrida, 'Interpretations at War: Kant, the Jew, the German', *Acts of Religion*, ed. Gil Anidjar (New York and London: Routledge, 2010), 137–90.

61 Paul Mendes-Flohr, *German-Jews: A Dual Identity* (New Haven, CT and London: Yale University Press, 1999), 86.

62 Rosenzweig, letter to his parents, 20 September 1917, in Glatzner, *Franz Rosenzweig*, 60.

63 Ibid., 205.

64 On Rosenzweig's warning of Jewish idolatry; that is, the danger it faces when it attempts to resolve (political) contradictions of relating to, and separating itself from, the world of nations, see Batnitzky, *Idolatry and Representation*, 169–87.

65 Hallo, one of the first reviewers of the *Star*, was to succeed Rosenzweig as head of the *Freies Jüdisches Lehrhaus* in Frankfurt.

66 Rosenzweig, *Der Mensch und sein Werk: Gesammelte Schriften 1:2* (Martinus Hijhoff, 1979), 887–8.

67 Derrida, 'Interpretations at War', 143.

68 Rosenzweig cited in Derrida, ibid., 142.

69 The phrase is Andrew Benjamin's. On the implications of the 'anoriginal' to the 'placed-ness' of the ethical encounter between the 'host' and 'the stranger', see Andrew Benjamin, 'Recovering Holiness and the Place of Others: Notes on *Vayikra* 19:34', *Parallax* 69 (October–December 2013): 36–48.

70 Rosenzweig, *Star*, 319.

71 Ibid., 173.

72 Rosenzweig in a letter to his parents, 18 December 1917, in Glatzer, *Franz Rosenzweig*, 64.

73 Ibid., 53–4.

74 For a related, albeit different, argument, see Louis P. Blond, 'Franz Rosenzweig: Homelessness in Time', *New German Critique*, 111 (Fall 2010): 27–58.

75 Rosenzweig, *Star*, 323.

76 Derrida, 'Force of Law', 997.

77 Rosenzweig, *Star*, 344.

78 Mosès, *Angel of History*, 51.

79 Rosenzweig, *Star*, 344.

80 Rosenzweig, *Star*, 322.

81 Judith Butler, *Parting Ways: Jewishness and the Critique of Zionism* (New York: Columbia University Press, 2012), 224.

82 On Rosenzweig's Judaism as it is distinguished by a particular 'structure of desire', see Santner, *Psychotheology of Everyday Life*, 110.

83 Ibid., 61.

84 The term is Heidegger's – itself borrowed from Kierkegaard and Luther.

85 Rosenzweig, *Star*, 174.

86 Ibid.

87 Ibid.

88 It is precisely because of the 'secular piety' of idealism – the extent to which knowledge usurps the place of the belief – that Rosenzweig dedicates the first part of *The Star* to the separation of the factual and speculative.

89 Rosenzweig, *Star*, 352.

90 Mòses, *Angel of History*, 28–9.

91 Rosenzweig in Mosès, *Angel of History*, 29.

92 Rosenzweig, *Star*, 358.

93 Rosenzweig, 'The New Thinking', 83–4.

94 Rosenzweig, '"Germ-Cell" of the Star', 63.

95 Rosenzweig, *Star*.

96 For his variations on this phrase, see Rosenzweig, *Star*, 368–9.

97 Butler, *Parting Ways*, 102.

98 Rosenzweig, 'On Miracles' in Glatzner, *Franz Rosenzweig*, 290.

99 Ibid., 289–90.

100 Ibid., 290.

101 For a brilliant analysis of Rosenzweig's miracle as it exposes a genuine break or 'emergency' in social and symbolic representation, see Eric L. Santner, 'Miracles Happen: Benjamin, Rosenzweig, Freud, and the Matter of the Neighbour', *The Neighbour*, 76–133. For an equally illuminating analysis of how Rosenzweig's miracle contrasts with the Schmittian model of political power and legal governance, see Bonnie Honig, 'The Miracle of Metaphor: Rethinking the State of Exception with Rosenzweig and Schmitt', *Diacritics* 37:2/3 (2007): 78–102.

102 Walter Benjamin, *The Arcades Project*, trans. Howard Eiland and Kevin McLaughlin (Cambridge, MA and London: The Belknap Press, 1999).

103 Ibid., 435.

104 Rosenzweig in Glatzer, *Franz Rosenzweig*, 53.

105 Benjamin, *Arcades Project*, Convolute 1°2, 846.

106 Benjamin, *Arcades Project*, N 1, 2. 456.

107 For her account of Rosenzweig as a key progenitor of this move, see Rose, *The Broken Middle*, 247–76. While Rose gives him short-shrift, Rosenzweig's influence on a variety of contemporary (postmodern) philosophers is clear, even if sometimes only briefly acknowledged. For example, although Levinas wrote only two essays and two shorter pieces on him, the preface to *Totality and Infinity* (1961) declares its debt to the *Star* to be 'too often present in this book to be cited'. For in-depth comparative studies between the two, see Robert Gibbs, *Correlations in Rosenzweig and Levinas* (Princeton, NJ: Princeton University Press, 1992) and Richard A. Cohen, *Elevations: The Height of the Good in Rosenzweig and Levinas* (Chicago,

IL: University of Chicago Press, 1994). Similarly, while Rosenzweig's influence on Derrida is arguably most evident in *Spectres of Marx: The State of the Debt, the Work of Mourning and the New International* (1993) – in particular, the concept of 'the messianic without messiancism' – references to him occur throughout Derrida's writings. See, for example, the long footnote in Derrida's *Monolingualism and the Other; or The Prosthesis of Origin* (Stanford, CA: Stanford University Press, 1996), 79–84 and various references in *Interpretations at War: Kant, the Jew, the German* (1989). For a more recent account of the general impact (and, at times, dismissal) of German-Jewish modernism in the writings of Maurice Blanchot, Giorgio Agamben, Alain Badiou and Slavoj Žižek, see Vivian Liska, *German-Jewish Thought and Its Aftermath: A Tenuous Legacy* (Bloomington, IN: Indiana University Press, 2017).

108   Rosenzweig, *Star*, 352.

109   Benjamin, Thesis VIII of 'Theses on the Philosophy of History', *Illuminations*, trans. Harry Zohn (London: Fontana/Collins), 259.

110   'Surely there is nothing more Jewish than a lack of transition' is how Rosenzweig, writing of Hermann Cohen, describes the immediacy of contradiction. In Derrida, 'Interpretations at War', 144.

111   The phrase is Emmanuel Levinas' in Levinas, 'Nameless', *Proper Names*, trans. Michael B. Smith (London: The Athlone Press, 1996), 123.

Chapter 2

1   For a summation of the opposing interpretations of Scene Five, Act Two, see Chapter 5 of Michael Cherlin, *Schoenberg's Musical Imagination* (Cambridge: Cambridge University Press, 2007).

2   Arnold Schoenberg, *Moses und Aron: Oper in drei Akten* (London: Schott, 1985).

3   Deuteronomy 4:15.

4   Adorno, 'Sacred Fragment: Schoenberg's Moses und Aron', *Quasi Una Fantasia: Essays on Modern Music*, trans. Rodney Livingstone (London: Verso, 1992), 226. See also Adorno, 'Arnold Schoenberg 1874–1951', *Prisms*, trans. Samuel and Sherry Weber (Cambridge: MIT Press, 1983), 147–72.

5   Exodus 4:10.

6   Schoenberg, *Moses and Aaron*.

7   Exodus 20:4.

8   Against the stricter terms of Maimonides for whom idolatory refers to the making of any and all images, the emphasis here is more in line with Rosenzweig's argument that what is prohibited is not the image itself but rather a certain valuation of it; that is, one that in assuming the fixity of the image produces a certain *type* of worship. On this, see Leora Batnitzky, *Idolatory and Representation: The Philosophy of Franz Rosenzweig Reconsidered* (Princeton, NJ: Princeton University Press, 2000), 17–31.

9   On problems concerning forbidden representations of the Shoah, see Jean-Luc Nancy, *The Ground of the Image*, trans. Jeff Fort (New York: Fordham University Press, 2005), 15–27.

10 On the degree to which the cherubim function metonymically and therefore do not lead to an error in the conception of God, see Moshe Halbertal and Avishai Margalit, *Idolatory*, trans. Naomi Goldblum (Cambridge, MA, and London: Harvard University Press, 1992), 48–9.

11 Nancy, *The Ground of the Image*, 30–3.

12 Isaiah 46:7.

13 Rosenzweig in Glatzer, *Franz Rosenzweig*, 53.

14 To 'put the immobile statue in movement' is the phrase Levinas uses in thinking together the visual and conceptual within an ethics of intersubjective relations. Levinas, 'Reality and Its Shadow', *The Levinas Reader*, ed. Seán Hand (Oxford: Oxford University Press, 1989), 142.

15 Brecht cited in Benjamin, *Understanding Brecht*, trans. Anna Bostock (London: NLB, 1973), 110.

16 While various deployments of theological, and specifically messianic, motifs appear in different periods of Benjamin's writings – albeit not in *The Arcades Project* where, according to Michael W. Jennings' accounting, the term 'messianic' appears only seven times and this in relation to French utopian socialists – they are always used in specific, localized contexts. On the 'situational' nature of Benjamin's theology as it supports particular political commitments, see Jennings, 'The Will to Apokatastasis: Media, Experience, and Eschatology in Walter Benjamin's Late Theological Politics', *Walter Benjamin and Theology*, ed. Colby Dickinson and Stéphane Symons (New York: Fordham University Press, 2016), 93–109.

17 Benjamin, *One-Way Street and Other Writings*, trans. Edmund Jephcott and Kingsley Shorter (London and New York: Verso, 1979), 51.

18 Benjamin cited in 'Translator's Forward', *The Arcades Project*, x.

19 Benjamin, 'Exposè of 1939', *Arcades*, 14.

20 'Let two mirrors reflect each other; then Satan plays his favourite trick, and opens here in his way [...] The perspective on infinity. Be it now divine, now satanic: Paris has a passion for mirrorlike perspectives.' Benjamin, 'Paris Arcades II', *Arcades*, c°,2.

21 Otto Rühle cited in Benjamin, *Arcades*, G5, 1, 181.

22 Karl Marx, *Capital*, Vol. 1, trans. Ben Fowler (New York: Vintage, 1977), 163.

23 Benjamin, *Arcades*, J65a, 6, 345.

24 Eric L. Santner, *On Creaturely Life: Rilke, Benjamin, Sebald* (Chicago, IL: Chicago University Press, 2006), 17.

25 Ibid., 81.

26 Benjamin, *Arcades*, Q1, 1, 527.

27 For a clear summation of this in Adorno's concept of 'Natural History', first formulated for a 1932 lecture in which he adapts Lukacs' concept of 'second nature', see Adorno, 'The Idea of Natural History', *Telos*, 60 (1984): 111–24.

28 Benjamin, *Selected Writings, Vol 4, 1938–1940*, ed. Howard Eiland and Michael W. Jennings (Cambridge, MA: The Belknap Press, 2003), 183.

29 Adorno in a letter to Benjamin, August 1935, *Arcades* N5,2, 466.

30 Benjamin, 'Central Park', *Selected Writings*, Vol. 4, 183.

31 One such fragment reads: 'The book on the Baroque exposed the seventeenth century to the light of the present day. Here, something analogous must be done for the nineteenth-century, but with greater distinctiveness'; see Benjamin, *Arcades*, N1a, 2, 459.

32 Benjamin, 'Central Park', *Selected Writings*, 183.

33 Benjamin, in response to 1935 letter from Adorno, *Arcades*, N5,2, 466.

34 Isaiah, 46:7.

35 Jonathan Boyarin, *Storm from Paradise: The Politics of Jewish Memory* (Minneapolis: University of Minnesota Press, 1992), 41.

36 Desiderius Erasmus, *The Collected Works of Erasmus*, Vol. 6, ed. John W. O'Malley (Toronto: University of Toronto Press, 1988), 66.

37 Benjamin, 'Exposé of 1939', *Arcades*, 14–15.

38 See Benjamin, *Origins*, 35–6.

39 See Rebecca Comay, 'Materialist Mutations of the Bilderverbot', *Walter Benjamin and Art*, ed. Andrew Benjamin (New York and London: Continuum Press, 2005), 32–59. The ancient topos of the 'blue distance' or '*Fernblick ins Blau*' – literally, 'the far-gaze into the blue' – appears in various formulations in Benjamin. See, for example,

Selected Writings, Vol 1, 1913–1926, ed. Marcus Bullock and Michael W. Jennings (Cambridge, MA: Belknap Press, 1996), 397–40, where it relates to the logic of the dream in Ludwig Klages's '*Lebensphilosophie*'.

40   Willy Spühler cited in Benjamin, *Arcades*, M2, 7, 420.

41   Comay, 'Materialist Mutations of the Bilderverbot', 43. Comay reads Adorno's understanding of the Bilderverbot with and against Benjamin's, in a series of compelling entanglements and antinomies. In relating the biblical image-ban to Benjamin's dialectical image, her reading has been influential to my own account.

42   Benjamin, 'Expose of 1935', *Arcades*, 11.

43   Benjamin, *Arcades*, M20a, 2, 454.

44   Ibid., P2, 1, 519.

45   Benjamin, *Arcades*, E1a,1, 122.

46   Ibid., 877.

47   Labédollière, cited in Benjamin, *Arcades*, E2a, 6, 126.

48   Ibid., c°, 1, 877.

49   Ibid., M17a, 2, 448.

50   Ibid., N5, 2, 466.

51   Benjamin, *Origin*, 233.

52   Benjamin, *Arcades*, J48, 6, 315.

53   Santner, *Creaturely Life*, 88.

54   Following Benjamin's discussions with Gershom Scholem during their years in Switzerland, 1919–23 marks the period of his engagement with Ernst Bloch's *Spirit of Utopia* and Rosenzweig's *Star of Redemption* both of which surface in his 'Theologico-Political Fragment' and 'The Task of the Translator.' It is only in 1939–40, with his engagement with Scholem's *Major Trends in Jewish Mysticism*, that the messianic explicitly reappears in 'Theses on the Philosophy of History'.

55   Benjamin's phrase, first used in his 1934 essay on Franz Kafka, refers, more generally, to the small, 'unforceful' nature of the messianic moment. See Benjamin, 'Franz Kafka: On the Tenth Anniversary of His Death', *Selected Writings*, Vol. 2, Part 2, trans. Rodney Livingstone and others, ed. Michael W. Jennings, Howard Eiland, and Gary Smith (Cambridge, MA: The Belknap Press, 1999), 811.

56   Benjamin, 'Letter to Max Horkheimer', *The Correspondence of Walter Benjamin 1910–1940*, ed. Gershom Scholem and Theodor Adorno, trans. Manfred R. Jacobson and Evelyn M. Jacobson (Chicago, IL: University of Chicago Press, 1994), 612.

57 With my focus on the city as a site of the Judaic injunction, I am less concerned with the 'image-sphere' (*Bildraum*) of the modern media – that is, Benjamin's concerns with the technical/conceptual apparatuses of montage, Surrealist dream-theory, the 'optical unconscious' of photography, the borderline of auratic decline and displacement – and rather with the issue of urban space itself.

58 Benjamin, *Selected Writings*, Vol. 4, 397.

59 Benjamin, *Arcades*, 877.

60 Ibid.

61 Ibid.

62 Baudelaire cited by Benjamin, *Arcades*, M14a, 1, 443.

63 On traumatic excitation as it produces and overwhelms the shields of the ego, see Freud, 'Beyond the Pleasure Principle', *Beyond the Pleasure Principle and Other Writings*, trans. John Reddick (London: Penguin, 2003), 43–102; and Georg Simmel, 'The Metropolis and Mental Life', *Georg Simmel: On Individuality and Social Form*, ed. Donald Levine (Chicago, IL: University of Chicago Press, 1971).

64 'It is very significant that our own bodies are in so many respects inaccessible to us. We cannot see our faces, our backs, nor our entire heads – in other words, the noblest parts of our body; we cannot lift ourselves up with our own hands, cannot embrace ourselves, and so on. We plunge into the world of perception feet-first, as it were, not headfirst.' Benjamin, *Gesammelte Schriften*, Vol. 6 (Frankfurt: Suhrkamp, 1972), 67.

65 Benjamin, *Arcades*, R2a, 3, 542 and 878.

66 Ibid., 883. These questions are, of course, also emblematic of the destruction of the aura which Benjamin examines most explicitly in 'The Work of Art in the Age of Mechanical Reproduction', *Illuminations*, trans. Harry Zohn (London: Collins/Fontana, 1973), 219–55.

67 Here I use, and adapt, Nancy's idea of representation as an intensive rather than reproductive operation. 'Rather than subjecting representation to prohibition or prevention, this representation […] is forbidding in itself. […] Instead of throwing itself outside of itself and outside of presence in the furor of the act, this representation hollows presence out and retains it within itself,' Nancy, *The Ground of the Image*, 38.

68 On this, see Lyotard's psychoanalytic reading of the difference between Greek tragedy, exemplified by Sophocles' Oedipus, and Hebraic unrepresentability, manifest in Shakespeare's Hamlet. 'Oedipus fulfills his desire in non-recognition; Hamlet unfulfills his desire in representation.' Jean-François Lyotard, 'Jewish Oedipus', trans. S Hanson, *Genre* 10:3 (1977): 395–411.

69 Benjamin, *Arcades*, R1, 6, 538 and 877.

70 Benjamin, *Origin*, 31.

71 Gabriel Bounoure cited in Benjamin, *Arcades*, M15, 4, 445.

72 Benjamin, *Arcades*, J34, 3, 290.

73 Ibid., M1a, 3, 418–19.

74 Raymond Escholier cited in Benjamin, *Arcades*, M6a, 1, 429.

75 Benjamin, 'Short Shadows (II)', *Selected Writings*, Vol. 2, Part 2, 699.

76 Winfried Menninghaus, 'Walter Benjamin's Variations of Imagelessness', *For Walter Benjamin: Documentation, Essays and a Sketch*, ed. Ingrid and Konrad Scheurmann (Bonn: Arbeitskreis selbständiger Kultur-Institute, 1993), 166. The term 'imagelessness' correlates to a number of similar concepts modified by 'los', for example, the 'expressionlessness' (also the 'intentionlessness') of 'pure' language which Benjamin develops in his theory of translation.

77 Theodor Adorno, 'A Portrait of Walter Benjamin', *Prisms*, trans. Samuel and Sherry Weber (Cambridge, MA: MIT Press, 1981), 240.

78 George Didi-Huberman, *Confronting Images: Questioning the Ends of a Certain History of Art* (Philadelphia, PA: Pennsylvania State University Press, 2009), 167.

79 Theodor Adorno, *Negative Dialectics*, trans. E.B. Ashton (New York: Continuum, 1973), 207.

80 Exodus 33: 18–23.

81 See Benjamin, 'Goethe's Elective Affinities', *Selected Writings*, Vol. 1, 350–2.

82 For a distinct, but related, discussion on the 'veiled' and 'unveiled', see Comay, 'Materialist Mutations', 34–5.

83 Benjamin, *Origin*, 36.

84 On the interdependence of visibility and invisibility and its adjunct of speech and silence – the philosophical and art-historical archive, here, is voluminous – see among many others, Maurice Merleau-Ponty, *The Visible and Invisible*, trans. Alphonso Lingis (Evanston, IL: Northwestern University Press, 1968); Maurice Merleau-Ponty, *The Primacy of Perception*, ed. James Edie (Evanston, IL: Northwestern University Press, 1964); Maurice Blanchot, *The Gaze of Orpheus and other Literary Essays*, ed. P. Adam Sydney (New York: Station Hill, 1981); Roland Barthes, *Camera Lucida: Reflections on Photography*, trans. Richard Howard (New York: Hill & Wang, 1981); Jacques Derrida, *Memoirs of the Blind: The Self-Portrait and Other Ruins*, trans. Pascale-Anne Brault and Michael Naas (Chicago, IL: University of Chicago Press, 1993); Jean-François Lyotard, *Discourse, Figure*, trans. Anthony Hudek and Mary Lydon (Minneapolis: University of Minnesota Press, 2010).

85 Maurice Blanchot, 'Renè Char and the Thought of the Neutral', *The Infinite Conversation*, trans. Susan Hanson (Minneapolis and London: University of Minnesota Press, 1969), 300.

86 Blanchot 'Speaking Is Not Seeing', *Infinite Conversation,* 29.

87 Ibid., 30.

88 In 'From a Short Speech on Proust Given on my Fortieth Birthday', Benjamin expresses a similar idea to Blanchot. '[Proust's images] do not come unsummoned; rather, it is a matter of images that we have never seen before remembering. This is clearest in the case of images in which we see ourselves as we do in dreams. We stand before ourselves just as we once stood in an originary past [*Urvergangenheit*] that we never saw.' Benjamin, *Gesammelte Schriften*, Vol. 1, Part 3, 1064.

89 Blanchot, 'Speaking Is Not Seeing', *Infinite Conversation*, 30.

90 Benjamin, 'Goethe's Elective Affinities', *Selected Writings*, Vol. 1, 351.

91 While the ontology of the present (and its relation to potential and action) is much discussed in Benjaminian scholarship, Andrew Benjamin gives a particularly compelling set of interrelated readings. See Andrew Benjamin, 'The Meaning of Time in the Moral World', *Working with Walter Benjamin: Recovering a Political Philosophy* (Edinburgh: Edinburgh University Press, 2103), 46–68; 'Time and Task: Benjamin and Heidegger Showing the Present' *Walter Benjamin's Philosophy*, 216–50; 'Boredom and Distraction: The Moods of Modernity' *Walter Benjamin and History*, ed. Andrew Benjamin (London and New York: Continuum, 2005), 156–70.

92 Benjamin, 'On the Concept of History', *Selected Writings*, Vol. 4, 397.

93 Benjamin in Stéphane Mosès, *The Angel of History*, 102.

94 Gershom Scholem, *On Jews and Judaism in Crisis: Selected Essays*, ed. Werner J. Dannhauser (New York: Schocken Books, 1976), 235.

95 Benjamin, 'The Destructive Character', *One Way Street*, 157–8.

96 Irving Wohlfarth, 'No-man's-land: On Benjamin's Destructive Character', *Walter Benjamin's Philosophy: Destruction and Experience*, ed. Andrew Benjamin and Peter Osborne (New York and London: Routledge, 1994), 162.

97 'In remembrance we have an experience that forbids us to conceive of history as fundamentally atheological, little as it may be granted us to try to write it with immediately theological concepts.' Benjamin, *Arcades*, N8, 1, 471.

98 Benjamin letter to Scholem, August 1934, *The Correspondence of Walter Benjamin and Gershom Scholem 1932–1940*, ed. Gershom Scholem (New York: Schocken Books, 1989), 135.

Chapter 3

1. Isaiah Berlin, 'The Origins of Israel', *The Power of Ideas*, ed. Henry Hardy (London: Chatto and Windus, 2000), 143.

2. Although under constant surveillance – with Gumilyov shot for alleged anti-Bolshevik conspiracy and Lev, their son, arrested and deported in 1937 and again in 1949 – it is unclear, according to György Dalos, whether Akhmatova was ever officially subject to a Central Committee publication ban between 1925 and 1940. See Dalos, *The Guest from the Future: Anna Akhmatova and Isaiah Berlin*, trans. A Wood (New York: Farrar, Strauss and Giroux, 1988), 22–5.

3. Most notoriously, Berlin was reproached for opposing the appointment of Isaac Deutscher, the Polish-born Marxist historian and fellow refugee, to a chair at the University of Sussex. For an in-depth account of their highly public intellectual and political hostilities, see David Caute, *Isaac and Isaiah: The Covert Punishment of a Cold War Heretic* (New Haven, CT: Yale University Press, 2015).

4. Berlin, 'Meeting with Russian Writers in 1945 and 1956', *Personal Impressions*, ed. H. Hardy (London: Hogarth Press, 1980), 156–210.

5. Anna Akhmatova, *The Complete Poems of Anna Akhmatova*, trans. Judith Hemschemeyer, ed. Roberta Reeder (Boston, MA: Zephyr Press, 1990), 409.

6. Michael Ignatieff, *Isaiah Berlin: A Life* (London: Chatto and Windus, 1998), 168. While Ignatieff's authorized biography of Berlin's is, arguably, the most well-known account, see also Arie M. Dubnov, *Isaiah Berlin: The Journey of a Jewish Liberal* (New York: Palgrave Macmillan, 2012).

7. Positing this relationship flies in the face of Berlin and Freud's knowledge of each other. In October 1938, Berlin took tea with Freud in the garden of Maresfield Gardens, London. According to Ignatieff, the meeting did little to change Berlin's life-long antipathy to Freud, about whom he never writes and little of whose work he read in any depth.

8. For a fascinating argument which, albeit without the Freudian content included here, looks at the 'dilemmatic spaces' inherent in a liberal consciousness of belonging, see Bonnie Honig, 'Difference, Dilemmas, and the Politics of Home', *Social Research* 61:3 (1994): 563–97. For a more psychoanalytic understanding of the transitional object in debates over immigration and liberal democracy, see also Honig, *Democracy and the Foreigner* (Princeton, NJ: Princeton University Press, 2001), 41–72.

9. Martin Jay, *The Dialectical Imagination: A History of the Frankfurt School and the Institute of Social Research 1923–1959* (Boston: Little, Brown and Company, 1973), 86.

10. See, Wilhelm Reich, *The Mass Psychology of Fascism* (London: Penguin, 1946); Reich, *The Function of the Orgasm* (London: Souvenir, 1983); and Herbert Marcuse, *Eros and Civilisation* (Boston, MA: Beacon Press, 1966).

NOTES

11 Berlin's refusal to come out in opposition to the Vietnam War is, perhaps, the clearest indictor of his general antipathy to 1960s activism. For a revealing account of Berlin's relationship with the Washington technocrats who oversaw the war – an account which takes equal issue with his biographer, Michael Ignatieff, for barely mentioning it – see Christopher Hitchens, 'Moderation or Death', *London Review of Books*, 26 November 1988. For Berlin's own position on Vietnam, see his symposium paper in *Authors Take Sides on Vietnam*, ed. C. Woolfe and J. Bagguley (London: Peter Owen, 1967), 60–1.

12 Berlin to Jean Floud, March 1969, cited in Ignatieff, *Isaiah Berlin*, 253; emphasis in the original. Reacting with voluble distaste to the student protests on American and European campuses, Berlin delivered a lecture on the dangers of political agitation to Columbia University's Humanist Group in the Spring of 1968.

13 Stephen E. Aschheim, *At the Edges of Liberalism: Junctions of European, German, and Jewish History* (Basingstoke: Palgrave Macmillan, 2012), 18.

14 Slavoj Žižek, 'Tolerance as an Ideology', *Critical Inquiry* 34 (2008): 660–82.

15 Lionel Trilling, *The Liberal Imagination* (New York: NYRB Classics, 2008), xxi.

16 Osip Mandelstam, 'My Time', *Complete Poetry of Osip Emilevich Mandelstam*, trans. Burton Raffel and Alla Burago (Albany, NY: SUNY Press, 1973), 130.

17 Mark Lilla, 'Wolves and Lambs', *The Legacy of Isaiah Berlin*, ed. Mark Lilla, Ronald Dworkin and Robert B. Silvers (New York: NYRB, 2001), 33.

18 Bernard Williams cited in Steven Lukes, 'The Singular and the Plural: On the Distinctive Liberalism of Isaiah Berlin', *Social Research* 61:3 (1994): 690.

19 Russell Jacoby, *Picture Imperfect: Utopian Thought for an Anti-Utopian Age* (New York: Columbia University Press, 2005), 68–9.

20 Lilla, 'Wolves and Lambs', 32.

21 Berlin, 'The Pursuit of the Ideal', *The Crooked Timber of Humanity: Chapters in the History of Ideas*, ed. Henry Hardy (London: Pimlico, 2003), 19.

22 Berlin, 'Giambattista Vico and Cultural History', *Crooked Timber*, 68.

23 Berlin, *Freedom and Its Betrayal: Six Enemies of Human Liberty*, ed. Henry Hardy (London: Pimlico, 2003), 153.

24 Ibid., 2.

25 Berlin, 'Nationalism: Past Neglect and Present Power', *Against the Current: Essays in the History of Ideas*, ed. Henry Hardy (London: Hogarth Press, 1980), 348.

26 Berlin, 'The Pursuit of the Ideal', *Crooked Timber*,47.

27 Berlin, *Freedom and Its Betrayal*, 67.

28 Ibid., 69.

29 Berlin, 'Two Concepts of Liberty', *Liberty*, 172.

30 Berlin, 'Herzen and His Memoirs', *Against the Current*, 211.

31 On Berlin's highly selective reading of Herzen's agrarian socialism and commitment to a thorough-going social restructuring, see Russell Jacoby, 'Isaiah Berlin – With the Current', *Salmagundi* 55 (1982): 232–41. For a similar criticism of Berlin's 'proprietary' reading of the diverse figures essayed in *The Crooked Timber*, see Perry Anderson's review, *London Review of Books*, 12:24 (1990): 3–7.

32 Lilla, 'Wolves and Lambs', 33.

33 Berlin, *Russian Thinkers* (Harmondsworth, Middx: Penguin,1978), 92.

34 Immanuel Kant cited in Berlin, *Russian Thinkers*, 92. While Berlin adopts Kant's aphorism as a personal mantra (he uses it in correspondence as early as 1933 and later adapts it to various contexts), the 1784 thesis from which it derives tells an opposite story. 'Only in such a preserve as civic union, these same passions subsequently do their most good: It is just the same with trees: each needs the others, since each in seeking to take the air and sunlight from others must strive upward, and thereby each realizes a beautiful, and straight nature, while those that live in isolated freedom put out branches at random and grow stunted, crooked, and twisted. ' – Kant, 'Idea for a Universal History from a Cosmopolitan Point of View', *On History*, trans. Lewis Beck White, Robert E. Anchor and Emil L. Fackenheim (Indianapolis, IN: Bobbs-Merill, 1963), 17.

35 Berlin, 'The Apotheosis of the Romantic Will: The Revolt against the Myth of an Ideal World', *Crooked Timber*, 211.

36 Berlin, 'Two Concepts of Liberty', *Liberty*, 216.

37 Aileen Kelly, 'Introduction', *Russian Thinkers*, xvii.

38 Herzen, *Childhood, Youth and Exile*, trans. J. D. Duff (Oxford: Oxford University Press, 1980), xxiv. The text comprises Parts I and II of Herzen's *My Past and Thoughts* (written 1852–3). Berlin's 'Introduction' is a reworked version of 'Herzen and Bakunin on Individual Liberty', *Russian Thinkers*, 82–113.

39 Berlin, 'Herzen and Bakunin', *Russian Thinkers*, 94.

40 Ibid.

41 Ibid.

42 Ibid., 94.

43 Sigmund Freud, 'Beyond the Pleasure Principle', *The Standard Edition of the Complete Psychological Works of Sigmund Freud, Volume XVIII (1920–1922)*, ed. James Strachey (London: Vintage, 2001), 38. Hereafter, *SE*.

44 Ibid., 44.

45 Herzen cited in Berlin, 'The Pursuit of the Ideal', *Crooked Timber*, 16.

46 For Herzen's conversations and dialogues on the period of 1847–51, see *From the Other Shore and the Russian People and Socialism: An Open Letter to Jules Michelet*, trans. Moura Budberg and Richard Wollheim (London: Weidenfeld and Nicolson, 1956).

47 Berlin 'Introduction', *Childhood, Youth and Exile*, xxiv.

48 Berlin, 'Two Concepts of Liberty', *Liberty*, 217.

49 Berlin, 'The Pursuit of the Ideal', *Crooked Timber*, 18.

50 Berlin, 'Introduction', *Childhood, Youth, Exile*, xxiv.

51 Berlin, *Freedom and Its Betrayal*, 18.

52 Berlin, 'Alleged Relativism in Eighteenth Century European Thought', *Crooked Timber*, 87.

53 Slavoj Žižek, 'Tolerance as an Ideology', *Critical Inquiry*, 662.

54 Ibid., 660.

55 Lukes, 'The Singular and the Plural', *Social Research*, 687–718.

56 Berlin, 'Two Concepts of Liberty', *Liberty*, 213–14.

57 Berlin, 'The Pursuit of the Ideal', *Crooked Timber*, 17.

58 Ibid.

59 Berlin, *Russian Thinkers*, 200.

60 Berlin, 'Introduction', *Childhood, Youth and Exile*, xxiv.

61 Ibid., xxv.

62 Santner, *On the Psychotheology of Everyday Life*, 14.

63 Kelly, 'A Revolutionary without Fanaticism', *The Legacy of Isaiah Berlin*, 18.

64 Freud, 'Beyond the Pleasure Principle', *SE*, 31.

65 Berlin, *The Jewish Chronicle*, 21 September 1951, 17. The article is reprinted in *Hebrew University Garland*, ed. Norman Bentwich (London: Constellation Books, 1952).

66 For John Gray, Berlin is 'almost alone among liberal theoreticians of the twentieth century [...] who continues this older liberal tradition, which associated itself with the human need for a common culture, and recognised its principle political embodiment in modern times in the nation-state.' See Gray, *Isaiah Berlin: An Interpretation of His Thought* (Princeton, NJ: Princeton University Press, 2013), 134–5.

67 For a lively polemic against Berlin's Herderian conceptions of Judaism, see Brian Barry, 'Isaiah, Israel and Tribal Realism', *Times Literary Supplement*, No. 9, 2001. For other engagements, see Yael Tamir, *Liberal Nationalism: Studies in Moral, Political and Legal Philosophy* (Princeton, NJ: Princeton University Press, 1993); John Gray,

Isaiah Berlin: An Interpretation of His Thought (1996); Avishai Margalit, 'The Crooked Timber of Nationalism', in *The Legacy of Isaiah Berlin* (New York: New York Review Books, 2001), 147–60.

68 Berlin, *The Roots of Romanticism* (Princeton, NJ: Princeton University Press, 1999), 60.

69 Berlin, *Three Critics of the Enlightenment: Vico, Hamann, Herder*, ed. Henry Hardy (Princeton, NJ: Pimlico and Princeton University Press, 2000), 181–2.

70 On his distinction between nationalism as a natural need for collective fate and solidarity and the pathology of a severe and fanatical particularism, see, in particular, Berlin, 'Nationalism: Past Neglect and Present Power', *Against the Current*, 333–55.

71 Berlin, 'Benjamin Disraeli, Karl Marx and the Search for Identity', *Against the Current*, 252–86. As an illustration of the antagonism between Berlin and Isaac Deutscher, noted above, see the latter's more self-reflexive and politically optimistic treatment of Heine and Marx's Judaism in Deutscher, 'Message of the Non-Jewish Jew', *Non-Jewish Jew and Other Essays* (Oxford: Oxford University Press, 1968).

72 Berlin, 'A Nation among Nations', *Jewish Chronicle*, 4 May 1973, 32.

73 For a reading of this poem as both a critique of assimilation and lampoon of poetic modernism, see Dubnov, *Isaiah Berlin*, 48–52.

74 Berlin, 'Benjamin Disraeli, Karl Marx and the Search for Identity', *Against the Current*, 260.

75 Ibid.

76 Ibid., 280.

77 Dubnov, *Isaiah Berlin*, 9.

78 Ibid., 260.

79 Ibid., 283. The description, as Berlin notes, is from Act One, Scene Three, of Sheridan's libretto for the comic opera *The Duenna* (1775).

80 Berlin cited in Ignatieff, *Isaiah Berlin*, 253.

81 Berlin, *Russian Thinkers*, 200.

82 Michael P. Steinberg, *Judaism Musical and Unmusical* (Chicago, IL: University of Chicago Press, 2007), 38–56.

83 See, for example, Michael Molnar, 'John Stuart Mill Translated by Sigmund Freud' *History and Psychoanalysis* 1:2 (1999): 195–205 and Aner Govrin, 'Some Utilitarian Influences in Freud's Early Writings' *History and Psychoanalysis* 6:1 (2004):5–21.

84 Freud, 'Family Romance', *SE*, Vol. 9, 235–41.

85 Steinberg, *Judaism Musical and Unmusical* (Chicago, IL: University of Chicago Press, 2007), 47.

86 Ibid., 56.
87 Ibid., 47.
88 See especially Berlin, 'John Stuart Mill and the Ends of Life', *Liberty*, 218–51.
89 Freud, *Civilisation and Its Discontents*, trans. David Mclintock (London: Penguin Books, 2004), 29–30.
90 Berlin, 'Two Concepts', *Liberty*, 215.
91 Ibid., 217.
92 Ibid., 212.
93 Freud, 'The Economic Problem of Masochism', *SE*, Vol. 19, 166.
94 George Crowder, *Isaiah Berlin: Liberty and Pluralism* (Cambridge: Polity Press, 2004), 147.
95 Ibid., 146.
96 Kelly, 'A Revolutionary without Fanaticism', *Legacy of Isaiah Berlin*, 29.
97 Santner, *Psychotheology of Everyday Life*, 38.
98 Ibid.
99 Ibid., 40. Santner's phraseology draws on his reworking of Gershom Scholem's well-known description of Kafka in his correspondence with Walter Benjamin. See Gershom Scholem, Letter to Benjamin, 20 September 1934, *The Correspondence of Walter Benjamin and Gershom Scholem 1932–1940*, trans. Gary Smith and Andre Lefevre (New York: Schocken Books, 1989), 142. See also the description of the Kafkaesque subject in Žižek, *The Sublime Object of Ideology* (London: Verso, 1989), 44.
100 Santner, *Psychotheology of Everyday Life*, 39.
101 Ibid., 22.
102 Ibid., 42.
103 Ibid., 21.
104 Helene Cixous, *Three Steps on the Ladder of Writing*, trans. Sarah Cornell and Susan Sellers (New York: Columbia University Press, 1993), 205.
105 Freud, 'Mourning and Melancholia', *SE*, Vol. 14, 237–58.
106 Ibid., 257.
107 Ibid., 243.
108 Berlin, 'Meeting with Russian Writers', *Personal Impressions*, 198–9.
109 Ibid., 202.

110 Berlin, *Russian Thinkers*, 22.

111 For a wonderful analysis of the psychic contradictions at the heart of political resistance – that is, resistance as it moves between 'negation and position, from affirmation to refusal, until the very distinction becomes unclear'- see Rebecca Comay, 'Resistance and Repetition: Freud and Hegel', *Research in Phenomenology* 45 (2015): 237–66.

112 Ibid., 238.

113 Berlin, *Personal Impressions*, 207.

114 This is not to ignore Akhmatova's immediate predicament or to see her allegiance to a pre-Soviet past as devoid of political motivation. It is rather to refract Berlin's account of her resistance through the logic of his own politics.

115 Akhmatova, 'I Am Not One of Those Who Left the Land', *Poems of Anna Akhmatova*, trans. Stanley Kunitz and Max Hayward (Boston: Houghton Mifflin Harcourt, 1962), 75–6.

116 Freud, 'The Ego and the Id', *SE*, Vol. 19, 3–66.

117 Steinberg, *Judaism Musical and Unmusical*, 56.

118 Freud, 'Remembering, Repeating, and Working Through', *SE*, Vol. 12, 145–56.

119 Berlin, *Russian Thinkers*, 200.

Chapter 4

1 Isaac Deutscher, 'The Non-Jewish Jew', *The Non-Jewish Jew and Other Essays*, trans. with an introduction by Tamara Deutscher (London: Verso, 2017), 25–6.

2 Ibid., 26.

3 Ibid.

4 Ibid., 27.

5 Arendt's study chiefly draws on the Varnhagen papers in the Berlin State Library and on the letters and diary entries in the three-volume *Rahel, ein Buch des Andenkens* (1834) prepared by Rahel's husband, Karl August Varnhagen von Ense, a liberal diplomat in post-Napoleonic Prussia.

6 Gilles Deleuze and Felix Guattari, 'Conceptual Personae', *What Is Philosophy?*, trans. Graham Burchell and Hugh Tomlinson (London: Verso, 1994), 61–84.

7. Coined and developed by the Portuguese poet and writer Fernando Pessoa, the concept is most often associated with Søren Kierkegaard, whose more than a dozen heteronyms, each with their own biographies, rhetorical, or even musical and theatrical styles, populate his philosophical and religious writings.
8. The use of the personal first name is Arendt's convention.
9. Deleuze and Guattari, *What Is Philosophy*, 64.
10. Letter from Jaspers to Arendt, March 1930 in *Hannah Arendt-Karl Jaspers Correspondence: 1926–1969*, ed. Lotte Kohler and Hans Saner, trans. Robert and Rita Kimber (San Diego, CA, New York and London: Harcourt Brace & Company, 1992), 10.
11. Arendt, *Rahel*, 105
12. Deleuze and Guattari, *What Is Philosophy?* 69.
13. Letter from Arendt, March 1930, *Correspondence*, 11.
14. Arendt, *Rahel*, 172.
15. This statement is not uncontested. Among those who accuse Arendt's portrait of being a retrospective projection, see Käte Hamburger's 1933–4 essay revised and republished as 'Rahel und Goethe', *Rahel Gesammelte Werke* 10, ed. Konrad Feilchenfeldt, Uwe Schweikert, und Rahel E. Steiner (Munich: Mattes and Seitz, 1983), 179–204; and Heidi T. Tewarson, *Rahel Varnhagen: The Life and Work of a German-Jewish Intellectual* (Lincoln: University of Nebraska Press, 1998).
16. Arendt, *Rahel*, xiii.
17. Arendt, 'On Humanity in Dark Times: Thoughts about Lessing', *Men in Dark Times* (New York and London: Harcourt Brace & Company, 1968), 19.
18. 'The Greek word for law, *nomos*, derives from *nemein*, which means to distribute, to possess (what has been distributed), and to dwell. The combination of law and hedge in the word *nomos* is quite manifest in a fragment of Heraclitus … ("the people should fight for the law as for a wall").' In Arendt, *The Human Condition*, 2nd Edition (Chicago, IL, and London: University of Chicago Press, 1998), 63, f. 62.
19. Ibid., 194.
20. Ibid.
21. Ibid., 63–4.
22. In its double function of founding and joining, Arendt's city-wall recalls Heidegger's famous formulation of the bridge: 'A boundary is not that at which something stops but, as the Greeks recognised, the boundary is that from which something *begins its essential unfolding*. That is why the concept is that of *horismos*, that is, the horizon, the boundary. Space is in essence that for which room has been made, that which is let into its bounds. That for which room is made is always granted and hence is

joined, that is gathered, by virtue of a location, that is, by such a thing as a bridge. *Accordingly, spaces receive their essential being from locations and not from "space"'*. Martin Heidegger, 'Building, Thinking, Dwelling', *Basic Writings*, ed. David Farrell Krell (New York: Harper & Row, 1977), 332.

23 For recent developments of this theme, see Judith Butler, Zeynep Gambetti and Leticia Sabsay, eds. *Vulnerability in Resistance* (Durham and London: Duke University Press, 2016).

24 Arendt, *Arendt-Jaspers Correspondence*, 29.

25 Arendt, 'We Refugees', *The Jewish Writings*, ed. Jerome Kohn and Ron H. Feldman (New York: Schocken Books, 2007), 274.

26 Jacques Rancière, *Dissensus: On Politics and Aesthetics* (New York: Bloomsbury, 2010), 50.

27 Together with his criticisms of its early drafts, Jaspers remained ambivalent about the biography right up until its 1957 publication. In a letter dated 23 August 1952, he identifies the problem of the whole endeavour: 'This work still seems to me to be your own working through of the basic question of Jewish existence, and in it you use Rahel's reality as a guide to help you achieve clarity and liberation for yourself.' He also objects to what he sees as Arendt's moralizing judgement: 'Your view of Rahel, is I feel loveless [...] You have to permit Rahel her errors, just as you have to permit Goethe, his errors; and to have to perceive those errors in the context of the individual's stature, as the darker sides of truth.' In *Arendt-Jaspers Correspondence*, 192–6.

28 Arendt, *Arendt-Jaspers Correspondence*, 11.

29 On this, see Arendt, 'Zionism Reconsidered', *Jewish Writings*, 343–74.

30 Lisa Ditsch, 'On Friendship in Dark Times', *Feminist Interpretations of Hannah Arendt*, ed. Bonnie Honig (University Park: The Pennsylvania State University Press, 1995), 294.

31 See Max Weber, *Ancient Judaism*, trans. and ed. Hans H. Gerth and Don Martindale (New York: The Free Press, 1967); and Weber, *The Sociology of Religion*, trans. Ephraim Fischoff (Boston: 1963). For a reading of the various obscurities and contradictions in Weber's formulation, see Arnaldo Momigliano, 'A Note on Max Weber's Definition of Judaism as a Pariah-Religion', *History and Theory* 8:3 (October 1980): 313–18.

32 See Bernard Lazare, *Job's Dungheap: Essays in Jewish Nationalism and Social Revolution*, trans. Harry L. Bisse (New York: Schocken, 1948).

33 Arendt, 'The Jew as Pariah: A Hidden Tradition', *The Jewish Writings*, ed. Jerome Kohn and Ron H. Feldman (New York: Schocken, 2007), 275–97.

34 Arendt, *The Human Condition*, 181.

35 Arendt, 'Jew as Pariah', 283.

36 Ibid., 288.

37 Ibid., 290.

38 Kafka in Arendt, 'Jew as Pariah', 290.

39 Ibid., 290–1.

40 Ibid., 290.

41 The phrase is Till van Rahden's. See van Rahden, *Jews and Other Germans: Civil Society, Religious Diversity and Urban Politics in Breslau, 1860–1925*, trans. Marcus Brainard (Madison: University of Wisconsin Press, 2008).

42 Although Rahel was among the most prominent of those emancipated Prussian Jews who emerged as key figures in the intellectual and artistic life in the late eighteenth century – the period between 1790 and 1806 would be called *Rahelzeit* – other leading Jewish salonnières include: Dorothea von Schlegel, daughter of Moses Mendelsohn and wife to poet and critic Friedrich von Schlegel; Henriette Herz whose habitués included Alexander von Humboldt and the theologian Friedrich Schleiermacher; the novelist Rebecca Friedländer and Amalie Beer, mother to the operatic composer Giacomo Meyerbeer. On the cultural and social history of these salons, see Deborah Hertz, *Jewish High Society in Old Regime Berlin* (New Haven, CT: Yale University Press, 1988) and Dagmar Barnouw, *Visible Spaces: Hannah Arendt and the German-Jewish Experience* (Baltimore, MD: Johns Hopkins University Press, 1990). On the salon as a specifically 'female public sphere', see Seyla Benhabib, *The Reluctant Modernism of Hannah Arendt* (Lanham, MD: Rowman & Littlefield, 2003), 14–21. For a counter-argument to Benhabib, see Bonnie Honig, 'Towards an Agonistic Feminism: Hannah Arendt and the Politics of Identity', *Feminist Interpretations of Hannah Arendt*, 135–66. For a more general history of the salons from 1780s Berlin to 1930s America, see Emily D. Bilski and Emily Braun, eds. *Jewish Women and Their Salons: The Power of Conversation* (New Haven, CT and London: Yale University Press, 2005).

43 Emancipation of the Jews in the German-speaking world began in 1782 with the Edict of Toleration (*Toleranzedikt*) issued by the Hapsburg Emperor, Joseph II, allowing them to practise all branches of commerce, access state secondary schools and attend universities. With the German states slow to follow, the first Jews in the German-speaking world to enjoy full civil rights were those in territories west of the Rhine, brought under the Napoleonic Code in 1789. Following the defeat of Napoleon and the reorganizations of the Congress of Vienna in 1815, the rights of Jews in different German territories varied widely. In Prussia, the 1823 Law for the Estates of the Provinces restricted the vote to those 'in communion' with a Christian Church. Jews throughout the Austro-Hungarian Empire only received full civil rights in 1867; a similar measure was enacted by North German Federation in 1869. With the founding of the German Empire, the civil rights of all German Jews were finally enacted into law in 1871.

44 Arendt, *Rahel*, 7.

45 Ibid., 180.

46 Ibid., 4.

47 Ibid., 7.

48 Ibid. 177.

49 Ibid., 6.

50 Immanuel Kant, 'What Is Enlightenment?', *Kant's Political Writings*, 2nd Edition, trans. H. R. Nisbet, ed. by Hans Reiss (Cambridge: Cambridge University Press, 1991), 54–60.

51 Arendt, *Rahel*, 7.

52 Ibid., 8.

53 Jean-Luc Nancy, *The Inoperative Community*, ed. Peter Connor (Minnesota: University of Minnesota Press, 1991), xxxvii.

54 Arendt, *Rahel*, 8.

55 Ibid.

56 Ibid., 9.

57 Ibid., 21.

58 Ibid., xvi.

59 Ibid., 177.

60 Ibid., 96–7.

61 Ibid. 177.

62 Ibid., 10.

63 Ibid., 6.

64 Ibid.

65 On the 'subjective in-between', see Arendt, *The Human Condition*, 181–8.

66 Arendt, *Rahel*, 182.

67 Ibid., 20–1.

68 Arendt, 'The Enlightenment and the Jewish Question', *The Jewish Writings*, 11.

69 Arendt, 'On Humanity in Dark Times', *Men in Dark Times*, 31.

70 Gotthold Ephraim Lessing cited in Arendt, 'On Humanity in Dark Times', *Men in Dark Times*, 12. The phrase refers to the leitmotif of Lessing's *Nathan the Wise*

on which Arendt draws in her acceptance of the Lessing Prize of the Free City of Hamburg, 1959.

71 Arendt, *Rahel*, 21.

72 Arendt, 'The Enlightenment and the Jewish Question', *The Jewish Writings*, 16.

73 See Paul Mendes-Flohr, *German Jews: A Dual Identity* (New Haven, CT, and London: Yale University Press, 1999), 5. Other variants of this well-known phrase include the Zionist leader Kurt Blumenfeld's self-description as a 'Zionist by grace of Goethe'. See Arendt, *Arendt-Jaspers Correspondence*, 198.

74 Arendt, *The Human Condition*, 176. For the first study to focus exclusively on Arendt's natality, see Patricia Bowen-Moore, *Hannah Arendt's Philosophy of Natality*. (New York: St. Martin's Press, 1989). For various other readings, see Françoise Collin. 'Birth as Praxis', in *The Judge and the Spectator: Hannah Arendt's Political Philosophy*, ed. Dana R. Villa and J. J. Hermsen (Leuven, Belgium: Peeters, 1999), 97–110; Ann O'Byrne, *Natality and Finitude* (Bloomington: Indiana University Press, 1989); Stephan Kampowski, *Arendt, Augustine, and the New Beginnings* (Grand Rapids: Eerdmans, 2008); Jeffrey Champlin, 'Born Again: Arendt's "Natality" as Figure and Concept', *The Germanic Review* 88:2 (2013): 150–64; John Kiess, *Hannah Arendt and Theology* (London: Bloomsbury, 2016).

75 Arendt, *Human Condition*, 9.

76 Ibid., 177.

77 As frequently argued, the interferences of natality might be taken as Arendt's tacit yet insistent critique of Heidegger's principal theme of mortality, of being-towards-death. 'The life span of man running toward death would inevitably carry everything human to ruin and destruction if it were not for the faculty of interrupting it ... [A] faculty which is inherent in action is an ever-present reminder that men, though they must die, are not born in order to die but in order to begin', *The Human Condition*, 246.

78 Ibid., 177.

79 Francois Collin, 'Birth as Praxis', *The Judge and the Spectator: Hannah Arendt's Political Philosophy*, eds. Joke J. Hermsen and Dana R. Villa (Leuven, Belgium: Peeters, 1999), 97–110.

80 Ibid., 180–1.

81 Arendt, *Rahel*.

82 Arendt, *Human Condition*, 178.

83 Arendt, '"What Remains? The Language Remains": A Conversation with Günter Gaus', *Essays in Understanding*, 12.

84 On the impossibility of laying claim to a neutralized identity, see, in particular, Arendt's 'In Humanity in Dark Times: Thoughts on Lessing', 3–31. For a subtle reading which shows Arendt refusing the honour of the Lessing Prize on the basis of

its (resurrected) humanism and, simultaneously, on the basis of her refugee status, see Lisa Disch 'On Friendship in 'Dark Times', 285–312.

85 Arendt, *The Human Condition*, 176.

86 Arendt, 'Enlightenment and the Jewish Question', 16.

87 Arendt, *Rahel*, 21.

88 For a related argument about the twofold function of the political 'in-common', see Jean-Luc Nancy, *The Inoperative Community*, ed. Peter Connor, trans. Peter Connor, Lisa Garbus, Michael Holland and Simona Sawhney (Minnesota: University of Minnesota Press, 1991), 1–42. On the interrelationship of place, commonality, law and justice in context of the Greek philosophical and literary tradition, see also Andrew Benjamin, *Place, Commonality and Judgement: Continental Philosophy and the Ancient Greeks* (London and New York: Continuum, 2012).

89 While Arendt's discussion of natality as action begins with her early engagement of St. Augustine's creation theology (explored in the second part of her doctoral dissertation) it was shaped decisively by contemporary events. The role of the workers' councils in the 1956 Hungarian Revolution, the civil rights protest movements and anti-Vietnam War demonstrations of the 1960s, all offer instances of action rooted in the newness of possibility.

90 Arendt, *Men in Dark Times*, 18.

91 Arendt, *Rahel*, 1.

92 Ibid.

93 Rahel cited in Arendt, *Rahel*, 185.

94 Ibid., 184

95 Ibid., 183–4.

96 Arendt, 'On Humanity in Dark Times', *Men in Dark* Times, 18.

97 Before the mid-1940s, Arendt's essays on Zionism and the Jewish State mostly share ground with supporters of *Brit Shalom* and the Ihud, the latter a small bi-nationalist party founded by Judah Leon Magnes, president of the Hebrew University, Martin Buber, and Henrietta Szold, organizer of Youth Aliyah and founder of the Hadassah Hospital. As envisioned by Arendt, the Jewish state would be structured on a council system of joint Jewish-Arab governance: 'Local self-governing and mixed Jewish-Arab municipal and rural councils, on a small-scale and as numerous as possible, are the only realistic political measures that can eventually lead to the political emancipation of Palestine.' In Arendt, 'To Save the Jewish Homeland', *The Jewish Writings*, 401. Palestine would thus not be a sovereign state but a new autonomous polity. In 1948, with the United Nations Resolution recognizing partition and the founding of the Jewish State and again in 1950, after the establishment of Israel by force of arms, Arendt's account of official Zionist policy merges with her critique of national sovereignty drawn from European political history.

98 Arendt, 'Herzl and Lazare', *The Jewish Writings*, 339.

99 See Arendt, 'The Jewish State: Fifty Years after, Where Have Herzl's Politics Led', *The Jewish Writings*, 375–87.

100 Arendt, 'To Save a Jewish Homeland', *The Jewish Writings*, 396–7.

101 Ibid.

102 Arendt, 'Zionism Reconsidered', *The Jewish Writings*, 343. First published in the journal *Menorah*, the essay is Arendt's response to the demand adopted by the American Zionist Congress in October 1944 for 'a free and democratic Jewish commonwealth …. [which] shall embrace the whole of Palestine, undivided and undiminished' – ibid. The demand represented, for her, the final victory of the Revisionist programme, presaging decades of escalating state violence.

103 Ibid., 344.

104 Arendt, 'To Save the Jewish Homeland', *Jewish Writings*, 399.

105 Or a 'Jewish homestead', as Arendt rephrases it in 'Zionism Reconsidered', *Jewish Writings*, 345. The clear cross-reference, here, is with the Jeffersonian vision; specifically, his model of directly incorporating the smallest units of self-government – precincts, wards or local 'elementary republics'– into a federated system, which Arendt explores in *On Revolution* (1963).

106 Arendt, 'What Is Freedom?' *Between Past and Future* (London and New York: Penguin Books, 1977), 151.

107 Arendt, 'Peace or Armistice in the Near East', *The Jewish Writings*, 436.

108 Ibid., 435.

109 Ibid., 436. On the problem of the causations of 'self-evident truth', see, in particular, Arendt, 'What Is Freedom', *Between Past and Future*, 143–72.

110 Arendt, *Origins of Totalitarianism*, 296.

111 'With sovereignty, the pariah people has not ceased to be a pariah – it has created a pariah state'. Ron H. Feldman, 'Introduction', *The Jewish Writings*, lxiii.

112 Arendt, 'The Jew as Pariah', *Jewish Writings*, 276.

113 Arendt, 'Herzl and Lazare', *The Jewish Writings*, 338–42.

114 Lazare, 'Antisémitisme et revolution' cited in Löwy, *Redemption and Utopia*, 193.

115 See Lazare 'Jewish Nationalism', *Job's Dungheap*, 54–79.

116 Arendt, 'Herzl and Lazare', *The Jewish Writings*, 339.

117 Lazare cited in Nelly Wilson, *Bernard Lazare: Antisemitism and the Problem of Jewish Identity in Late Nineteenth-century France* (Cambridge: Cambridge University Press, 1978), 232–3.

118 Lazare's Symbolist tale, 'L'Eternal Fugitif', the Eternal Fugitive (*c.* 1891), is a retelling of Moses and the Golden Calf. While written during his 'anti-Semitic' period – Lazare's political writings chart a lifetime of dramatic shifts from his early Catholic mysticism and perception of Judaism as a prosaic, and implicitly bourgeois religion, to his rediscovery of Jewish messianism and involvement in the Zionist movement – the parable has been seen to presage Lazare's pioneering role in Dreyfus's defence. For an overview of Lazare's 'careering' allegiances, see Michael Löwy, 'A French Exception', *Redemption and Utopia: Jewish Libertarian Thought in Central Europe* (London and New York: Verso, 2017), 178–99.

119 Against Bonnie Honig who sees Arendt's pariah as an individuated figure whose independence works against its political resources, I suggest that Lazare gives us an example of the pariah closer to Honig's own idea of the agonistic political agent than her critique apparently allows. Indeed, this chapter owes much to Honig's arguments in 'Towards an Agonistic Feminism', *Feminist Interpretations of Hannah Arendt*, 135–66.

120 Arendt, 'Herzl and Lazare', *The Jewish Writings*, 340. As Arendt notes, it was largely the Christian socialist Charles Péguy's portrait of his friend and mentor included in the posthumous 1928 edition of *Le fumier de Job* (later translated either as *Job's Dungheap* or as *The Manure of Job*), which introduced Lazare to a French audience. Together with Wilson and Löwy's excellent studies, see Annette Aronowicz, *Jews and Christians on Time and Eternity: Charles Péguy's Portrait of Bernard-Lazare* (Stanford, CA: Stanford University Press, 1988); and Evlyn Gould, *Dreyfus and the Literature of the Third Republic: Secularism and Tolerance in Zola, Barrès, Lazare and Proust* (Jefferson, NC, and London: McFarland & Company, 2012).

121 Arendt, 'Jewish History, Revised', *Jewish Writings*, 303. The two are not unconnected. As Löwy notes, the archive of Lazare's unpublished papers contain several references to a planned essay on Sabbatai Sevi. See Löwy, *Redemption and Utopia*, 197–8.

122 Arendt, 'Jewish History, Revised', *The Jewish Writings*, 303.

123 On Sabbatai Sevi, see the 'Eighth Lecture', in Gershom Scholem, *Major Trends in Jewish Mysticism* (New York: Schocken Books, 1995). For his massive study of the Sabbatian movement up to the death of Sabbatai and Nathan of Gaza, see Scholem, *Sabbatai Sevi: The Mystical Messiah 1926–1667* (Princeton, NJ: Princeton University Press, 2016).

124 For a sustained argument on how Arendt's theory of nativity and action do not have any significant theological dimensions, see Dana R. Villa, *Arendt and Heidegger: The Fate of the Political* (Princeton, NJ: Princeton University Press, 1996).

125 Arendt, 'Jewish History, Revised', *The Jewish Writings*, 310.

126 For a similar reading, see Judith Butler, *Parting Ways: Jewishness and the Critique of Zionism* (New York: Columbia University Press, 2012): 122–3.

127 Arendt, 'Jewish History, Revised', 305.

128 Scholem cited in ibid., 304.

129 Ibid., 307.

130 Ibid., 309. Working off unpublished documents of Sabbatai Sevi's closest followers, Scholem himself diagnoses anti-Halakhic radicalism as, in part, the ideation of a mental affliction, seeing Sabbatai's 'exaltations, enthusiasm, and euphoria' – and alternating fits of melancholia – as signs of a 'manic-depressive psychosis'. Scholem ascribes a more intellectually and theologically coherent role to Nathan of Gaza who emerges, in his account, as the real centre of the messianic movement. See *Major Trends*, 290–9.

131 Arendt, 'Jewish History, Revised', 311.

132 See Scholem, 'Seventh Lecture', *Major Trends*, 244–86.

133 Ibid., 284.

134 Arendt, 'Jewish History, Revised', *Jewish Writings*, 309.

135 Ibid., 311.

136 Ibid.

137 Arendt, 'The Jewish State: Fifty Years After', *Jewish Writings*, 387.

138 Arendt, 'On Humanity in Dark Times', 31.

139 Arendt, 'Dedication to Karl Jaspers', *Essays in Understanding*, 212. The dedication first appeared in *Sechs Essays* (Heidelberg: Lambert Schneider, 1948).

140 Ibid., 215.

141 Ibid.

142 See, especially, Giorgio Agamben, 'Beyond Human Rights', *Means without Ends*, trans. Vincenzo Binetti and Cesare Casarino (Minneapolis: University of Minnesota Press, 2000), 15–28.

143 Arendt, 'Dedication to Karl Jaspers', *Essays in* Understanding, 215.

144 Agamben, 'Beyond Human Rights', 24.

145 Theodor Adorno, 'Refuge for the Homeless', *Minima Moralia: Reflections on Damaged Life*, trans. E. F. N. Jephcott (London: Verso, 1978), 38–9.

146 Adorno, 'Refuge for the Homeless', 39.

147 On the significant differences between Adorno and Arendt on this problem, including Adorno's devaluation of the public sphere as a site of critical possibility, see Dana Villa, 'Genealogies of Total Domination: Arendt, Adorno, and Auschwitz', *New German Critique* 34:1 (2007): 1–45.

148 The phrase is an adaption of Jean-François Lyotard's, *The Inhuman: Reflections on Time*, trans. Geoffrey Bennington and Rachel Bowlby (Stanford, CA: Stanford University Press, 1991), 202.

149 Arendt, 'Dedication to Karl Jaspers', *Essays in Understanding*, 215.

Chapter 5

1. Immanuel Kant, *Anthropology from a Pragmatic View*, ed. and trans. Robert B. Louden (Cambridge: Cambridge University Press, 2006), 110.

2. Ibid., 216.

3. Jean François Lyotard, 'Scapeland', *The Lyotard Reader*, ed. Andrew Benjamin (Oxford: Blackwell, 1992), 212–19.

4. Ibid., 217.

5. Kant, *Anthropology from a Pragmatic View*, 213.

6. Lyotard, 'Scapeland', 213.

7. Ibid., 218.

8. Paul Ricoeur, *History, Memory, Forgetting*, trans. Kathleen Blamey and David Pellauer (Chicago, IL: University of Chicago Press, 2004), 21.

9. For an adjacent account of landscape (*paysage*) defined by a phenomenology of infinite estrangement, see Jean-Luc Nancy, 'Uncanny Landscape', *The Ground of the Image*, trans. Jeff Fort (New York: Fordham University Press, 2005), 51–62.

10. Lyotard, 'Scapeland', 215.

11. Ibid., 217.

12. Maurice Blanchot, *The Work of Fire*, trans. Charlotte Mandell (Stanford, CA: Stanford University Press, 1995), 9.

13. Maurice Blanchot, *The Space of Literature*, trans. Anne Smock (Lincoln: University of Nebraska Press, 1982), 48. On Blanchot's non-dialectical 'neutral' or 'neuter' as a way of approaching, but never reconciling, the 'unknown', see Blanchot, 'René Char and the Thought of the Neutral', *The Infinite Conversation*, 298–306.

14. Kafka, *Diaries*, trans. Joseph Kresh, Martin Greenberg and Hannah Arendt (New York: Schocken Books, 1964), 330.

15. Sebald's affinity with the eighteenth-century natural historian and Alaskan explorer, George Wilhelm Steller, and to the nineteenth-century poet and landscape painter, Adalbert Stifter, is particularly notable. On the relation of Sebald's prose to Stifter, see Eva Juhl, 'Die Wahrheit über das Unglück: Zu W. G. Sebald', *Die Ausgewanderten: Resien im Diskurs*, ed. Anne Fuchs and Theo Harden (Heidelberg: C. Winter, 1995), 640–59. Steller appears as the protagonist in the second of Sebald's prose poems, 'And if I Remained by the Outermost Sea', *After Nature*, trans, Michael Hamburger (London: Penguin, 2002), 43–76. For sustained examinations of Sebald's use of travel-writing genres and stylistics, see especially, John Zilcosky, 'Sebald's Uncanny Travels: The Impossibility of Getting Lost', *W.G. Sebald – A Critical Companion*, ed.

J. J. Long and Anne Whitehead (Edinburgh: Edinburgh University Press, 2004), 102–20; Zilcosky, 'Writing Travel', *Writing Travel: The Poetics and Politics of the Modern Journey*, ed. John Zilcosky (Toronto: University of Toronto Press, 2008), 3–24; Bianca Theisen, 'Prose of the World: W. G. Sebald's Literary Travels', *Germanic Review* 79:3 (2004):163–79.

16 Sebald, *The Emigrants*, trans. Michael Hulse (London: The Harvill Press, 1997), 151.

17 Massimo Cacciari, *Posthumous People: Vienna at the Turning Point*, trans. Rodger Friedman (Stanford, CA: Stanford University Press, 1996), 6.

18 Sebald, *After Nature*, 99.

19 Ibid.

20 Also known as *The Man Who Disappeared* (*Der Verschollene*), *Amerika* is Kafka's incomplete novel, posthumously edited and published by Max Brod in 1927. 'The Nature Theatre of Oklahoma' was intended as its concluding chapter.

21 Sebald, *After Nature*, 99.

22 On 'un-archivability' as it annuls both memory and forgetting, see Giorgio Agamben, *Remnants of Auschwitz: The Witness and the Archive*, trans. Daniel Heller-Roazen (New York: Zone Books, 2002), 137–71.

23 'This entire subterranean, hidden, mute, undiscovered loneliness that we call life but might as well be called death unless we knew what will *become* of us and that is only after death that we will come into *our* life and come alive – oh, very much alive, we posthumous people!' Nietzsche, *The Gay Science*, ed. Bernard Williams, trans. Josefine Nauckhoff (Cambridge: Cambridge University Press, 2001), 230. For a wonderful application of Nietzsche's description to a reading of the cultural habitus of Ludwig Wittgenstein, Peter Altenberg, Robert Walser, Adolf Loos, Gustav Klimt, see Cacciari, *Posthumous People*.

24 Sebald, *The Rings of Saturn*, trans. Michael Hulse (London: Vintage, 2002), 172.

25 On the various modes of blindness in, and being blindsided by, Sebald's fiction, see Carol Jacobs, *Sebald's Vision* (New York: Columbia University Press, 2015), 1–17.

26 Sebald and Jan Peter Tripp, *Unrecounted*, trans. Michael Hamburger (London: Penguin, 2005), 88.

27 Sebald, *Austerlitz*, trans. Anthea Bell (London: Penguin, 2001), 29–31.

28 Sebald, 'The Undiscover'd Country: The Death Motif in Kafka's *The Castle*', *Journal of European Studies* 2 (1972): 22–34. See also Sebald, 'The Law of Ignominy: Authority, Messianism and Exile in *The Castle*', in *On Kafka: Semi-Centenary Perspectives*, ed. Franz Kuna (Paul Elek: London, 1976), 42–58 and *The Undiscover'd Country: W.G Sebald and the Poetics of Travel*, ed. Markus Zisselsberger (Rochester, NY: Camden House, 2010).

29 This is Sebald's own translation of Adorno in Sebald, 'The Undiscover'd Country': 23. See also Adorno, 'Schubert', *Can One Live after Auschwitz: A Philosophical Reader*, ed. Rolf Tiedemann (Stanford, CA: Stanford University Press, 2003), 299–313.

30 Kafka, *The Castle*, trans. Mark Harman (New York: Schocken Books, 1999), 21.

31 Sebald, *The Emigrants*, trans. Michael Hulse (London: Harvill Press, 1997), 23.

32 Adorno cited in Sebald, 'The Un'discover'd Country', 23.

33 Adorno, 'Notes on Kafka', *Prisms*, trans. Samuel and Shierry Weber (Cambridge: MIT Press, 1983), 246.

34 For a discussion of ash as a paradigm of the trace, the effacement and therefore as a substance which both preserves and loses memory, see David Farrell Krell's reading of Derrida's 1985 journal article 'Feu la cendre' ['Fire, the Ash'] in Krell, *On Memory, Reminiscence, and Writing: On the Verge* (Bloomington: Indiana University Press, 1990), 309–14. For a Benjaminian reading of the uncanny evidentiary nature of dust and ash in Sebald, see Santner, *On Creaturely Life: Rilke, Benjamin, Sebald*, 97–106.

35 'From the outset, the now legendary and in some respects genuinely admirable reconstruction of the country after the devastation wrought by Germany's wartime enemies, a reconstruction tantamount to a second liquidation in successive phases of the nation's own past history, prohibited any backward view'. Sebald, *On the Natural History of Destruction*, trans. Anthea Bell (New York: Random House, 2003), 6–7.

36 In contrast to prominent voices of his own generation who, from the 1960s onwards, document their National Socialist heritage in explicitly existential and political ways (e.g. Peter Schneider, Uwe Timm, Peter Handke and the cinema of Alexander Kluge and Rainer Maria Fassbinder), Sebald's more allusive exploration starts with *After Nature* in 1988. It is only with the 1999 publication of 'Luftkrieg und Literatur' – first presented as a lecture series in Zurich in 1997, reproduced in *The New Yorker* and published in English as 'Air War and Literature' in *On the Natural History of Destruction* in 2003 – that Sebald insists on specifying the facts of the Second World War. He refers, here, not to any silence over the crimes of the Third Reich but to the 'self-anaesthesia' of the Allied fire-storming of German cities in 1943–5, and the post-war economic restructuring which seemed to suppress those events. While he takes account of some of Hans Magnus Enzenberger's writings, Kluge's pseudo-documentary account of *The Air Raid on Halberstadt on 8 April 1945* and Hans Erich Nossak's *The End: Hamburg 1943*, Sebald's diagnosis of a collective cultural insensibility is conclusive. 'The darkest aspects of the closing act of the destruction, experienced by the vast majority of the German population, remained such a shameful family secret encumbered with a kind of taboo that one could not perhaps even confess to oneself' – *On the Natural History*, 10.

37 On the idea of de-sheltering (*désabritement*), especially as it relates to, but differs from, Heidegger's *alèthéia* ('unconcealedness'), see Maurice Blanchot, *Writing the Disaster*, trans. Ann Smock (Lincoln: University of Nebraska Press, 1986), 94–5.

38 Bruns, *Blanchot: The Refusal of Philosophy*, 220.

39 Giorgio Agamben, *Homo Sacer: Sovereign Power and Bare Life*, trans. Daniel Heller-Roazen (Stanford, CA: Stanford University Press, 1998), 132; see also Agamben, *Means without Ends: A Note on Politics*, trans. Cesare Casarino and Vincenzo Binetti (Minneapolis and London: University of Minnesota Press, 2000), 22.

40 Agamben, *Homo Sacer*, 136–43.

41 Sebald, *Austerlitz*, trans. Anthea Bell (London: Penguin Books, 2001), 261–2.

42 Bertolt Brecht, 'Ten Poems from *A Reader for Those Who Live in Cities*', *Bertolt Brecht Poems, 1913–1956*, ed. John Willett and Ralph Manheim (London: Methuen, 1976).

43 Ibid., 131–2.

44 Benjamin, 'Commentary on Poems by Brecht', *Selected Writings, Volume 4, 1938–40*, ed. Howard Eiland and Michael W. Jennings (Cambridge, MA: The Belknap Press, 2003), 232. For a longer extract of the 1935 letter from Arnold Zweig to Brecht, see Erdmut Wizisla, *Benjamin and Brecht: The Story of a Friendship*, trans. Christine Shuttleworth (London and New York: Verso, 2016), 134.

45 Ibid., 232–3.

46 Ibid., 233.

47 Ibid., 236.

48 Zweig letter to Brecht cited in Wizisla, *Benjamin and Brecht*, 134.

49 On this, see Blanchot's account of Claude Lanzmann's *Shoah*: 'This is what the genocide of the Jews was: not only the annihilation of all Jews, but the annihilation of that annihilation itself. Nobody was meant to know, neither those carrying out the orders, nor those giving them, nor the supreme instigator, nor finally the victims who should have disappeared in the ignorance and the absence of their own disappearance.' Blanchot, 'N'oubliez pas', *Blanchot's Epoch, Paragraph*, 30: 3 (2007): 35.

50 Sebald, *The Rings of Saturn*, 177–8.

51 Sebald, *Vertigo*, trans. Michael Hulse (London: The Harvill Press, 1999), 33–5. For an account of similar urban wanderings in Kafka's *The Trial* and Thomas Mann's *Death in Venice*, see John Zilcosky, 'Sebald's Uncanny Travels: The Impossibility of Getting Lost', 217–43.

52 On the significance of 'generation' in the history of post-war German literature, see, among others, Sigrid Weigel, '"Generation" as a Symbolic Form: On the Genealogical Discourse of Memory since 1945', *The Germanic Review* 77:4 (2002), 264–7.

53 Sebald, *On the Natural History of Destruction*, 70–1.

54 Originally developed in her influential *Family Frames: Photography, Narrative and Postmemory* (Cambridge, MA: Harvard University Press, 1997), the concept of postmemory is given more extended treatment in Hirsch, *The Generation of*

Postmemory: Writing and Visual Culture after the Holocaust (New York: Columbia University Press, 2012). On the practice and ethics of postmemory in Sebald, see, among others, Richard Crownshaw, 'Reconsidering Postmemory: Photography, the Archive and Post-Holocaust in W.G. Sebald's *Austerlitz*', *Mosaic* 37:4 (2004): 215–36; J. J. Long, 'History, Narrative and Photography in W.G. Sebald's *Die Ausgewanderten*', *Modern Language Review* 98:1 (2003): 117–37. See also Santner, *Creaturely Life*, 160–7.

55 Hirsch, *The Generation of Postmemory*, 107.

56 Sebald, *Austerlitz*, 31.

57 Sebald, *The Rings of Saturn*, 178–9.

58 Sebald, *On the Natural History of Destruction*, 71.

59 My term 'born-afterwardsness' is an open reformulation of the peculiar unevenness of psychic temporality that Freud calls *nachträglich* (and Lacan *après-coup*). 'I am working on the assumption that our psychical mechanism has come into being by a process of stratification: the material present in the form of memory-traces being subjected from time to time to a *rearrangement* in accordance with fresh circumstances – to a *re-transcription*' (Freud letter to Willem Fleiss, 6 December 1896, *SE*, Vol. 1, 233.

60 Shoshana Felman, 'Camus' *The Plague*, or a Monument to Witnessing', *Testimony: Crises of Witnessing in Literature, Psychoanalysis, and History*, ed. Shoshana Felman and Dori Laub (New York: Routledge, 1992), 94.

61 Blanchot, *Writing the Disaster*, 42.

62 Arendt, *Between Past and Future*, 7. Arendt borrows this phrase from the last chapter of Tocqueville's *Democracy in America*, which, she suggests, not only anticipates Char's aphorism but also Kafka's 'HE', the last in the series of *Notes from the Year 1920*, later published as *The Great Wall of China*, 1946.

63 Ibid., 5–6.

64 Ibid., 47.

65 Arendt, *Between Past and Present*, 6.

66 Ibid.

67 Blanchot, *Faux Pas*, 213.

68 Sebald, *Natural History of Destruction*, 7.

69 Ibid., 76–7.

70 In this Sebald's project skews Heidegger, especially Heidegger's re-translation of Heraclites's Fragment 119: 'Ethos means abode, dwelling place. The word names the open region in which the human being dwells. The open region of his abode allows

Epilogue

1. Bertolt Brecht, *Bertolt Brecht's Refugee Conversations*, ed. Tom Kuhn, trans. Romy Fursland (London: Methuen Drama, 2019), 64. Conceived as a series of episodic dialogues between two characters – Ziffel, a physicist, and Kalle, a metal worker, both in enforced exile from Nazi Germany – the work was published only after Brecht's death, partially in 1957 and 1958 and then more fully in 1961. Although produced several times as a theatrical two-hander, *Refugee conversations* remains essentially an experiment in satire and narrative form.

2. Explicitly citing Hegel's *The Science of Logic*, Ziffel characterizes the Hegelian dialectic as an irascible married couple: ' Each [concept] is married to its opposite and they conduct their business as a couple, bring lawsuits as a couple, carry our raids and break-ins as a couple [...] and a completely discordant, querulous couple at that! [...] They can't live with each other and they can't live without each other.' In Brecht, *Refugee Conversations*, 63.

3. See Santner, *The Psychotheology of Everyday Life*, especially, 45, 64, 112–15.

4. Jacqueline Rose, *The Question of Zion* (Princeton, NJ: Princeton University Press, 2005), xiv. See also Rose, *The Last Resistance* (London: Verso, 2007), 39–62 and 214–23.

5. Judith Butler, *Parting Ways: Jewishness and the Critique of Zionism*, 1–28 and 205–24.

6. Ibid., 6.

7. I've borrowed the phrase from the title of Anna Freud's famous 1967 paper on the process of childhood grief. See 'About Losing and Being Lost', *Selected Writings*, ed. Richard Elkins and Ruth Freeman (London: Penguin, 1998), 94–105.

8. Edward Said, *Freud and the Non-European* (London: Verso, 2003), 66.

9. On the idea of a negative phenomenology as it relates to the apophatic dimension of representation, see Jean-Luc Marion, *Negative Certainties*, ed. Stephen E. Lewis (Chicago, IL: University of Chicago Press, 2015.

10. Jean Améry, *At the Mind's Limits*, trans. Sidney Rosenfeld and Stella P. Rosenfeld (Bloomington: Indiana University Press, 1980), 96.

11. Steinberg, *Judaism Musical and Unmusical*, 56.

12 Here I riff off Agamben's understanding of the 'cut of Apelles' which, in his reading of Paul, refers to the division of the very division of Jew/Greek, Jew/non-Jew. See Agamben, *Time That Remains*, 44–58.

13 Rose, *Broken Middle*, 310.

14 On the Agambian (and Benjaminian) understanding of this kind of spacing, see Andrew Benjamin, *Place, Commonality and Judgement*, 136–58.

15 Rosenzweig in Mosès, *System and Revelation*, 204.

16 Ibid., 207.

17 Ibid.

18 Rosenzweig, *Franz Rosenzweig: His Life and Thought*, 157–8.

19 Rosenzweig, *The New Thinking*, 91.

20 In his wonderful essay on the nature of the miracle in Rosenzweig, Benjamin and Freud, Santner makes a similar case for understanding Rosenzweig's 'New Thinking' less as a form of theological thought than one which exposes secularity's own investments in fantasies of (ultimate or executive) exception. See Santner, 'Miracles Happen: Benjamin, Rosenzweig, Freud, and the Matter of the Neighbour', 76–133.

21 On justice as the 'disjointure' of time, see, in particular, Jacques Derrida, *Spectres of Marx*, trans. Peggy Kamuf (London: Routledge, 1994).

BIBLIOGRAPHY

Adorno, Theodor W. *Can One Live after Auschwitz: A Philosophical Reader*, ed. Tiedemann, Rolf, Stanford: Stanford University Press, 2003.
Adorno, Theodor W. 'The Idea of Natural History', *Telos*, 60 (1984): 111–24.
Adorno, Theodor W. *Minima Moralia: Reflections on Damaged Life*, trans. Edmund Jephcott, London: Verso, 1978.
Adorno, Theodor W. *Negative Dialectics*, trans. Ernst Basch Ashton, New York: Continuum, 1973.
Adorno, Theodor W. *Prisms*. trans. Samuel and Sherry Weber, Cambridge: MIT Press, 1981.
Adorno, Theodor W. *Quasi Una Fantasia: Essays on Modern Music*, trans. Rodney Livingstone, London: Verso, 1992.
Agamben, Giorgio. *Homo Sacer: Sovereign Power and Bare Life*, trans. Daniel Heller-Roazen, Stanford: Stanford University Press, 1998.
Agamben, Giorgio. *Means without Ends*, trans. Vincenzo Binetti and Cesare Casarino, Minneapolis: University of Minnesota Press, 2000.
Agamben, Giorgio. *Remnants of Auschwitz: The Witness and the Archive*, trans. Daniel Heller-Roazen, New York: Zone Books, 2002.
Agamben, Giorgio. *The Time That Remains: A Commentary on the Letter to the Romans*, trans. Patricia Dailey, Stanford: Stanford University Press, 2005.
Akhmatova, Anna. *The Complete Poems of Anna Akhmatova*, trans. Judith Hemschemeyer, ed. Roberta Reeder, Boston: Zephyr Press 1990.
Akhmatova, Anna. *Poems of Anna Akhmatova*, trans. Stanley Kunitz and Max Hayward, Boston: Houghton Mifflin Harcourt, 1962.
Améry, Jean. *At the Mind's Limits*, trans. Sidney Rosenfeld and Stella Rosenfeld, Bloomington: Indiana University Press, 1980.
Anderson, Perry. 'England's Isaiah', *London Review of Books*, 12:24, 1990.
Arendt, Hannah. *Essays in Understanding: 1930–1954*, ed. Jerome Kohn, New York: Schocken Books, 1994.
Arendt, Hannah. *The Human Condition*, 2nd Edition. Chicago: University of Chicago Press, 1998.
Arendt, Hannah. *The Jewish Writings*, ed. Jerome Kohn and Ron Feldman, New York: Schocken Books, 2007.
Arendt, Hannah. *The Origins of Totalitarianism*, New York: Schocken Books, 2004.
Arendt, Hannah. *Men in Dark Times*, London: Harcourt Brace & Company, 1968.
Arendt, Hannah. *Between Past and Future*, London: Penguin, 1977.
Arendt, Hannah. *Rahel Varnhagen: The Life of a Jewess*, London: Leo Baeck Institute, 1957.
Arendt, Hannah. *On Revolution*, London: Penguin, 1963.

Aronowicz, Annette. *Jews and Christians on Time and Eternity: Charles Péguy's Portrait of Bernard-Lazare*, Stanford: Stanford University Press, 1988.

Aschheim, Stephen. *At the Edges of Liberalism: Junctions of European, German, and Jewish History*, Basingstoke: Palgrave Macmillan, 2012.

Assmann, Jan. *Moses the Egyptian: The Memory of Egypt in Western Monotheism*, Cambridge: Harvard University Press, 1997.

Barnouw, Dagmar. *Visible Spaces: Hannah Arendt and the German-Jewish Experience*, Baltimore: Johns Hopkins University Press, 1990.

Barry, Brian. 'Isaiah, Israel and Tribal Realism', *Times Literary Supplement*, 9 (2001).

Barthes, Roland. *Camera Lucida: Reflections on Photography*, trans. Richard Howard, New York: Hill & Wang, 1981.

Batnitzky, Leora. *Idolatory and Representation: The Philosophy of Franz Rosenzweig Reconsidered*, New Jersey: Princeton University Press, 2000.

Benhabib, Seyla. *The Reluctant Modernism of Hannah Arendt*, Oxford: Rowman & Littlefield, 2003.

Benjamin, Andrew. *Place, Commonality and Judgement: Continental Philosophy and the Ancient Greeks*, London: Continuum, 2012.

Benjamin, Andrew. *The Plural Event*, London: Routledge, 1994.

Benjamin, Andrew. 'Recovering Holiness and the Place of Others: Notes on *Vayikra* 19:34', *Parallax*, 19:4 (2013): 36–48.

Benjamin, Andrew, ed. *Walter Benjamin and Art*, London: Continuum Press, 2005.

Benjamin, Andrew, ed. *Walter Benjamin and History*, London and New York: Continuum, 2005.

Benjamin, Andrew. *Working with Walter Benjamin: Recovering a Political Philosophy*, Edinburgh: Edinburgh University Press, 2013.

Benjamin, Andrew and Peter Osborne, eds. *Walter Benjamin's Philosophy: Destruction and Experience*, London: Routledge, 2013.

Benjamin, Walter. *The Arcades Project*, trans. Howard Eiland and Kevin McLaughlin, Cambridge: Harvard University Press, 1999.

Benjamin, Walter. *Berlin Childhood around 1900*, trans. Howard Eiland, Cambridge: The Belknap Press of Harvard University Press, 2006.

Benjamin, Walter. *The Correspondence of Walter Benjamin 1910–1940*, ed. Gershom Scholem and Theodor Adorno, trans. Manfred R. Jacobson and Evelyn M. Jacobson, Chicago: University of Chicago Press, 1994.

Benjamin, Walter. *Illuminations*, trans. Harry Zohn, London: Collins/Fontana, 1973.

Benjamin, Walter. *One-Way Street and Other Writings*, trans. Edmund Jephcott and Kingsley Shorter, London: Verso, 1979.

Benjamin, Walter. *The Origin of German Tragic Drama*, trans. John Osborne, London: Verso, 1998.

Benjamin, Walter. *Reflections: Essays, Aphorisms, Autobiographical Writings*, trans. Edmund Jephcott, New York: Schocken, 1986.

Benjamin, Walter, *Selected Writings, Volume 1, 1913–1926*, ed. Marcus Bullock and Michael W. Jennings, Cambridge, MA: The Belknap Press of Harvard University Press, 2004.

Benjamin, Walter, *Selected Writings, Volume 2, Part 1, 1927-1930*, ed. Michael W. Jennings, Howard Eiland and Gary Smith, Cambridge, MA: The Belknap Press of Harvard University Press, 2005.
Benjamin, Walter. *Selected Writings, Volume 3, 1935-1938*, ed. Howard Eiland and Michael W. Jennings, Cambridge: The Belknap Press of Harvard University Press, 2006.
Benjamin, Walter. *Selected Writings, Volume 4, 1938-1940*, ed. Howard Eiland and Michael W. Jennings, Cambridge: The Belknap Press of Harvard University Press, 2006.
Benjamin, Walter. *Understanding Brecht*, trans. Anna Bostock, London: NLB, 1973.
Benjamin, Walter and Theodore Adorno. *The Complete Correspondence, 1928-40*, trans. Nicholas Walker, Cambridge: Polity Press, 1999.
Bentwich, Norman, ed. *Hebrew University Garland*. London: Constellation Books, 1952.
Berlin, Isaiah. *The Crooked Timber of Humanity: Chapters in the History of Ideas*, ed. Henry Hardy, London: Pimlico, 2003.
Berlin, Isaiah. *Freedom and Its Betrayal: Six Enemies of Human Liberty*, ed. Henry Hardy, London: Pimlico, 2003.
Berlin, Isaiah. *Personal Impressions*, ed. Henry Hardy, London: Hogarth Press, 1980.
Berlin, Isaiah. *The Power of Ideas*, ed. Henry Hardy, London: Chatto and Windus, 2000.
Berlin, Isaiah. *The Roots of Romanticism*, Princeton: Princeton University Press, 1999.
Berlin, Isaiah. *Russian Thinkers*, London: Penguin, 1994.
Berlin, Isaiah. *Against the Current: Essays in the History of Ideas*, ed. Henry Hardy, London: Hogarth Press, 1980.
Berlin, Isaiah. *Three Critics of the Enlightenment: Vico, Hamann, Herder*, ed. Henry Hardy, Princeton: Princeton University Press, 2000.
Bernstein, Richard. *Freud and the Legacy of Moses*, Cambridge: Cambridge University Press, 1998.
Bilski, Emily and Emily Braun, eds. *Jewish Women and Their Salons: The Power of Conversation*, London: Yale University Press, 2005.
Bion, Wilfred Ruprecht. *Cogitations*, New York: Routledge, 1994.
Blanchot, 'N'oubliez pas', *Blanchot's Epoch, Paragraph*, 30:3 (2007): 35.
Blanchot, Maurice. *The Gaze of Orpheus and Other Literary Essays*, trans. Lydia Davis, New York: Barrytown: Station Hill, 1981.
Blanchot, Maurice. *The Infinite Conversation*, trans. Susan Hanson, London: University of Minnesota Press, 1969.
Blanchot, Maurice. *The Space of Literature*, trans. Anne Smock, Lincoln: University of Nebraska Press, 1982.
Blanchot, Maurice. *The Work of Fire*, trans. Charlotte Mandell, Stanford: Stanford University Press, 1995.
Blanchot, Maurice. *Writing the Disaster*, trans. Ann Smock, Lincoln: University of Nebraska Press, 1986.
Blond, Louis. 'Franz Rosenzweig: Homelessness in Time', *New German Critique*, 37:3 (2010): 27-58.
Bowen-Moore, Patricia. *Hannah Arendt's Philosophy of Natality*, New York: St. Martin's Press, 1989.
Boyarin, Jonathan. *Storm from Paradise: The Politics of Jewish Memory*, Minneapolis: University of Minnesota Press, 1992.

Brecht, Bertolt. *Bertolt Brecht Poems, 1913–1956*, ed. John Willett and Ralph Manheim, London: Methuen 1976.

Brecht, Bertolt. *Bertolt Brecht's Refugee Conversations*, ed. Tom Kuhn, trans. Romy Fursland, London: Methuen Drama, 2019.

Bruns, Gerald. *Blanchot: The Refusal of Philosophy*, London: Johns Hopkins University Press, 1997.

Butler, Judith. *Parting Ways: Jewishness and the Critique of Zionism*, Columbia University Press: New York, 2012.

Butler, Judith, Zeynep Gambetti and Leticia Sabsay, eds. *Vulnerability in Resistance*, London: Duke University Press, 2016.

Cacciari, Massimo. *Posthumous People: Vienna at the Turning Point*, trans. Rodger Friedman, Stanford: Stanford University Press, 1996.

Caute, David. *Isaac and Isaiah: The Covert Punishment of a Cold War Heretic*, New Haven: Yale University Press, 2015.

Champlin, Jeffrey. 'Born Again: Arendt's 'Natality' as Figure and Concept', *The Germanic Review*, 88:2 (2013): 150–64.

Cherlin, Michael. *Schoenberg's Musical Imagination*, Cambridge: Cambridge University Press, 2007.

Cixous, Helene. *Three Steps on the Ladder of Writing*, trans. Sarah Cornell and Susan Sellers, New York: Columbia University Press, 1993.

Cohen, Hermann. *Reason and Hope: Selections from the Jewish Writings of Hermann Cohen*, ed. and trans. Eva Jospe, New York: W. W. Norton, 1971.

Cohen, Hermann. *Religion of Reason out of the Sources of Judaism*, ed. Simon Kaplan, New York: Frederick Ungar Publishing, 1971.

Cohen, Joseph. *Le Spectre Juif de Hegel*, Paris: Galilée, 2005.

Cohen, Richard. *Elevations: The Height of the Good in Rosenzweig and Levinas*, Chicago: University of Chicago Press, 1994.

Comay, Rebecca. 'Materialist Mutations of the *Bilderverbot*', in ed. Andrew Benjamin *Walter Benjamin and Art*, London: Continuum Press, 2005, 32–59.

Comay, Rebecca. *Mourning Sickness: Hegel and the French Revolution*. Stanford: Stanford University Press, 2011.

Comay, Rebecca. 'Resistance and Repetition: Freud and Hegel', *Research in Phenomenology*, 45:2 (2015): 237–66.

Crownshaw, Richard. 'Reconsidering Postmemory: Photography, the Archive and Post-Holocaust in W.G. Sebald's *Austerlitz*', *Mosaic*, 37:4 (2004): 215–36.

Dalos, Gyorgy. *The Guest from the Future: Anna Akhmatova and Isaiah Berlin*, trans. Antony Wood, New York: Farrar, Strauss and Giroux, 1988.

Deleuze, Gilles and Felix Guattari. *What Is Philosophy?* trans. Graham Burchell and Hugh Tomlinson, London: Verso, 1994.

Derrida, Jacques. *Archive Fever: A Freudian Impression*, London: The University of Chicago Press, 1995.

Derrida, Jacques. 'Force of Law: The "Mystical Foundation of Authority"', trans. Mary Quaintance, *Cardozo Law Review*, 11 (1990): 920–1045.

Derrida, Jacques. *Glas*, Paris: Galilée, 1973.

Derrida, Jacques. 'Interpretations at War: Kant, the Jew, the German', in ed. Gil Anidjar *Acts of Religion*, New York and London: Routledge, 2010, 135–88.
Derrida, Jacques. *Memoirs of the Blind: The Self-Portrait and Other Ruins*, trans. Pascale-Anne Brault and Michael Naas, Chicago: University of Chicago Press, 1993.
Derrida, Jacques. *Monolingualism and the Other; or the Prosthesis of Origin*, Stanford, CA: Stanford University Press, 1996.
Derrida, Jacques. *Spectres of Marx: The State of the Debt, the Work of Mourning and the New International*, trans. Peggy Kamuf, London: Routledge, 1994.
Deutscher, Isaac. *Non-Jewish Jew and Other Essays*, Oxford: Oxford University Press, 1968.
Dickinson, Colby and Stéphane Symons, eds. *Walter Benjamin and Theology*, New York: Fordham University Press, 2016.
Didi-Huberman, Georges. *Confronting Images: Questioning the Ends of a Certain History of Art*, trans. John Goodman, Pennsylvania: Penn State University Press, 2009.
Dubnov, Arie M. *Isaiah Berlin: The Journey of a Jewish Liberal*, New York: Palgrave Macmillan, 2012.
Erasmus, *The Collected Works of Erasmus*, Vol. 6, ed. John W O'Malley, Toronto: University of Toronto Press, 1988.
Eva Juhl, 'Die Wahrheit über das Unglück: zu W. G. Sebald', in eds. Anne Fuchs and Theo Harden, *Die Ausgewanderten: Resien im Diskurs*, Heidelberg: C. Winter Universitätsverlag, 1995, 640–59.
Fackenheim, Emil. *The Religious Dimension in Hegel's Thought*, Bloomington: Indiana University Press, 1971.
Felman, Shoshana and Dori Laub. *Testimony: Crises of Witnessing in Literature, Psychoanalysis, and History*, New York: Routledge, 1992.
Freud, Anna. *Selected Writings*, ed. Richard Elkins and Ruth Freeman, London: Penguin, 1998.
Freud, Sigmund. *Moses and Monotheism*, trans. Katherine Jones, New York: Vintage Books, 1955.
Freud, Sigmund. *Beyond the Pleasure Principle and Other Writings*, trans. John Reddick, London: Penguin, 2003.
Freud, Sigmund. *The Standard Edition of the Complete Psychological Works of Sigmund Freud, Volume XVIII (1920–1922)*, ed. James Strachey, London: Vintage, 2001.
Gibbs, Robert. *Correlations in Rosenzweig and Levinas*, New Jersey: Princeton University Press, 1992.
Glatzer, Nahum, ed. *Franz Rosenzweig: His Life and Work*, Cambridge: Hackett Publishing, 1998.
Gordon, Peter Eli. *Rosenzweig and Heidegger: Between Judaism and German Philosophy*, Berkeley: University of California Press, 2005.
Gould, Evlyn. *Dreyfus and the Literature of the Third Republic: Secularism and Tolerance in Zola, Barrès, Lazare and Proust*, London: McFarland & Company, 2012.
Govrin, Aner. 'Some Utilitarian Influences in Freud's Early Writings', *History and Psychoanalysis*, 6:1 (2004): 5–21.
Gray, John. *Isaiah Berlin: An Interpretation of His Thought*, Princeton: Princeton University Press, 2013.

Halbertal, Moshe and Avishai Margalit. *Idolatory*, trans. Naomi Goldblum, London: Harvard University Press, 1992.
Hamburger, Käte. 'Rahel und Goethe', in eds. Konrad Feilchenfeldt, Uwe Schweikert und Rahel E. Steiner, *Rahel Gesammelte Werke 10*, Munich: Mattes and Seitz, 1983, 179–204.
Hand, Seán, ed. *The Levinas Reader*, Oxford: Oxford University Press, 1989.
Handelman, Susan. *Fragments of Redemption: Jewish Thought and Literary Theory in Benjamin, Scholem, and Levinas*, Bloomingron: Indiana University Press, 1991.
Handelman, Susan. *The Slayers of Moses: The Emergence of Rabbinic Interpretation in Modern Literary Theory*, Albany: SUNY Press, 1982.
Hegel, Georg Wilhelm Friedrich. *Early Theological Writings*, ed. T. M. Knox, Philadelphia: University of Pennsylvania Press, 1975.
Hegel, Georg Wilhelm Friedrich. *The Philosophy of Right*, trans. T. M. Knox, Oxford: Oxford University Press, 1952.
Heidegger, Martin. *Basic Writings*, ed. David Farrell Krell, New York: Harper & Row, 1977.
Hertz, Deborah. *Jewish High Society in Old Regime Berlin*, New Haven: Yale University Press, 1988.
Herzen, Alexander. *Childhood, Youth and Exile*, trans. J. D. Duff, Oxford: Oxford University Press, 1980.
Herzen, Alexander. *From the Other Shore and the Russian People and Socialism: An Open Letter to Jules Michelet*, trans. Moura Budberg and Richard Wollheim, London: Weidenfeld and Nicolson, 1956.
Hirsch, Marianne. *Family Frames: Photography, Narrative and Postmemory*, Cambridge: Harvard University Press, 1997.
Hirsch, Marianne. *The Generation of Postmemory: Writing and Visual Culture after the Holocaust*, New York: Columbia University Press, 2012.
Hitchens, Christopher. 'Moderation or Death', *London Review of Books*, 11:20 (1988).
Hollander, Dana. *Exemplarity and Chosenness: Rosenzweig and Derrida on the Nation of Philosophy*, California: Stanford University Press, 2008.
Hollander, Dana. 'Franz Rosenzweig on Nation, Translation and Judaism', *Philosophy Today*, 38:4 (1994): 380–9.
Honig, Bonnie. *Democracy and the Foreigner*, Princeton: Princeton University Press 2001.
Honig, Bonnie. 'Difference, Dilemmas, and the Politics of Home', *Social Research*, 61:3 (1994): 563–97.
Honig, Bonnie, ed. *Feminist Interpretations of Hannah Arendt*, Pennsylvania: Pennsylvania State University Press, 1995.
Honig, Bonnie. 'The Miracle of Metaphor: Rethinking the State of Exception with Rosenzweig and Schmitt', *Diacritics*, 37:2/3 (2007): 78–102.
Ignatieff, Michael. *Isaiah Berlin: A Life*, London: Chatto and Windus, 1998.
Jacobs, Carol. *Sebald's Vision*, New York: Columbia University Press, 2015.
Jacoby, Russell. 'Isaiah Berlin – With the Current', *Salmagundi*, 55 (1982): 232–41.
Jacoby, Russell. *Picture Imperfect: Utopian Thought for an Anti-Utopian Age*, New York: Columbia University Press, 2005.
Jay, Martin. *The Dialectical Imagination: A History of the Frankfurt School and the Institute of Social Research 1923–1959*, Boston: Little, Brown and Company, 1973.

Kafka, Franz. *The Castle*, trans. Mark Harman, New York: Schocken Books, 1999.
Kafka, Franz. *Diaries*, trans. Joseph Kresh, Martin Greenberg and Hannah Arendt, New York: Schocken Books, 1964.
Kafka, Franz. *Selected Writings*, ed. Michael W. Jennings, Howard Eiland and Gary Smith, trans. Rodney Livingstone and Others, Cambridge: The Belknap Press of Harvard University Press, 1999.
Kampowski, Stephan. *Arendt, Augustine, and the New Beginnings*, Grand Rapids: Eerdmans, 2008.
Kant, Immanuel. *Anthropology from a Pragmatic View*, ed. and trans. Robert Louden, Cambridge: Cambridge University Press, 2006.
Kant, Immanuel. *On History*, trans. Lewis Beck White, Robert Anchor and Emil Fackenheim, Indianapolis: Bobbs-Merill, 1963.
Kiess, John. *Hannah Arendt and Theology*, London: Bloomsbury, 2016.
Kohler, Lotte and Hans Saner, eds. *Hannah Arendt-Karl Jaspers Correspondence: 1926–1969*, trans. Robert and Rita Kimber, London: Harcourt Brace & Company, 1992.
Krell, David Farrell. *On Memory, Reminiscence, and Writing: On the Verge*, Bloomington: Indiana University Press, 1990.
Kuna, Franz ed. *On Kafka: Semi-Centenary Perspectives*, London: Paul Elek, 1976.
Lacan, Jacques. *Anxiety: The Seminar of Jacques Lacan, Book X*, ed. Jacques Alain Miller, trans. A. R. Price, Cambridge: Polity Press, 2014.
Lazare, Bernard. *Job's Dungheap: Essays in Jewish Nationalism and Social Revolution*, trans. Harry L. Bisse, New York: Schocken, 1948.
Leibowitz, Nehama. *New Studies in Shemot, Exodus*, trans. Areh Newman, Jerusalem: World Zionist Organisation, 1976.
Levinas, Emmanuel. *Difficult Freedom: Essays in Judaism*, trans. Seán Hand, Baltimore: The Johns Hopkins University Press, 1997.
Levinas, Emmanuel. *Existence and Existents*, trans. Alphonso Lingis, The Hague: Martinus Nijhoff, 1978.
Levinas, Emmanuel. *Otherwise than Being or beyond Essence*, trans. Alphonso Lingis, The Hague: Martinus Nijhoff, 1981.
Levinas, Emmanuel. *Proper Names*, trans. Michael B. Smith, Stanford: Stanford University Press, 1996.
Levinas, Emmanuel. *Totality and Infinity: An Essay on Exteriority*, trans. Alphonso Lingis, The Hague: Martinus Nijhoff, 1979.
Lilla, Mark, Ronald Dworkin and Robert Silvers, eds. *The Legacy of Isaiah Berlin*, New York: New York Review Books, 2001.
Liska, Vivian. *German-Jewish Thought and Its Aftermath: A Tenuous Legacy*, Bloomington: Indiana University Press, 2017.
Long, John. 'History, Narrative and Photography in W.G. Sebald's *Die Ausgewanderten*', *Modern Language Review*, 98:1 (2003): 117–37.
Long, John and Anne Whitehead, eds. *W.G. Sebald – A Critical Companion*, Edinburgh: Edinburgh University Press, 2004.
Löwy, Michael. *Redemption and Utopia: Jewish Libertarian Thought in Central Europe*, London: Verso, 2017.

Lukes, Steven. 'The Singular and the Plural: On the Distinctive Liberalism of Isaiah Berlin', *Social Research*, 61:3 (1994): 687–717.
Lyotard, Jean-François. *Discourse, Figure*, trans. Anthony Hudek and Mary Lydon, Minneapolis: University of Minnesota Press, 2010.
Lyotard, Jean-François. *The Inhuman: Reflections on Time*, trans. Geoffrey Bennington and Rachel Bowlby, Stanford: Stanford University Press, 1991.
Lyotard, Jean-François. 'Jewish Oedipus', trans. S Hanson, *Genre*, 10:3 (1977): 395–411.
Lyotard, Jean-François. 'Scapeland', in ed. Andrew Benjamin *The Lyotard Reader*, Oxford: Blackwell, 1989, 212–19.
Mandelstam, Osip. *Complete Poetry of Osip Emilevich Mandelstam*, trans. Burton Raffel and Alla Burago. Albany: SUNY Press, 1973.
Marcuse, Herbert. *Eros and Civilisation*, Boston: Beacon Press, 1966.
Marion, Jean-Luc. *Negative Certainties*, ed. Stephen Lewis, Chicago: University of Chicago Press, 2015.
Meineke, Friedrich. *Cosmopolitanism and the Nation State*. Princeton: Princeton University Press. 1970.
Mendes-Flohr, Paul. *German Jews: A Dual Identity*, London: Yale University Press, 1999.
Mendes-Flohr, Paul, ed. *The Philosophy of Franz Rosenzweig*, London: University Press of New England for Brandeis University Press, 1988.
Menninghaus, Winfried, 'Walter Benjamin's Variations of Imagelessness', in eds. Ingrid and Konrad Scheurmann, *For Walter Benjamin: Documentation, Essays and a Sketch*, Bonn: Arbeitskreis selbständiger Kultur-Institute, 1993, 166–79.
Merleau-Ponty, Maurice. *The Primacy of Perception*, ed. James Edie, Evanston: Northwestern University Press, 1964.
Merleau-Ponty, Maurice. *The Visible and Invisible*, trans. Alphonso Lingis, Evanston: Northwestern University Press, 1968.
Molnar, Michael. 'John Stuart Mill Translated by Sigmund Freud', *History and Psychoanalysis*, 1:2 (1999): 195–205.
Momogliano, Arnaldo. 'A Note on Max Weber's Definition of Judaism as a Pariah-Religion', *History and Theory*, 8:3 (1980): 313–18.
Mosès, Stéphane. *The Angel of History: Rosenzweig, Benjamin, Scholem*, trans. Barbara Harshav, California: Stanford University Press, 2009.
Mosès, Stéphane. *System and Revelation: The Philosophy of Franz Rosenzweig*, trans. Catherine Tihanyi, Detroit: Wayne State University Press, 1992.
Nancy, Jean-Luc. *The Ground of the Image*, trans. Jeff Fort, New York: Fordham University Press, 2005.
Nancy, Jean-Luc. *The Inoperative Community*, ed. Peter Connor, trans. Peter Connor, Lisa Garbus, Michael Holland and Simona Sawhney, Minnesota: University of Minnesota Press, 1991.
Nietzsche, Friedrich. *The Gay Science*, ed. Bernard Williams, trans. Josefine Nauckhoff, Cambridge: Cambridge University Press, 2001.
O'Byrne, Ann. *Natality and Finitude*, Bloomington: Indiana University Press, 1989.
Pines, Shlomo. *The Guide for the Perplexed*, Chicago: University of Chicago Press, 1963.

Rabinbach, Anson. 'Critique and Commentary/Alchemy and Chemistry', *New German Critique*, 17 (1979): 7–9.
Rabinbach, Anson, 'Between Enlightenment and Apocalypse: Benjamin, Bloch and Modern German Messianism', *New German Critique*, 34 (1985): 78–124.
Rabinbach, Anson. *In the Shadow of Catastrophe: German Intellectuals between Apocalypse and Enlightenment*, Berkeley: University of California Press, 1997.
Rancière, Jacques. *Dissensus: On Politics and Aesthetics*, New York: Bloomsbury, 2010.
Reich, Wilhelm. *The Function of the Orgasm*, London: Souvenir, 1983.
Reich, Wilhelm. *The Mass Psychology of Fascism*, London: Penguin, 1946.
Ricoeur, Paul. *History, Memory, Forgetting*, trans. Kathleen Blamey and David Pellauer, Chicago: University of Chicago Press, 2004.
Rose, Gillian. *Broken Middle*, Oxford: Blackwell, 1992.
Rose, Gillian. *Judaism and Modernity: Philosophical Essays*, Oxford: Blackwell, 1993.
Rose, Gillian. *Mourning Becomes Law: Philosophy and Representation*, Cambridge: Cambridge University Press, 1996.
Rose, Jacqueline. *The Last Resistance*, London: Verso, 2007.
Rose, Jacqueline. *The Question of Zion*, Princeton: Princeton University Press, 2005.
Rosenzweig, Franz. *Cultural Writings of Franz Rosenzweig*, ed. and trans. Barbara E. Galli, New York: Syracuse University Press, 2000.
Rosenzweig, Franz. *Der Mensch und sein Werk: Gesammelte Schriften 1:2*, Dordrecht: Martinus Hijhoff, 1979.
Rosenzweig, Franz. *Franz Rosenzweig: His Life and Thought*, presented by Nahum N. Glazer. New York: Schocken Books, 1961.
Rosenzweig, Franz. *Franz Rosenzweig's 'The New Thinking'*, trans. Alan Udoff and Barbara E. Galli, New York: Syracuse University Press, 1999.
Rosenzweig, Franz. *Hegel und der Staat*, Berlin: Scientia Verlag, 1982.
Rosenzweig, Franz. *Philosophical and Theological Writings*, ed. and trans. Paul Franks and Michael Morgan. Cambridge: Hackett Publishing, 2000.
Rosenzweig, Franz. *The Philosophy of Franz Rosenzweig*, ed. Paul Mendes-Flohr, Hanover and London: University Press of New England for Brandeis University Press, 1988.
Rosenzweig, Franz. *The Star of Redemption*, trans. Barbara Galli, Madison: University of Wisconsin Press, 2005.
Said, Edward. *Freud and the Non-European*, London: Verso, 2003.
Santner, Eric L. On *Creaturely Life: Rilke, Benjamin, Sebald*, Chicago: University of Chicago Press, 2006
Santner, Eric L. 'Miracles Happen: Benjamin, Rosenzweig, Freud, and the Matter of the Neighbour', in eds. Slavoj Žižek, Eric L. Santner and Kenneth Reinhard, *The Neighbour: Three Inquiries in Political Theology*, Chicago: University of Chicago Press, 2005, 76–133.
Santner, Eric L. *On the Psychotheology of Everyday Life: Reflections on Freud and Rosenzweig*, London: University of Chicago Press, 2001.
Scholem, Gershom. *The Correspondence of Walter Benjamin and Gershom Scholem 1932–1940*, trans. Gary Smith and Andre Lefevre, New York: Schocken Books, 1989.
Scholem, Gershom. *On Jews and Judaism in Crisis: Selected Essays*, ed. Werner Dannhauser, New York: Schocken Books, 1976.

Scholem, Gershom. *Major Trends in Jewish Mysticism*, New York: Schocken Books, 1995.
Scholem, Gershom. *Sabbatai Sevi: The Mystical Messiah 1926-1667*, Princeton: Princeton University Press, 2016.
Sebald, Winfried Georg. *Austerlitz*, trans. Anthea Bell, London: Penguin, 2001.
Sebald, Winfried Georg. *The Emigrants*, trans. Michael Hulse, London: The Harvill Press, 1997.
Sebald, Winfried Georg. *After Nature*, trans. Michael Hamburger, London: Penguin, 2002.
Sebald, Winfried Georg. *The Rings of Saturn*, trans. Michael Hulse, London: Vintage, 2002.
Sebald, Winfried Georg. *On the Natural History of Destruction*, trans. Anthea Bell, New York: Random House, 2003
Sebald, Winfried Georg. 'The Undiscover'd Country: The Death Motif in Kafka's *The Castle*', *Journal of European Studies*, 2 (1972): 22-34.
Sebald, Winfried Georg. *Vertigo*, trans. Michael Hulse, London: The Harvill Press, 1999.
Sebald, Winfried Georg and Jan Tripp. *Unrecounted*, trans. Michael Hamburger, London: Penguin, 2005.
Simmel, Georg. *Georg Simmel: On Individuality and Social Form*, ed. Donald Levine, Chicago: University of Chicago Press, 1971.
Steinberg, Michael. *Judaism Musical and Unmusical*, Chicago: University of Chicago Press, 2007.
Strauss, Leo. *Natural Right and History*, Chicago: University of Chicago Press, 1971.
Strauss, Leo. *Philosophy and Law: Essays toward the Understanding of Maimonides and His Predecessors*, trans. Fred Baumann, Philadelphia: Jewish Publication Society, 1987.
Tamir, Yael. *Liberal Nationalism: Studies in Moral, Political and Legal Philosophy*, Princeton: Princeton University Press, 1993.
Tewarson, Heidi. *Rahel Varnhagen: The Life and Work of a German-Jewish Intellectual*, Lincoln: University of Nebraska Press, 1998.
Theisen, Bianca. 'Prose of the World: W. G. Sebald's Literary Travels', *Germanic Review*, 79:3 (2004): 163-79.
Trilling, Lionel. *The Liberal Imagination*, New York: NYRB Classics, 2008.
van Rahden, Till. *Jews and Other Germans: Civil Society, Religious Diversity and Urban Politics in Breslau, 1860-1925*, trans. Marcus Brainard, Madison: University of Wisconsin Press, 2008.
Villa, Dana. *Arendt and Heidegger: The Fate of the Political*, Princeton: Princeton University Press, 1996.
Villa, Dana. 'Genealogies of Total Domination: Arendt, Adorno, and Auschwitz', *New German Critique*, 34:1 (2007): 1-45.
Villa, Dana and Joke Hermsen, eds. *The Judge and the Spectator: Hannah Arendt's Political Philosophy*, Leuven: Peeters, 1999.
Walser, Michael. *Exodus and Revolution*, New York: Basic Books, 1985.
Walser, Michael. *In God's Shadow: Politics in the Hebrew Bible*, London: Yale University Press, 2012.
Weber, Max. *Ancient Judaism*, ed. and trans. Hans Gerth and Don Martindale, New York: The Free Press, 1967.
Weber, Max. *The Sociology of Religion*, trans. Ephraim Fischoff, Boston: Beacon Books, 1963.

Weigel, Sigrid. '"Generation" as a Symbolic Form: On the Genealogical Discourse of Memory since 1945', *The Germanic Review*, 77:4 (2002): 264–67.

Wilson, Nelly. *Bernard Lazare: Antisemitism and the Problem of Jewish Identity in Late Nineteenth-Century France*, Cambridge: Cambridge University Press, 1978.

Wizisla, Erdmut. *Benjamin and Brecht: The Story of a Friendship*, trans. Christine Shuttleworth London: Verso, 2016.

Wolin, Richard. *Walter Benjamin: An Aesthetic of Redemption*, Berkeley: University of California Press, 1994.

Woolfe, C. and J. Bagguley, eds., *Authors Take Sides on Vietnam*, New York: Simon & Schuster, 1967.

Yerushalmi, Yosef Hayim. *Freud's Moses: Judaism Terminable and Interminable*, London: Yale University Press, 1991.

Yovel, Yirmiyahu. *Dark Riddle: Hegel, Nietzsche and the Jews*, Philadelphia: Pennsylvania University Press, 1988.

Zilcosky, John, ed. *Writing Travel: The Poetics and Politics of the Modern Journey*, Toronto: University of Toronto Press, 2008.

Zisselsberger, Markus, ed. *The Undiscover'd Country: W.G Sebald and the Poetics of Travel*, New York: Camden House, 2010.

Žižek, Slavoj, 'Neighbours and Other Monsters: A Plea for Ethical Violence', in eds. Slavoj Žižek, Eric l. Santner and Kenneth Reinhard, *The Neighbour: Three Inquiries in Political Theology*, Chicago: University of Chicago Press, 2005, 134–90.

Žižek, Slavoj. *The Sublime Object of Ideology*, London: Verso, 1989.

Žižek, Slavoj. 'Tolerance as an Ideology', *Critical Inquiry*, 34:4 (2008): 660–82.

Zornberg, Aviva Gottlieb. *The Particulars of Rapture, Reflections on Exodus*, New York: Schocken Books, 2002.

INDEX

Adorno, Theodor W., on Schoenberg's *Moses und Aron* 48; on homelessness in relation to Arendt 139–40; on impossibility of dwelling 139–40; *Minima Moralia* 139; *Notes on Kafka* 151; on Schubert's *Winterreise* 150; on visual inaccessibility 67

Agamben, Giorgio 139, 153

Akhmatova, Anna 14, 74–6; contradictions of resistance in 106–7, 170; on 'Guest from the Future' 102–5; immovability of 105–7; Meeting with Berlin 74–6, 102, 105, 110; melancholic condition of 104–8; and Rahel Varnhagen 15, 170, *see also*, exile-as-melancholy

allegory, in Benjamin 39, 42–43; affinity with Rosenzweig's Judaism 44–5; city as 45, 63; as temporality 42–3; as 'undead life' 55–6; as 'un-mended middle' 43–4

Améry, Jean 169

Arendt, Hannah 11, 15; on artificiality of place 115, 131–2; on Auschwitz and failure of post-war national regeneration 138–40; Char in 161–2; and 'conceptual persona' 113–14, 117; *The Human Condition* 115–16, 126–7, 137; on in-common incompletion 116, 120, 128, 131, 133, 138, 170; and Jaspers 113, 117–18, 140, 198n27; 'The Jew as Pariah: A Hidden Tradition' 119–20, 133; 'Jewish History, Revised' 135, 137; on Jewish state 130–1, 134, 137–8, 202n97; 'The Jewish State; Fifty Years After' 137; and Lazare 119–20, 133–5, 204n118, 204n120; on Mendelssohn 124–5; on miseries of assimilation and limits of emancipation 121–5, 127–30, 135, 170; on natality 126–8, 131–2, 202n89; *The Origins of Totalitarianism* 116–17, 126; on the pariah 113–14, 116–20; *Between Past and Present* 161–2, *see also* assimilation; pariah; on the polis 114–16, 119, 132, 137, 139–40; on Rahel 15, 113–14, 116–18, 120–31, 140, 170; *Rahel Varnhagen: The Life of a Jewess* 112–14, 117, 120, 130; on Sabbatean theology 135–8; 'To Save a Jewish Homeland' 130–1; Scholem in 135–7

assimilation: as liberalism 12, 77, 92, 97, 109–10; Arendt rejection of 121–5, 127–30, 135, *see also* Berlin; Arendt; Steinberg; Berlin critique of 93–8; as mourning and incompletion 92–3, 99, 108–10; as reality principle or 'exile with a difference' 12, 99–101, 169; Rosenzweig on 28–9, 31

Benjamin, Walter 11, 22; angel of history 70; amplification and breakdown of the visual in 60–9; *The Arcades Project* 1, 40–2, 44, 52–65; Baudelaire as 'Jewish angel in' 60–61; city as Baroque allegory in 56, 58–9, 67; on city as spatial excess 62; on city as temporal disordering 40–3, 52, 61; commodity as 'undead life' in 52–6, 58–60, 64, 68, 70; *Critique of Violence* 21; 'The Destructive Character' 71, *see also* allegory; image; natural history; time; 'Exposé of 1939' 53, 57; on Haussmann 57, 58; idea of the image-ban in 52, 60–7, 70–1; idolatry of

INDEX

Haussmannian space in 57–60; natural history (*Naturgeschichte*) 22–3, 54, 56, 59, 63; *One-Way Street* 53; *The Origin of German Tragic Drama* 42, 56–7, 64, 68; relation to Exodus 33:18–23 68–70; Rosenzweig linked to 39, 42, 44–5; on spatiality of the anecdote 41–2; temporality of allegory in 42–4; 'Theses on the Philosophy of History' 23, 44–5, 59

Benjamin, Andrew, on 'anoriginal origin' 5, 32

Berlin, Isaiah 11–12; 'Benjamin Disraeli, Karl Marx and the Search for Identity' 94–5, see also Freud; and Akhmatova 14, 74–6, 98, 102, 105–7, 110, 170; antipathy to Freud in 78, 98, 190n7; critique of Jewish assimilation 93–7; 'flow of life' or concept of the middle in 85–6, 91–2, 105–6, 109–10; *Freedom and Its Betrayals* 82; Freudian 'death-instinct' in 86–8, 106; liberalism in 79, 81, 89, 91, 93–4, 98, 110; on French *philosophes* and German *Aukflärung* 81–4; on Herder 84, 90, 94; on Herzen's *Childhood, Youth and Exile* 85; 'Jewish Slavery and Emancipation' 93; 'The Origins of Israel' 73; *Personal Impressions* 75; pluralism in 12, 14–15, 74, 76, 80–1, 89–91, 96–104, 108; rejection of Arendt and Marcuse 78, 96; *Two Concepts of Liberty* 89, 100; use of Herzen in 73, 84–8, 97

Blanchot, Maurice 11, 15, 68, 146

Brecht, Bertolt, critique of depth in 52; *Reader for Those Who Live in Cities* 154–5; 'Refugee Conversations' 165

Butler, Judith 167

Cohen, Hermann, 'Deutschtum und Judentum' 29–31

Comay, Rebecca 57, 68, 186n41; on concept of resistance in 106

Derrida, Jacques 6, 11, 15, 21, 31

Deleuze, Gilles & Guattari, Felix, on 'conceptual persona' 113–14

Deutscher, Isaac, 'The Non-Jewish Jew' 111–12; Berlin's hostility to 190n3, 194n71; and pariah 116, 120

Didi-Huberman, Georges 67

Dubnov, Arie, M. 95

Exile, and *Exodus*/exodus 1–5, 13, 33, 37–8, 43–5, 50–2, 67–8; as alternative public space 114, 118, 138, 140, 158; as anoriginality 5, 10–12, 52, 166; Brechtian formulations of 155, 165, 173; and emanationism 135–7; as excess 76–8; as melancholy 104–9, 170; as necessary wound 167–8, *see also* assimilation; as the middle 14, 33; in relation to *nachgeboren* 15; and Santner's 'Egyptomania' 166–7; temporality of 32–4, 44, 51, 146, 163–4, 169, 171, 173; 'with a difference' 12, 109, 169

Freud, Sigmund 4, 12, 62; Berlin's antipathy to 78, 98, 190n7; *Civilization and Its Discontents* 77, 100; correlations with Berlin 76, 78, 86–8, 92, 100–2, 106–7; on death-instinct 87–9; *The Ego and the Id* 108–9; idea of self-cure in 12, 166–8; *Mourning and Melancholia* 104–6; on reality principle 99–104

Gordon, Peter Eli 179n49

Gray, John 93, 193n66

Hegel, Georg Wilhelm Friedrich 18, 20–1, 26, 36–7, 84, 179n51

Heidegger, Martin 11; Arendt's concept of natality as critique of 201n77; idea of founding and joining in 197n22; relation to Rosenzweig 177n9; Sebald's inversion of 210n70

Heine, Heinrich 94; Arendt on 119, 129; Berlin on 95, 97, 108; Deutscher on 112

Herder, Johann Gottfried 84; Berlin's reading of 94
Herzen, Alexander 73, 84, 86–8; Berlin's reading of 85, 87, 97, 192n31; correlation with Freud 87
Horkheimer, Max 60

Image, Judaic conception of 48–52, 184n8; as ante-aesthetic 66–7, 169; as broken mimesis 62; infraction or 'ban' internal to 51–2, 60–4, 66–8, 168–9; relation to exilic middle 69; as 'revealing/reveiling' 69–71; and Second Commandment 50–2, 63, 69, 70–1; as spatial and temporal prognostic 57–8

Jaspers, Karl, and Arendt 113, 117–18, 140, 198n27

Kafka, Franz, as pariah 119–20; Adorno on 150–1; Blanchot on 146; and Sebald 146–7, 151, 157
Kant, Immanuel, on *vesania* 142–4, 147
Kraus, Karl 8

landscape 12–14, 142–50, 155–7; as distance 144–8, 156–60, 162–3, 169; as negative phenomenology 169, *see also* Sebald; Lyotard
Lazare, Bernard 119–20; 133–5
Levinas, Emmanuel 3, 6, 11; on debt to Rosenzweig 182n107
liberalism, as self-limiting labour 12, 97; as loss 12, 74, 88, 91, 97, 99, 101–2, 110, *see also* Berlin; as spatial bearing 97
Lyotard, Jean François 6, 15; on 'Scapeland' 143–5, 150

Marx, Karl, Berlin on 84, 95–7, 108; in Benjamin 54
Mendelssohn, Moses 29
messianic 11, 18, 69, 76, 136–7, 184n16
middle city 7–10, Rosenzweig's version of 17–20, *see also* Rose, Gillian; non-national middle

Mill, John Stuart 93, in relation to Freud 98–9
Mosès, Stéphane 21, 36, 179n49

natural history 22–3, 54–6, 59
negative phenomenology 169, *see also* Lyotard on 'Scapeland'
non-national middle 9, 39, 166, 170, 172–3
Nancy, Jean-Luc 15, 50, 121

pariah, in Deutscher 111–12, 116, 120; in Arendt 113–14, 116–20; Bonnie Honig's critique of 204n119; concept of natality and 127–9, 133; 'The Jew as Pariah: A Hidden Tradition' 119–20, 133; as opposite of self-preservation 139, *see also* Arendt; as political agent 116–17; spatiality of 114, 116–18, 139–40; as state 133; in Weber 119
posthumous, Nietzsche on 148, 207n23; as place and present 13, 148–52, 157, 161–2, 164, 169, *see also* Sebald

Rabinbach, Anson 18
Rose, Gillian 5–8, 32, 39; on Athens and Jerusalem 5–8, 45; on 'broken middle' 7–10, 32;
Rose, Jacqueline 167
Rosenzweig, Franz 11, 15; on 'concept of 1800' 18–19; concept of the border in 20; on the disjunctive 'and' 30–3; 'Germ Cell' 19; on and against Hegel 18, 20–1, 26, 36–7; on and against Hermann Cohen 29–31; 'homeless in time' in 32–4; 41; myth of Wandering Jew in 26–7, 29; 'The New Thinking' 19, 24, 31; on Pharisean practice and contemporary German-Jewry 28–9; on *Star of Redemption* 14, 17, 20–4, 26, 30, 36–7, 42–4, 171–2; spatiality of the middle in 17–19, 25, 32–35, 37, 44; temporality of Day of Atonement and Day of Judgement in 34; temporality

of the middle in 19, 20, 25–6, 33–5; on temporality of the miracle 37–9; on 'theoretical beeline' 172–3, *see also* time; time of the state in 19, 21–4; on waiting 35–7
Rousseau, Jean-Jacques 80, 83, 122

Schlegel, Karl Wilhelm Friedrich 105, 122
Schoenberg, *Moses und Aron* 47–9, 51 See also image
Scholem, Gershom 18, 70–1, 135–7, 195n99, 205n130
Santner, Eric L., on 'sovereign temporality' 22; concept of 'Egyptomania' 166–7; reading of natural history and undead life 54–55, 59; on repetition compulsion 35; on trauma 103
Sebald, W.G. 12–13; *After Nature* 147; and Arendt's reading of Char 161–2; *Austerlitz* 147, 149, 153, 159; background of 141–2; Brecht's concept of erasure as precursor to 154–6; on Breendonk prison 149–50; 159; concept of distance in 144–8, 156–90, 160, 162–3, 169; concept of exile in 141–2, 146, 155, 158, 163, 165; *The Emigrants* 147, 151; landscape in 142–50, 152, 155, 157, 164, 169; as *nachgeboren* 15, 157–9, 160–2; *On the Natural History of Destruction* 152, 158, 208n35, *see also* trauma; posthumous, landscape; time; on posthumous place and present 13, 148–52, 157, 161–2, 164, 169; and post-war silence 146, 152, 155, 158, 163, 208n36; problem of memory in 142, 144, 152–4, 159–63; problem of time in 144, 148–53, 157–9, 161–4; relation to Holocaust literature 151–4; relation to Kafka's *Amerika* in 147–8; relation to Lyotard's 'Scapeland' and Kant's *vesania* in 142–7; *The Rings of Saturn* 148, 156; *Vertigo* 156–7
Steinberg, Michael P. 'exile *with a difference*' 12, 109, 169; Freudian reading of Mill in 98–9

time, Rosenzweig's 'new need for' 24–6; in Benjamin's city 40–2; as divine miracle 37–9; homelessness in 32–4, 41; of the middle 17–20, 26, 37–9; in Sebald 144, 148–53, 157–9, 161–4, *see also* trauma; of the state 21–7, 36–8; as relationality 24–6; as waiting and wandering 29, 35–7, 39
Trauma 103–4, 109, 167; as failure of transmission and testament 160–4; reopening wound of 119, 166–8

Varnhagen, Rahel 170, 112–14; and Akhmatova 15, 170, *see also* Arendt; and natality 126, 129; paradoxes of German-Jewish modernity in 120–7; as pariah 116–18, 127–9; as salonnière 113, 199n42

wandering Jew 10, 26–7, 29, 169

Žižek, Slavoj 27, 79, 90
Zornberg, Aviva 1, 3
Zweig, Arnold 154–5

CPSIA information can be obtained
at www.ICGtesting.com
Printed in the USA
LVHW052011220722
724181LV00014B/648